Somerville's Travels

AA

Editor: Donna Wood

Designer: Andrew Milne

Picture Researcher: Alice Earle

Image retouching and internal repro: Sarah Montgomery

Cartography provided by the Mapping Services Department
of AA Publishing

Map illustrations by Chapel Design & Marketing

Production: Stephanie Allen

Produced by AA Publishing

ISBN: 978-0-7495-6312-7

Published by AA Publishing (a trading name of AA Media Limited,
whose registered office is Fanum House, Basing View, Basingstoke
RG21 4EA; registered number 06112600).

A03955

Printed in China by C & C Offset Printing Co. Ltd

theAA.com/bookshop

Somerville's Travels

Journeys through the heart and soul of the British Isles

Christopher Somerville

AA

Locator Map

Contents

Foreword by Arthur Smith **8**

Introduction **10**

1 **Penwith Mist** **12**
Land's End to St Ives

2 **The Great Moors of the West** **26**
Ivybridge to Lynmouth across Dartmoor and Exmoor

3 **Mump, Tump, Moor and Tor** **38**
Muchelney to Glastonbury Tor across
the Somerset Levels

4 **The Oldest Road in Britain** **50**
The Harroway from Surrey to the Devon coast

5 **Mud, Marsh and Creek** **62**
Tilbury Fort to Canvey Island, Essex

6 **Capital Ring** **74**
Around London's Green Corridor

7 **Ancient Trackway of the Chiltern Hills** **86**
Goring to Ivinghoe Beacon

8 **The Great Flats of Fenland** **98**
Grantchester to King's Lynn

9 **The Rim of Gower** **108**
Three Cliffs Bay to Whiteford Sands

10 **Mystery and Magic in the Berwyn Hills** **120**
Llanrhaeadr-ym-Mochnant to Llangollen

11 **A Midlands Odyssey** **132**
Birmingham to Stoke-on-Trent by canal

12 **Mighty Tideway** **148**
River Humber from source to mouth

13 **The Great Sands of Lakeland** **158**
Morecambe Bay to Millom

14 **Spring in Upper Teesdale** **170**
Cauldron Snout to Middleton-in-Teesdale

15 **Tunes and Trails of Cheviot** **182**
Alwinton to the Scottish border and back

16 **Upheaval and Renewal in the Hills of
South Armagh** **192**
Newry to Crossmaglen around the Ring of Gullion

17 **The Road to the Isles** **206**
Corrour Station to Rannoch and Glen Nevis

18 **A Winter Wander on the Spey** **218**
Nethy Bridge to Spey Bay

19 **The Flow Country** **230**
Inverness to Forsinard

20 **Out Stack** **240**
Shetland, Yell and Unst to the prow of Britain

Index **252**

Acknowledgements **256**

Foreword
Arthur Smith

It must have been thirty years ago that I found myself lost in a thick mist somewhere in the Lake District with the rain pouring down, my map in soggy tatters, no compass and a whining girlfriend, who had been reluctant to join me even in the bright sunny morning in the valley. We were quite high up and, although I didn't tell her this, I was becoming fearful about not making it down before nightfall.

Suddenly, a tall man with a reassuring beard emerged from the torrential gloom. He had a handsome face and a cagoule that was far more sensible than either of ours, and he gave us an encouraging smile, pointed to a path I had not spotted, shared a brief conversation about Coleridge and then disappeared into the mist in the opposite direction. An hour and a half later the girlfriend and I were drying off in the pub, making up and relishing our adventure.

That rambling fairy godfather was Christopher Somerville, and the woman and I are now married ... Well no, not true, but when I think of that man I think of Christopher, whom I first met when he was the resident walking correspondent on Radio 4's *Excess Baggage*, a programme I presented at the time. A producer told me that his descriptions of the hikes he had done always drew a far greater response than any other item on the show. I haven't seen the hairy rover of late but he remains my amiable, if invisible, companion whenever I follow another excursion from his book *Walks in the Country near London*.

Christopher's talents as a writer, an historian, an anecdotalist and an observer of the natural world make him the very best in his field, a broad verdant field he has probably directed me to at some point in my past. The walks he has selected for this book are outstanding in their beauty and interest, and Christopher really brings them alive. We come across ancient stones, holy wells, abandoned tramways, eccentric lairds, poets, painters, animals and flowers. The routes are elegantly threaded with historical anecdotes, local tales, and geographical insights, while vivid reminiscences of Christopher's own past make it almost a new genre. The photographs serve as a further gorgeous invitation to dip into these romantic treks. You may find that on opening *Somerville's Travels* you are, like me, soon itching to pull your boots on once more.

Like the countryside it describes, this book is to be cherished.

Introduction

Mist curled up like gunsmoke around the cliffs of Land's End. Standing at the barrier below the First and Last House, making ready to step out into Chapter One of this book of twenty journeys through Britain, I couldn't resist a smile as I thought of the first time I'd waited at this cliff-top railing some thirty years before. It had been misty that morning, too. Back then I'd been a reluctant teacher and aspiring writer, about to tackle the first of fifty coastal walks for a book I was hoping and praying would liberate me forthwith from the classroom. It took a while longer, in the event, but the sense of freedom and exhilaration on that spring morning had stayed sharp in my blood ever since. So had the memory of how I'd eventually set off north along the coast path, shivering, unable to see more than a couple of feet in front of myself thanks to the flannel-coloured murk that had crept in from the sea. Now on this early spring morning in 2009, it looked once again like mist for breakfast, lunch and tea.

I set off into a Cornish mist at the start of these twenty journeys, and in a Shetland Isles mist I finished them. In between, I grew to think of this country as an endlessly mutating being or presence, slowly unveiling itself, slowly insinuating itself among my own fibres. Its form and character, nebulous and mysterious under many layers of ignorance when I started out to explore and to write about these islands more than thirty years ago, have gradually become clearer. Topped and tailed by ancient granites, fertile in its West Country pastures and East Anglian cornlands, ravaged about its middle by industrial depredation, rising into fells and moors towards the north, roughening and steepening into wild country and wilderness as it runs out to the Celtic fringes – these are the kind of broad-brush impressions left in the mind as one journeys through Britain. But the fine details that really bring the picture into sharp focus are those you can only gather at slow speed and under no pressure of time: the sea lavender in the Norfolk saltmarsh that you put under the hand lens to watch a resident spider stalking its lilac-hued territory; the Iron Age hillfort off the Hampshire trackway where you climb late on a winter's evening to find snow drifted in trenches dug two thousand years ago; the fierce *urk! urk!* of a great skua sweeping past an inch from the end of your nose as you invade its breeding ground on a windy headland at dawn in the outermost Northern Isles. It was the seductive pull of that slow-time journeying that made me rule out the motor car as a mode of progress, even more than the obvious green credentials of travelling car-free.

As for the journeys themselves: I threw the net as widely as I could. What I was after were iconic landscapes, the kind we all have in our minds as encapsulating some essential aspect of Britain. West Country coves and moors, the ancient trackways of the chalk downs, the lonely hills of mid-Wales; Midlands canals and industries, high Pennine country, the debatable lands of the Scottish borders; then something really wild and open in Scotland, something waiting to be discovered in Northern Ireland's forgotten corner of South Armagh; an ending in a high place as far north as I could go and looking still further north. I wanted to twist the

Whatever your means of taking these twenty journeys through
our tiny but remarkable archipelago, may you reach the end inspired
to go straight out and find twenty more of your own.

adventure a bit, too. I didn't want to write a guidebook, or a tourist board manifesto. These twenty journeys avoid as far as possible the best-known examples of each type of landscape. They are places I have come across by accident or inspired recommendation or just sheer good luck over years of wandering and writing. They have beckoned me round the corner and up the back way. They are places that have stirred me, that still raise the hairs on the back of my neck.

Cornwall was a mystery wrapped in a mist. Dartmoor and Exmoor provided a dip into the ragbag of memory, especially into the effect on a small boy of thrilling tales like *The Hound of the Baskervilles* and *Tarka the Otter*. The oldest roads in Britain marched me through the downlands of the South Country in broiling sun and in sub-zero snow and ice. Moody fascination defined the unregarded flatland and estuarine country of outer Thames, Great Ouse and Humber. Mid-Wales was all mist, thunder and majestic nonsense at the elbow of the ebullient writer and full-time egoist George Borrow. In the Midlands I travelled the canal system from ex-industrial heart to heart, Black Country to Potteries, encountering massive dereliction and dislocation as well as some of the funniest and driest folk in these islands. Wildness began to tinge the picture the further north I travelled: the present dangers of the vast sands of South Lakelands, a blood-soaked past in the hidden corners of the lonely Cheviots. A tinge of romance came courtesy of Wordsworth's sonnets in praise of the River Duddon country, set against the gritty realism

of Norman Nicholson's poetry only a few miles downriver. Then, the proper wildernesses of Rannoch Moor and the Flow Country, each with its nugget of warmth and gleam of human presence focused on a remote railway station; the hard times and blood-lettings, both legendary and all too real, of South Armagh, caught in the sublime setting of the Ring of Gullion. Finally, Unst at the northernmost tip of the Shetland archipelago, the remotest place of all, the 'brow of Britain', with nothing but the open sea between the bare rock stacks that close off our island chain and the Arctic ice a thousand miles to the north.

Sixteen of these twenty expeditions I made wholly or mostly on foot. Canal narrowboat, ferry, bicycle (always a pain and an effort for me, though mitigated here by the fascination of the Somerset Levels and Shetland landscapes I was pedalling through), local bus and branch line train were my other *modus wanderandi*. I have included details of maps, routes, helpful websites and useful reading tips for anyone wanting to go out and actually do any of these journeys. But you could just as easily kick back with a glass at your elbow and let me collect the blisters and bum-sores on your behalf. Whatever your means of taking these twenty journeys through our tiny but remarkable archipelago, may you reach the end inspired to go straight out and find twenty more of your own.

Christopher Somerville

Penwith Mist

It was a proper Penwith mist, a mist you could punch a fist through and watch trailing away from your sleeve. A hard winter in west Cornwall, a bare spring and the harsh granite tors of Land's End blotted out in the thickest sea mist of the year.

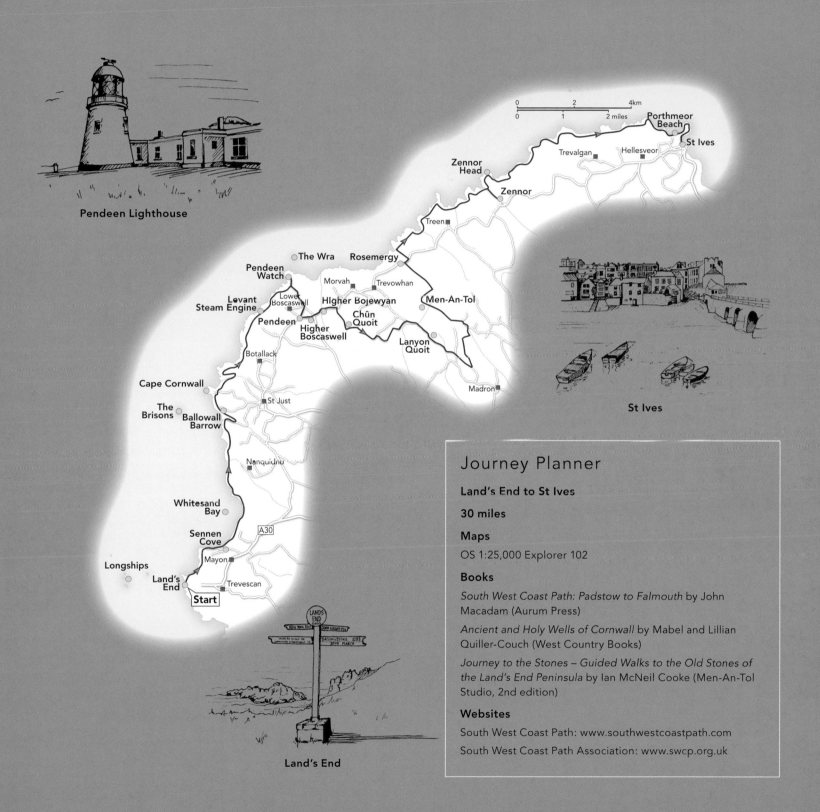

Pendeen Lighthouse

Porthmeor
Beach

St Ives

Trevalgan   Hellesveor

Zennor
Head

Zennor

Treen

The Wra   Rosemergy

Pendeen
Watch

Morvah   Trevowhan

Levant   Lower
Steam Engine   Boscaswell   Higher Bojewyan   Men-An-Tol

Pendeen   Chûn
Quoit

Higher
Boscaswell   Lanyon
Quoit

Botallack

Cape Cornwall   St Just   Madron

The
Brisons   Ballowall
Barrow   **St Ives**

Nanquidno

Whitesand
Bay

Sennen
Cove   A30

Mayon

Longships   Land's
End   Trevescan

Start

LANDS
END

Land's End

Journey Planner

Land's End to St Ives

30 miles

Maps

OS 1:25,000 Explorer 102

Books

South West Coast Path: Padstow to Falmouth by John
Macadam (Aurum Press)

Ancient and Holy Wells of Cornwall by Mabel and Lillian
Quiller-Couch (West Country Books)

*Journey to the Stones – Guided Walks to the Old Stones of
the Land's End Peninsula* by Ian McNeil Cooke (Men-An-Tol
Studio, 2nd edition)

Websites

South West Coast Path: www.southwestcoastpath.com

South West Coast Path Association: www.swcp.org.uk

Beside the First and Last House a talking telescope pointed out west, but there was no-one around this early in the morning to put a coin in the slot and set the commentary in motion. It would have been an empty gesture; there was, literally, nothing to see out there but the white wall of the mist. But there was plenty for ears to feed the imagination with as I leaned over the wall – the suck and sigh of waves on unseen rocks 200ft (60m) below, the heavy visceral throb of a marine diesel engine at sea somewhere not too far away, the rasping cries of jackdaws riding the cliff thermals. Birds of ill omen, their throaty voices were backgrounded by the mournful hooting of the Longships lighthouse. The map told me that the reef lay a mile due west, but it could as well have been 20, so diffused and wavery was the warning from its tower. When did Trinity House foghorns relinquish the sonorous bellow that all sailors learned to respect in favour of today's high, donkey-like bray? And another question, rather more practical – could I really negotiate these clifftop paths in such a pea-souper?

I zipped my collar to the throat, pulled on thermal gloves, stamped my boots a couple of times for courage and good luck, and set out into the ancient Hundred of Pennwydh. What Cornwall's westernmost region held for me was anyone's guess, especially in a fog forecast to linger around the toe-tip of Britain for the next couple of days. I took it very carefully for the first few minutes. But the coast path was wide and well surfaced, the cliff edges were obvious, and

there was a strange, cross-grained pleasure in walking alone within the white clouds.

W.H. Hudson came to the southwestern extremity of Cornwall in the early 1900s in order to research his book *The Land's End*, and the Argentine-born naturalist exactly caught the intense, if selfish, delight of the solitary walker who finds he has got this over-famous, overcrowded, over-commercialised spot all to himself:

> *Although the vague image of an imagined Land's End fades from the mind and is perhaps lost when the reality is known, the ancient associations of the place remain, and, if a visit be rightly timed, they may invest it with a sublimity and fascination not its own. I loitered many days near that spot in mid-winter, in the worst possible weather... I blessed the daily furious winds which served to keep the pilgrims away, and to half blot out the vulgar modern buildings with rain and mist from the Atlantic.*

At nightfall Hudson would fight the wind down to the piled tors at the very end of the promontory, in order to relish 'the raving of the wind among the rocks; the dark ocean – exceedingly dark except when the flying clouds were broken; the jagged isolated rocks, on which so many ships have been

shattered, rising in awful blackness from the spectral foam that appeared and vanished and appeared again; the multitudinous hoarse sounds of the sea, with throbbing and hollow booming noises in the caverns beneath.' I rolled his words around my palate as I trod the cliff path. 'Hoarse' was not a description I would ever have thought of applying to the sound of the sea, but it perfectly reflected what I was hearing here and now, the gullet noise of the invisible waves as they beat the rocks and subsided back into themselves with a greasy hiss.

Down in Sennen Cove the mist made a leached-out watercolour of pubs, hotels and knick-knack shops still shuttered against the winter, their salt-grey paint running with orange dribbles of rust. I took to the beach and walked the curve of Whitesand Bay over ribbed sands crunchy with shells. From the edge of the sea came the wail of gulls and a rising drumming of hooves. A solitary horsewoman appeared, cantering along the tideline, her long ponytail flying behind her. The rider as insubstantial as a figure in a Jack Yeats painting, the synchronised legs of the grey horse stretching and intermeshing, the floating tails of woman and beast, seemed like elements in a fable. A second or two and they were fading away again, the gentle wash of wavelets smoothing out the concussion of the hooves.

Tregiffian Vean cliff showed up where I hoped it would. Up on my path in the sky once more I steered due north through granite stacks and grassy headlands where the green spears of montbretia awaited the brilliant orange tips that summer would bring. A couple of miles along the cliffs and I had drawn level, so map and compass assured me, with The Brisons, a vicious pair of sea stacks a mile offshore. I stopped to listen and fancied I could hear, or perhaps feel, the thumping vibrations of big waves on solid rock out in the mist. Looking out on a clear day at the Longships or The Brisons, big upstanding rocks that tower from the sea,

Above left **The Longships lighthouse in the early 19th century, when ferocious Atlantic storms off Land's End could maroon the keepers for weeks on end**

Right **Not necessarily authentic: amateur archaeologist and maverick William Copeland Borlase added a wall or two to Ballowall Barrow**

it is hard to imagine how any navigator who was not half-cut or wholly inattentive could fail to give such obvious hazards a wide berth. In a thick coastal mist and foul weather you can better appreciate the danger. Factor in a complete lack of sophisticated navigational aids, a pitch-black night and a gale driving on to an unknown lee shore, and it's all too easy to see how sailing ships could be wrecked so swiftly and devastatingly and with such a huge loss of life.

In one of the most notorious wrecks of 1868, a gale-driven Liverpool brig bound for the Spanish Main struck The Brisons in a heavy fog at night and disintegrated. As day broke, watchers on the cliffs could see the captain, his wife and the eight-man crew clinging to a ledge on Great Brison. They hung on until a swell swamped the rock and washed them all off. One sailor had the presence of mind to scramble onto a piece of the wreck and keep clear of the reef by using a scrap of canvas as a sail. He was rescued by a brave fishing-boat crew from Sennen. All the rest drowned except the captain and his wife, who had been thrown by the waves onto the adjacent Little Brison. Although the revenue cutter was launched, it could not get near because of the ferocity of the sea. Man and woman were forced to remain on the shelterless rock for more than 24 hours, until the coastguard boat could approach near enough to fire a line by rocket. The captain was rescued exhausted but unharmed, but his wife did not survive the final ordeal of being dragged through the waves to the boat. Eight souls out of ten were lost; all the deaths happened in full view of the rescuers, not far away, who were powerless to do anything to help. Similar tragedies unfolded by the thousand all along the Cornish coast in days of sail, even after the lighthouses and their deep-throated foghorns were installed.

If I hadn't somehow blundered off the coast path at Carn Gloose, I'd never have happened upon Ballowall Barrow. The stone-walled burial mound shaped itself out of the mist a little way inland as I cast around for a clue. From the top of the outer wall I looked down into the heart of the structure, oval-shaped and deep, with stone-lined cists, or burial chambers, recessed within its walls. Excavating the barrow in 1878, William Copeland Borlase found pottery and burned human bone in the cists. Borlase, MP for East Cornwall and grandson of an eminent Cornish antiquarian, was able to do pretty much as he wished with what he found, especially in such an out-of-the-way place as Penwith. He felt free to add a few extra walls to Ballowall Barrow in order to funnel visitors around the monument. It was not the only liberty he took, once he had gained power and influence. A scandal involving bad debts and a jealous mistress ruined him in the 1890s, and he died disowned by his family, his learned achievements devalued. Towards the end of his life Borlase tried to recover from bankruptcy by working abroad as a manager of tin mines, a situation he would have appeared well qualified for simply by virtue of being a Cornishman.

The granite of west Cornwall lies thick with deposits of tin, and the industries involved with the mineral – mining and smelting – were a staple of Penwith all through the Middle Ages. Tin was certainly mined here in Roman times, and there is some evidence that the local industry was on its feet as far back as

the early Bronze Age, perhaps 4,000 years ago. Cornish tin mines, great and small, were legion: clangorous, dangerous holes known as 'wheals', where the water had to be pumped away continuously, industrial injuries were commonplace and death an everyday hazard. Local men who were not full-time farmers or fishermen expected to earn their bread in the tin mines. That all changed when cheap foreign tin became available in the early 1900s, and after limping on until the end of the century the home-grown industry finally came to an end in March 1998 with the closure of the 300-year-old South Crofty mine, the oldest in Europe.

Signs and scars of the tin mining industry lie all around. Opposite Ballowall Barrow a circular stone structure proved to be the cap of an old mineshaft filled nearly to the top with stones and sealed with a grid of iron bars. Other capped shafts poked out of the gorse and heather among spoil heaps half drowned in damp bracken. Beyond, overshadowing the crumbled ruin of a pumping engine house, rose a tall industrial chimney with a thick stone band around its neck. Hollows, heaps and deep holes made a treacherous ground

to be wandering fog-blind, and I was glad to stumble on a coast path sign and hear the crash of waves on unseen cliffs once more. I'd scarcely started north along the cliffs again when a gust of wind from the sea shredded the mist to reveal a slender tower planted on a promontory up ahead. A lighthouse? Strange that I hadn't heard the ass-like bray of a foghorn. 'Cape Cornwall,' the map told me. I looked more closely, and found a laconic 'Chy' hidden among the close-packed staves of the contour lines. Close to, the chimney revealed itself as made of brick, with a base handsomely encircled by brick pilasters. I put my back against its rough and comforting bulk, fetched a cheese and pickle sandwich out of the backpack and opened my notebook. The chimney, I read, was built to draw away the fumes from boilers that powered the pumps and winding gear of Cape Cornwall's tin and copper mine, a 'wet' one whose levels ran far out under the sea. As a sea mark for ships, the old chimney on its eminence has far outlived its original purpose (the Cape Cornwall mine operated only from 1839 until 1883), but its significance as a monument is even greater. For miles around, inland and out to sea, it draws attention to the place

where the Atlantic tides separate between those trending north towards the Irish Sea and those running south to make the turn eastwards into the English Channel – a marker of great movements among the dividing waters.

A bit of a kip on the Cape, a foot inspection, and I was ready for the afternoon's foray. It felt bizarre to be walking amid such famous coastal scenery, quite the wildest and most impressive for dozens of miles, and have it so comprehensively hidden from view. The crash and splatter of the sea on my left, the barking of a pent-up farm dog away inland and the occasional r-r-ronk of a raven overhead formed a kind of surround-sound system that accompanied me along the path until a familiar sight loomed ahead – the sturdy engine houses and jagged-topped chimneys of the Levant mine, pride of the Penwith coast, crammed between the moor and the sea at the brink of 300-ft (90-m) cliffs. I well remembered being shown over the site the year before by an elderly volunteer guide, a drily amusing man with a kaleidoscopic knowledge of the mine whose expression held a deep, almost religious joy as he stood forgetful of his guests and contemplated the power and glory of the great green-painted beam engine pounding away like the hind leg of a galloping dinosaur.

The Levant mine operated for over a hundred years, and developed during its lifetime a whole maze of shafts, tunnels and levels in the cliffs and under the sea floor. I leaned over precariously to scan with binoculars what the mist allowed me to see of the cliff face, and could make out a jagged black arch with the hint of iron bolts and rails at its mouth. One hundred and thirty thousand tons of copper came out of the Levant between its 1820 opening and its closure in 1930; nearly 25,000 tons of tin. How many men kept their families fed, how many were hurt or died in this one mine, was never recorded. The question could be asked in dozens of locations across Penwith, hundreds throughout west Cornwall – mines famous and obscure, mines remembered only in name, mines and miners unremembered. The whole tin-mining region is now protected and preserved as a UNESCO World Heritage Site, in recognition of its industrial importance, its landscape significance and the stunning impact it makes on anyone with two eyes and a bit of curiosity and imagination.

The high-pitched mooing of the foghorn on Pendeen Watch began to make itself heard as I walked on north, but I had got within a hundred yards of the squat white tower before I caught sight of it tucked down into the clifftop under its wind-vane arrow. It took scores of wrecks and centuries of pleading for Pendeen Watch lighthouse to be approved and built in the 1890s, a tremendous undertaking involving the levelling of the whole summit of the headland to accommodate the tower and its walled complex of store rooms, workshops and keepers' cottages. Another gap in the mist offered a glimpse over an angry-looking sea whipped by the wind into lines of foam. Out there lay The Wra reef, dark, jagged and deadly in a collar of lather. A crab boat was making for port – St Ives, probably, a few miles along the coast – with a bone in its teeth, a white slash of bow-wave. What with satellite-assisted navigation, up-to-the-minute charts on screen, sophisticated radio and depth-finding gear, there was no way this tough little vessel was going to run foul of The Wra. I watched it pitch and yaw until the vaporous curtain closed once more. Then, with a good few miles now under my belt and a

Left **Beautifully maintained by the National Trust, the historic buildings of the Levant tin and copper mine stand exposed and lonely on their cliff edge**

great desire to see something other than mist, I turned my back on the coast and headed down the lighthouse road towards where the map told me the village of Pendeen and its satellite hamlets of Boscaswell and Bojewyan must lie. A plate of food, a place to dry my boots and a nice laze by someone's fire seemed suddenly the only things on earth worth dreaming of.

Next morning I drew the curtains and looked out hopefully. Mist. Oh, God. Oh, well, then. Breakfast ahoy, and then ho for a day inland, a day for ancient stones and holy wells. I spread out the map. A blush-making embarrassment of archaeological riches. If there was one antiquity within a day's walk of Pendeen, there were dozens and dozens. I'd make a big circle, sticking to the lanes and field paths, and see what bumped up against me.

Out in the stone-walled lane to Chûn Downs, everything dripped. Every bracken frond held multiple strings of pearls, every spider web a sheik's fortune in diamonds. With the world beyond a hundred yards abolished by the mist, it was a day to take stock of small delights, whatever was near at hand and under the nose. A shrew scurried across the path, a tiny black sausage of damp fur on a blur of legs. Minuscule, scarlet-lipped trumpets of fungi sprouted from a bed of star moss on the wall. Celandine buds as hard and fat as wax cylinders, held in the warmth of my palms, refused to uncurl until the sun should come calling for them. I made slow progress, crouching on hands and knees to inspect long-leggity spiders, crawling on my stomach to try (unsuccessfully) to surprise a hare in his bent-grass form. Anyone would have taken me for a madman if they'd happened by. But no-one was about in the mist and wind.

Quite why the moors and farmlands of west Cornwall are so fantastically rich in monuments from our deep history, in stone tombs and stone circles, in standing stones and ancient settlements and venerable holy wells, is hard to fathom. The climate must certainly have been better several thousand years ago, and the region with its mineral riches and surrounding sea must have traded widely with the Continent. There was enough food, enough comfort, enough social equilibrium – in Stone and Bronze Age terms – to see a sizeable, stable population settled in what are nowadays Penwith's bleak uplands and barren moorlands. The inhabitants of ancient Pennwydh, however marginal their lives and meagre their resources by modern standards, were able to allot time, energy and manpower to the building of great tombs to honour their dead, great structures to house their ceremonies.

Whoever erected Chûn Quoit on the crest of the downs some five thousand years ago, for example, could call on considerable engineering and mathematical skills. The massive stone tomb loomed up before me like a giant fungoid organism, its great capstone resting on four fat legs planted in the moor as if they would never move till the world's end. The cap must weigh many dozens of tons, perhaps a hundred. How did people working with only wood, bone and stone manage to make this thing, or the great flat-topped 'altar' of Lanyon Quoit tomb a mile or so to the west? And why, when they could simply have scattered cremation ashes or tipped dead bodies over the cliffs? Wandering the moors from one tremendous site to another, losing my way in the white-out and finding it again, I wondered for how long people had been asking themselves these questions. Was such curiosity a function of the

Right **The ancient chambered tomb of Lanyon Quoit was blown down during a storm in 1815, and subsequently reconstructed in an inaccurate but dramatic 'altar' shape**

Far right **Yin and yang, male and female: the symbolism of Men-An-Tol, the 'Stone with the Hole', seems clear – but no-one really knows**

Right **Clootie trees, festooned with rags for prayers or spells, testify to a resurgence of interest in holy wells**

dawning of the Age of Enlightenment? Had folk really passed by Chûn Quoit for millennia without troubling themselves about who, when and why? 'Made by giants!' Did that satisfy enquiring human minds over all that time?

Down below Boswarthen I followed the old path through thickets of leafless hazels to Madron Well. Holy wells are ticklish things to find, but not quite as tricky as they used to be. In parallel with a recent decline in formal church attendance, there has been a great revival of interest in these ancient places of resort. Their sheltering trees are once more festooned with clooties, bits of rag and other items hung there for good luck. In the 17th and 18th centuries, though, when distrust of popish superstitions was strong throughout these islands, the holy wells that had been sanctified by early Christian missionaries and relied upon for cures and blessings by ordinary folk for the ensuing thousand years were widely neglected where they were not destroyed. But visits continued; belief persisted. After all, these mineral springs with their healing properties had been in use all across Britain through many millennia before the missionaries ever landed in their precarious coracles or made their way through the mountain passes. The hermits had put them under a spell. Faith in the wells endured, as Mabel and Lillian Quiller-Couch reported in 1894 in their little guidebook *Ancient and Holy Wells of Cornwall*:

> *In the near neighbourhood of Penzance, and about three-quarters of a mile from the church and church-town of Madron, the traveller will find the celebrated Madron Well. Children used to be taken to this well on the first three Sundays in May to be dipped in the water, that they might be cured of the rickets. At the present time people throw in two pins or pebbles to consult the spirit, or try for sweethearts. There is still an abundant supply of beautiful water in the well ... Here divination is performed on May mornings by rustic maidens anxious to know when they are to be married.*

I found Madron Well as I remembered it from a visit a few years ago: water welling from the roots of a clootie tree laden with cloth packages, linen strips, silver paper twists and a rotting pair of black lace knickers. Along the muddy path, hidden away among hawthorns and hazels, stood the moss-grown walls of an early medieval baptistry with its own clear spring. Here cripples would pass the night in prayer on 'May Thursday' in hopes of a cure, and lovers would soon be wed if the crossed pins they threw in should sink to the bottom without separating.

The baptistry was a place to sit and dream. When I got up again, I was amazed to discover the piskies had stolen half a day from me. But they hadn't yet rolled the fog away from west Cornwall. Back by Boswarthen I went, and on across the moors, seeing only what was within the penumbra immediately surrounding me. Nose to map and compass, I steered myself to the three enigmatic stones of Men-An-Tol, the 'Stone with the Hole'. No similar monument exists anywhere in these islands. In the presence of the three component stones, the questions surfaced once more. What did they think they were doing, the people who fashioned a stone wheel with a hole through the middle, set it up on its rim and erected a stocky standing column on either side? The yin and the yang of the Men-An-Tol seem explicit, at all events. Locals

Right **Granite gateposts, granite field walls, granite tors protruding through the green skin of turf on the coast path near Zennor: the harsh reality of Penwith's geological underpinnings is always close to the surface**

found their own uses for the stones: they would squeeze through the hole in the middle to ease backache, crawl from east to west nine times around the monument to mend their rheumatism, and cure tubercular children by passing them through the ring stone before dragging them on the grass three times from west to east.

Someone had placed a nosegay of celandine and primrose buds before the holed stone. I stroked the coarse granite – an impulse as irresistible as passing one's hand along the rough pelt of a dog – and then made north through Rosemergy to find the coast path. It was another 4 miles (6km) to Zennor, and the clearest thing I saw all the way was the lighted window of the Tinner's Arms when I limped in at nightfall. Wouldn't you know it? Next morning dawned crisp, cold and peerlessly clear. A wide horizon, and a sky the colour of a song thrush egg. Now I had a proper dilemma. Should I take the inland path to St Ives, the old corpse road over granite bar stiles that passed Tregerthen where D.H. Lawrence and Frieda lived and gloomed, Higher Tregerthen where Rupert Brooke's lover Ka Cox lost her reason and her life through her entanglement with occultist Aleister Crowley, 'the wickedest man in the world'? Or should it be the 5-mile (8-km) stretch along the cliffs, one of the loveliest pieces of coast in Britain? Mystery, misery and mayhem, or light, air and sea?

The coastal path proved fully as delightful as I'd been anticipating. Strange to relate, though, I wasn't really into it this morning. The sun-splashed tors of Zennor Head, the tinkling streams above Carn Porth and River Cove, the hunting peregrines and coconut-scented gorse – they passed me by like a painting. Lovely to look at, but oddly unreal compared with the fourth dimension I had been walking in for two days now, the silent, heavy world of the mist. It wasn't until I had reached St Ives and was sitting on deserted Porthmeor Beach in that snug little artists' town, my back against the sea wall, a beef-and-stilton pasty in hand, that things really clicked into focus once more.

You can take the boy out of the clouds, it seemed, but it takes a while longer to rub one's inner eye completely clear of Cornish mist.

The Great Moors of the West

Rain: solid, sheeting rain. Rain, and the sound of my father squelching after me and cursing under his breath. Sodden sheep giving us the evil eye from the heather. And mist beyond them. That was all I remembered of a purgatorial slog across Dartmoor and Exmoor in 1978, following the long-distance footpath that had been established, recently and rather shakily, as the Two Moors Way.

Journey Planner

Ivybridge to Lynmouth across Dartmoor and Exmoor

102 miles

Maps

OS 1:25,000 Explorers OL20, OL28, 113, 127, 114, OL9

Two Moors Way – Devon's Coast to Coast Guide available from local tourist offices

Books

The Hound of the Baskervilles by Sir Arthur Conan Doyle (Penguin Classics)

The Hound of the Baskervilles – Hunting the Dartmoor Legend by Philip Weller (Devon Books)

The Concise British Flora in Colour by William Keble Martin (Ebury Press/ Michael Joseph)

Field & Hedgerow by Richard Jefferies (currently out of print)

Tarka the Otter by Henry Williamson (Penguin Modern Classics)

Websites

Two Moors Way Association: www.twomoorsway.org.uk

Music

'Hellhound on my Trail' by Robert Johnson – The Complete Recordings (Columbia CD)

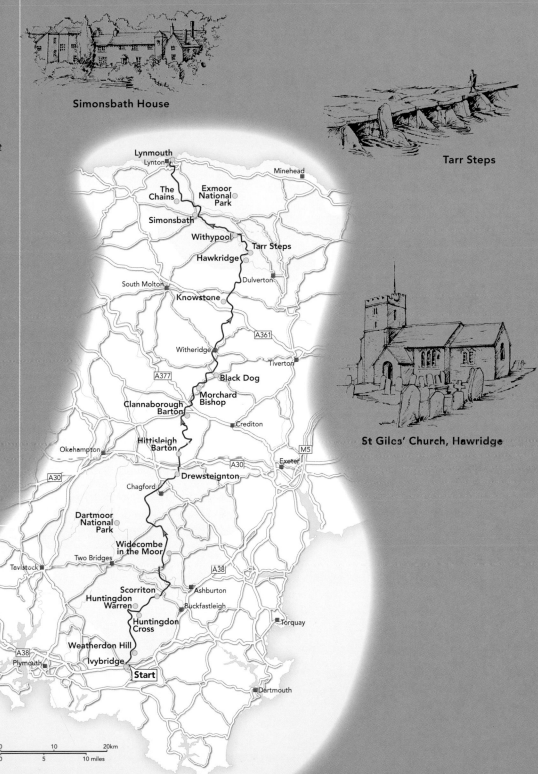

Simonsbath House

Tarr Steps

St Giles' Church, Hawridge

Those hundred-odd miles may have led through some of the most glorious landscapes in the southwest of England, but we never saw it through the stair rods of rain. Even now, 30 years on from that soaking July, I couldn't picture the two great West Country moors without seeing in my mind's eye a rain-blurred map, a fibbing compass and a permanent drip at the end of Dad's nose.

But had it really been that bad? I rummaged through the journal I'd kept, complete with beer stains, sweat splodges and amateurish sketches (Widecombe church with a Brillo-pad tree, the Mason's Arms at Knowstone with asymmetrical toytown cars outside). 'Day 1 – grey clouds, brisk wind. Day 2 – high cloud, blue sky. Day 3 – wide views, sunburnt faces…' So how had all those rainy memories been generated? I leafed through to the back of the book. Ah, yes, of course!

That final day across Exmoor! 'Mist creeping over the hilltops at Withypool… Horsen Farm, where rain began… Blue Gate: 20 yards visibility, mist, rain and wind… Simonsbath: rain still relentlessly falling…'

Now I remembered, all right. Our triumphant crossing of Exmoor, dear to me through breathless childhood readings of *Tarka the Otter*, had turned out to be a day of unadulterated mist and rain misery. We'd given up the open moor at Simonsbath, eaten our sandwiches at the Exmoor House Hotel in the company of a posse of Mother's Pride bread van drivers playing pool and drinking pints on their lunch break (it was 1978, after all), and then trudged the 7 miles (11km) over to Lynmouth along the B3223 in lashing rain and clinging mist, at imminent risk of being squashed by a succession of hooting cars.

The bloody awfulness of that one day had somehow drawn a rainy, foggy pall over the whole week. Re-reading snippets from the old notebook – an ancient verse about the 1638 lightning strike in Widecombe, the venerable landlady of the Drewe Arms at Drewsteignton, foxglove lanes near the Tarr Steps clapper bridge – it all sounded rather wonderful. Maybe a different season would bring better weather. I decided I'd go back for another bite at the cherry.

A cloudy March morning in Ivybridge, cold but clear, and a stony lane between high hedgebanks leading purposefully up onto the southernmost heights of Dartmoor. This was how I'd hoped it would be; hart's-tongue ferns in the banks, gleams of watery sun through the beech branches, sheep barging and baa-ing at the field gates as I passed. The northwest wind was sharp, but it brought good smells down from the moor – wet peat, wet bracken and the smell of cold water and granite, as much in the mind as in the nostrils.

The 360-odd square miles of Dartmoor are cut neatly into southern and northern halves by a pair of roads that cross each other at Two Bridges in the middle of the moor. Dad and I had started our expedition in Widecombe in the Moor, two days north of here in the farmland area between south and north Dartmoor. So the famous southern fastnesses of the Dark Moor, the sucking bogs, great castle-like tors and sudden, disorientating mists, were all unseen ground to me. However, if I hadn't ever set foot in these southerly swathes of the moor, I knew them almost as well as if I had, through the illimitable power of pure imagination. Like many a boy brought up in a TV-free house, I'd read my way round Britain by the age of 12. Dartmoor to me meant just one scenario: a hell-hound on my trail.

> I got to keep movin', I've got to keep movin'
> Blues fallin' down like hail, blues fallin' down like hail
> Lord, the days keep on worryin' me,
> There's a hellhound on my trail,
> Hellhound on my trail, hellhound on my trail...

I doubt if Delta blues maestro Robert Johnson ever read *The Hound of the Baskervilles*, but he certainly did catch the paranoia, the dread and the deadly fascination of phantom hounds and the power of their grip on the human psyche. What Arthur Conan Doyle unleashed in his wonderful Gothic fable, the 'gigantic hound' with its blazing jaws and unearthly howling, was enough to scare me rigid as I devoured the story under the bedclothes by the light of an illicit torch. Pleasurably, though. I knew everything was going to be all right, with Sherlock Holmes and Dr Watson on the trail of the diabolical hound and its wicked, scheming master. As for Dartmoor: that was the place where ponies were sucked into bogs, where the dreaded mist could lead a man fatally astray in the doomy wastes of the great Grimpen Mire.

Out through a gate and onto the moor. No mists, no bogs or spectral canines. Just the rising ridges of Western Beacon and Butterdon Hill, and the long green snake of the Redlake tramway curling round the flank of Weatherdon Hill beyond. The tramway was built in 1911 to transport workers and their materials between the South Dartmoor railway line and the

Left **The barren wastes of Fox Tor Mires near Dartmoor Prison, immortalised by Conan Doyle in *The Hound of the Baskervilles* as the dreaded Great Grimpen Mire where the villain Stapleton met his end**

Below **'Hist!' cried Holmes... 'Look out! It's coming!' Peter Cushing and Andre Morrell as Holmes and Watson, hunting the Hound of the Baskervilles on screen in 1959**

enormous china-clay pits at Redlake, 7 miles into the moor. It served the workings for 20 years until their closure, and has carried walkers deep into Dartmoor ever since. I trod the sinuous curves of its green trackbed with confidence. Rain came spattering across at intervals, curls of mist advanced and retreated on higher ground from time to time, but the old tramway kept pointing ahead like a crooked finger. I found I could let map and compass go hang. There was time to look around, to rejoice in the clean smell of the rain-washed moor and the constantly unreeling singing of the larks that went up their aerial staircases in jerky steps until they melted into the clouds and became pure song.

I pondered hounds as I went along. Robert Johnson was haunted and hunted by his fear of Hell. But then Johnson, so it was said, had gone down to the crossroads to meet the Devil one night and had sold his soul for the ability to play the blues as no man had done before or ever would again. The 19th-century mystic Francis Thompson fled like a hare from the love of God in his extraordinary poem 'The Hound of Heaven':

> I fled Him, down the nights and down the days;
> I fled Him, down the arches of the years;
> I fled Him, down the labyrinthine ways
> Of my own mind; and in the mist of tears
> I hid from Him, and under running laughter.

A clever psychologist could probably sort out exactly which neurotic anxieties Arthur Conan Doyle's creation represented in my own childhood nightmares. In many ways, though, it's good not to have the contents of one's psychological dustbin rummaged through too thoroughly. Anyone who makes it to late middle age will have collected a few hounds at his heels on the long trek there. Sufficient for me on this windy spring morning to recall the delicious shock of terror and fascination as the bane of the Baskervilles burst out of the mist and came galloping through my bedroom after the fleeing Sir Henry, while Holmes and Watson levelled their pistols behind my pillows and left the monster dead on my Noah's Ark rug.

The old tramway curved past the waste heaps and deep, dark pool of the abandoned china-clay works at Leftlake Mires and forged on across the empty, treeless moor, gaining height gradually. Looking at the map I found I had climbed about 700ft (200m) this morning, a hardly creditable fact. The gentle slope of the trackbed in the monotonous landscape of the moor had deceived me. In these dun brown wastes the giant spoil tip at Redlake stood out from miles away, a blackened cone 100ft (30m) tall, more like a volcano than a man-made object. Runs of piping 7 miles long, laid beside the tramway, had carried the china-clay slurry down to Ivybridge from settling pits near the clay diggings. Dozens of workers, plastered in pale clay, lived rough lives out here. Redlake had been noisy, dusty, smelly, dirty. Today there was only the movement of wind in the grass and larks against the clouds.

Now the Two Moors Way kissed the Redlake tramway goodbye, wriggled through a gap and made off across the moor as a faint path. I followed it, nose to map. Then I remembered the

Right **Tramways were built all across Dartmoor during the 19th century in the rush to extract tin, granite and china clay**

Far right **William Keble Martin and his brothers incised and set up this altar cross in their home-made open-air chapel at 'Mattins Corner' under Huntingdon Warren**

Satmap Global Positioning System in my backpack. Gadgets and myself don't normally mix, but my wife Jane had set this ingenious machine up carefully before I set out, explaining which buttons to push and which to leave alone. I switched it on, and after a few seconds a map appeared on its tiny screen, followed by a line of red dots which leaped athletically from Ivybridge up to the very spot where I was standing and paused there, like a pack of dogs looking eagerly at their master. 'Can we go on, then? Please?' Faithful hounds, they followed me all the way for the rest of the day. Or perhaps I was following them. A zen riddle, if ever there was one.

The path led steeply down to an old clapper bridge across the River Avon, then on over squelchy ground in the lee of the domed hill of Huntingdon Warren. Moorland slopes walled in the valley, and a deep silence lay there. During the 19th century a warrener had run a farm in this isolated place, maintaining a living larder of thousands of rabbits in the pillow mounds he built all over the hill. There were altercations with poachers so nasty that lookouts had to be posted around the wall that encircled the place.

Down by the river stood the ancient Huntingdon Cross, chest-high, stumpy and short-armed, a ragged testament in the wilderness. And further up the bank I found crumbled walls in a little hollow, with a plain cross cut into a stone set up on end – all that remains of an informal and remarkable moorland chapel. William Keble, Arthur and Jack Martin, sons of the Vicar of Dartington, were keen outdoor types and devout Christians, and here in 1909 they established 'Mattins Corner', a place to give thanks in the open air during their camping expeditions to Huntingdon Warren. Keble Martin was a talented and passionate botanist and artist, and fame eventually found him at the advanced age of 88 when his beautiful and learned *The Concise British Flora in Colour* was published in 1965.

The rain came on now with proper Dartmoor gusto. I put up my hood and turned away eastwards. In an hour or so I'd be down in Scorriton; that night I'd be crushed to smithereens in the pub quiz at the Tradesmen's Arms, victim of a lack of knowledge of reality TV. For now it was enough to trudge the moorland track and watch the drops pearling on the fine gauze of spider webs among the heather.

From Scorriton onwards the sun decided to put its hat on and make an effort. The next few days passed before me in a pleasant haze. The route of the Two Moors Way – what I could recall of it – appeared hardly to have deviated in three decades, and I followed it half-dreaming in easy weather.

Mornings seemed mostly to be for the woods, for some reason; afternoons for the more open ground, though there wasn't much of that as I crossed the long stretch of country between Dartmoor and Exmoor. Lanes were tight and steep, hemmed in by tall hedgebanks where the multiple tongues of foxglove leaves, large and pale, showed where the deep pink bells would be nodding in high summer for travellers on the Two Moors Way. I remembered seeing the distant ancestors of those foxgloves three decades before, bowed under the weight of raindrops, in the lane that led to the tucked-away ford of Forda, and cracking heartless jokes at my father's expense about digitalis and old men's coronaries. When we'd walked these valleys together all that time ago, Dad would have been only a year older than I was now, I realised with a shock as I puffed up the hills around Morchard Bishop and Black Dog – much fitter, too, leaner and more abstemious. A proper walker. And what had I turned into, meanwhile?

Hmmmm… that didn't quite bear thinking about. Would my father, striding down the lane today from Hittisleigh Barton or poking around Clannaborough's simple little church under its lightning-shattered oaks, recognise me as a chip off the old block? I hoped so. But there was no asking him now.

Puffed white clouds were sailing eastwards in a very blue sky as I came to Hawkridge at sandwich time on the fourth day out, with the pale purple dome of Exmoor now suddenly dominant across the forward skyline. Thinking of Dad, I ducked into St Giles's Church, to find one side of the barley-sugar rim of the Norman font rubbed smooth by seven centuries of clergymen as they rested their bellies against the stonework to baptise – how many Exmoor infants? Hundreds of thousands, at least.

No tourists had ventured to Tarr Steps this early in the year. No-one paddled around or photographed the celebrated clapper bridge whose ingeniously piled slabs have carried travellers across the brown tides of the River Barle for three thousand years. I passed across and entered paradise – by some called the Barle Valley. These 4 miles of winding, deep-cut river valley, utterly lost in a cleft of the moor, took me most of that afternoon to thread. Wind rushed overhead, the bare trees sighed, the peaty river chuckled, a green light filtered down. I could not have felt more thoroughly sunk in depths and shadows if I had been treading the bottom of the sea. Richard Jefferies came here in the 1880s, drifting and dreaming and writing what would be collected together as *Field & Hedgerow*. Was there ever such a super-observantly honest yet poetic recorder of the minutiae of nature in English settings? Has any writer ever meditated so profoundly upon the structure of the colour brown?

Left **Pennywort, seen growing here in a drystone wall near Tarr Steps (pictured right). It's locally known as bachelor's buttons, cups-and-saucers, dimplewort, money-penny, pancakes, penny caps, penny plates and penny pies**

Rush! rush! like a mighty wind in the wood. It draws me on to the deep green pool inclosed about by rocks – a pool to stand near and think into. The purple rock, dotted with black moss; the white rock; the thin scarlet line; the green water; the overhanging tree; the verdant moss upon the bank; the lady fern – are there still. But I see also now a little pink somewhere in the water, much brown too, and shades I know no name for. The water is not green, but holds in solution three separate sets of colours. The confervae on the stones, the growths beneath at the bottom waving a little as the water swirls like minute seaweeds – these are brown and green and somewhat reddish too. Under water the red rock is toned and paler, but has deep black cavities. Next, the surface, continually changing as it rotates, throws back a different light, and thirdly, the oaks' yellow-green high up, the pale ash, the tender ferns drooping over low down confer their tints on the stream. So from the floor of the pool, from the surface, and from the adjacent bank, three sets of colours mingle. Washed together by the slow swirl, they produce a shade – the brown of the Barle – lost in darkness where the bank overhangs.

That night in Withypool, tucked way down in its cleft of the moor, a pink sky in the west promised a final day to expunge the memory of that purgatory of mist and rain 30 years ago. But by the time I woke, some joker had run round the horizon and painted fiery red all over the east. I didn't need Richard Jefferies to pick the bones out of that particular colour. It was on with the waterproofs and out up the infant Barle, disbelieving fury gathering under my bonnet, rain and wind once more in my face. Rain? No, sleet. What the bloody hell? Not again! Splashing down to Simonsbath, I cursed the moor. I could almost see Dad's bootmarks in the wet road surface, and hear his muffled sniff and mutter.

But things got better. They generally do. A pint of Guinness in the Simonsbath House Hotel (new name, new decor, no smell of damp, no Mother's Pride drivers) and I walked out into one of those sparkling transformations that descend like magic on the uncertain days between winter and spring.

The long tuffets of moor grass, bleached to silver by the winter's snow and rain, seemed to coruscate as the wind shook them. The Hoar Oak Water sparkled and leapt from ledge to rock, breaking and reforming. The path, slick with the morning's rain, slid and squelched underfoot.

Above **Otter romps in the 1979 film** *Tarka the Otter*

Above right **Henry Williamson's writing hut, built by the author at Ox's Cross above his home village of Georgeham**

Left **Led by Deadlock the hound, the otter hunters chased Tarka under Rolle Bridge in the final act of Henry Williamson's epic wildlife drama**

If Conan Doyle and his demonic hound had fixed the flavour of Dartmoor once and for all in my boyhood consciousness, it was Henry Williamson and his charming otter Tarka that informed my vision of Exmoor for ever more. Dartmoor the Dark, all cold peat and granite harshness; Exmoor the Fair, with the lightness and warmth of its underlying sandstone and its tree-lined coasts. Dartmoor of treeless, mist-wrapped wastes and jagged horizons; Exmoor of leafy combes and high ridges smoothly cut against the sky. I must have read *Tarka the Otter*, or had it read to me, half a dozen times before I ever set eyes on Exmoor. Whatever the moor had looked like, I would have seen it through Williamson spectacles – rose-tinted ones, at that. Tarka to me was the very spirit of Exmoor; even more so because of the realism Williamson insisted on infusing into every corner of his tale. Tarka went hungry; he lost his mate and his son; he knew terror and anguish; he bled and suffered. At the end of the story he died, drowning in the estuary of the Two Rivers in the act of dragging down to death his personal nemesis – a hound. There were no concessions to a child's supposed sensibilities, and I wanted none. I loved Tarka, vibrantly alive or tragically dead.

Nowadays a Tarka Trail circles Exmoor. The Two Moors Way runs to meet it at The Chains, high in the wildest part of the moor, and the two paths make their way down to the coast together. Tarka came this way, fat with frogs from Pinkworthy Pond, journeying down the goyal, or valley, of the Hoar Oak Water, the loneliest, bleakest cleft in the moor. Bright sunshine of absolute clarity bathed the goyal this afternoon, a rare delight. The long tuffets of moor grass, bleached to silver by the winter's snow and rain, seemed to coruscate as the wind shook them. The Hoar Oak Water sparkled and leapt from ledge to rock, breaking and reforming. The path, slick with the morning's rain, slid and squelched underfoot. I came a tremendous tumble somewhere along the way within sight of the sea, falling headlong into the grass. There was muck on my hands, and water in my eyes. I didn't care. This was what Dad and I would have seen and savoured, had we been blessed with an afternoon like this: mud on the boots, the sea up ahead, a jumping stream and a golden moor.

3

Mump, Tump, Moor and Tor

The angel stared down at me from the shadows. She wore a tight-fitting, scaly jerkin cut as low as her stomach, revealing a pert pair of bare, apple-shaped breasts. Her apple cheeks continued the theme.

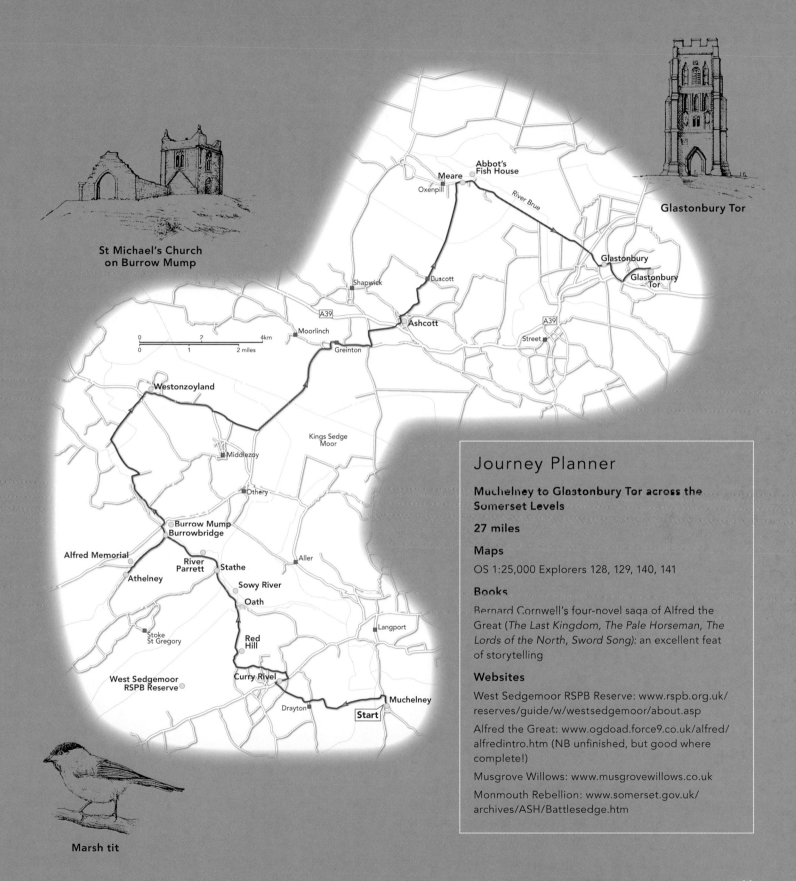

St Michael's Church
on Burrow Mump

Glastonbury Tor

Abbot's
Fish House

Meare

Oxenpill

River Brue

Glastonbury

Glastonbury
Tor

Shapwick

Duscott

A39

Moorlinch

Ashcott

Street

A39

0   ½   4km
0   1   2 miles

Greinton

Westonzoyland

Kings Sedge
Moor

Middlezoy

Othery

Burrow Mump
Burrowbridge

Alfred Memorial

Aller

River
Parrett

Stathe

Athelney

Sowy River

Oath

Stoke
St Gregory

Red
Hill

Langport

West Sedgemoor
RSPB Reserve

Curry Rivel

Drayton

Muchelney

Start

Marsh tit

Journey Planner

Muchelney to Glastonbury Tor across the Somerset Levels

27 miles

Maps

OS 1:25,000 Explorers 128, 129, 140, 141

Books

Bernard Cornwell's four-novel saga of Alfred the Great (*The Last Kingdom, The Pale Horseman, The Lords of the North, Sword Song*): an excellent feat of storytelling

Websites

West Sedgemoor RSPB Reserve: www.rspb.org.uk/ reserves/guide/w/westsedgemoor/about.asp

Alfred the Great: www.ogdoad.force9.co.uk/alfred/ alfredintro.htm (NB unfinished, but good where complete!)

Musgrove Willows: www.musgrovewillows.co.uk

Monmouth Rebellion: www.somerset.gov.uk/ archives/ASH/Battlesedge.htm

Perhaps the painter who depicted her thus scantily clad some time in the early 1600s – a daring gesture in those uncertain days of deadly religious intolerance – did really have apples in mind. The low peat moors of the Somerset Levels around the abbey and hamlet of Muchelney are *cordon bleu* cider country, after all; and what could be more enjoyable to picture than a village artist hard at work, his head full of Muchelney maidens, with a little smackerel of something in a nice cool jar at his elbow for extra inspiration?

I let myself out of the Church of St Peter and St Paul and wandered down the lane past the medieval Priest's House of grey mudstone. The strong sunlight of early summer picked out the glow of golden oolitic limestone, quarried from Ham Hill to frame the doorway and windows. The monastic communities of Middle Ages England may have been founded in poverty and chastity, but they knew how to make themselves comfortable in an age of domestic squalor and shabbiness. The remains of the monastery behind the church lay mostly at knee height, but the ante-rooms and kitchen of the monks' refectory, their cloister arches and their reredorter, or privy, stood in impressive, beautifully fitted stonework of gold and grey. It was a theme I was to find repeated all across the Somerset Levels, on the hillocks that locals call mumps, tumps and tors, and on low rises of ground above the moors, nowadays flat green fields but back then a maze of tidal marshes and fens – the skilful handiwork of the monks and their craftsmen as they built and maintained their citadels of prayer among the devil-haunted mires.

The devil for me this morning resided in my mode of transport. 'I'll do this journey by bike,' I'd gaily announced, thinking of the flat terrain of the Levels and forgetting all about the generally disastrous conjunction of a modern bicycle saddle – unyielding, narrow, anatomically divisive – with my tender posterior. Yes, Levels roads are easy, mostly, where they are not potholed or flooded or rising up unexpected hills that a glance at the map would never lead you to anticipate. I won't go on about it. Suffice it to say that it was a very, very sore and weary man who hobbled up Glastonbury Tor at the end of the day with the gait of a rodeo rider straddling two broncos at once – bucking broncos, at that.

With the bike gears crackling like bacon under a grill I set off from Muchelney along the lane to Curry Rivel. Hay meadows lay on either hand, dark green and ready for cutting, pale lemon-yellow where they had been freshly mown. There were smells of silage, of river mud, of cut grass and cow dung. The lane verges were riotously overgrown, twin linear forests of cow parsley whose frothy white blooms are known to Somerset children as 'gypsy lace'. Beyond Curry Rivel I topped Red Hill and went sailing down between orchid banks onto the Levels proper, the great boat-shaped nature reserve of West Sedgemoor. There are few wet meadow systems left in Britain, and the Somerset Levels represent the

Far left **A pair of juicy apples, just ripe for the picking – now what exactly did the painter of Muchelney's angels have in mind?**

Left **Unyielding, narrow, anatomically divisive – the author entrusts his tender posterior to a bicycle seat to explore the Somerset Levels**

Above **Dour grey mudstone for the walls, beautiful golden hamstone for the window and door frames: a contrast effectively employed wherever the monks built in this region**

largest – an ancient tidal flood plain drained over the centuries, where sodden peat underlies species-rich grasslands whose fields are separated from each other by the 'wet hedges' of water-filled ditches – rhynes, as they are called around here. Birdlife is abundant, waterlife teems; dragonflies, bees, darters and flies put a drowsy humming into the peculiarly thick air of the fields and damp carr woodlands all summer long. Nineteenth-century peat cutting, 20th-century drainage nearly did for the integrity of this delicately balanced ecosystem. Twenty-first-century chemical agriculture and over-development might finish the job. But for now the Levels remain as they are, partly exploited, partly preserved, wholly fascinating if you like a forkful of subtlety and a pinch of mystery in your landscape.

The road to Oath lay long and straight. On the right, chemically fertilised grassland of uniform bright green, the occasional rogue flowerhead standing out like a jewel in a setting of dross. On the left, the moor reserve; cows chin-deep in grasses of a dozen species and hues, all spangled white, pink and yellow with buttercups, dandelion clocks, orchids and milkmaids. The willows along the road had been freshly pollarded, the white stumps of their severed rods as raw and damp as new wounds. A row of these club-shaped trees stood aslant, half- sunk in the soft peat of a rhyne bank, all in line like old sergeants waiting at a casualty clearing station, their lopped limbs neatly stacked on the ground in front of them. I stopped the bike and leaned it against a willow too old and spread for pollarding, to hear a marsh tit among the leaves giving out a shrill but sweet *tee-too*!

The road led on through Oath and Stathe, theoretical places too scattered and sparse to be called villages. Twin watercourses were my guides: the snaky, rushy, half-choked River Parrett,

and its shadow sister the man-made Sowy River, straight, wide and clean. If there's one thing the Somerset Levels have in natural superabundance, it is water. How to maintain it there in useful but not overwhelming quantities, how to shepherd and safeguard and cage this wild and precious element, has been the study and preoccupation of 20 generations. Sluices, rhynes, ditches and banks, locks and gates, pumps and weirs – these are the Levels' circulatory system, with engineers as the physicians who keep it all going round and round, on and on. Back in AD878 when the King of Wessex, Alfred the Great, was skulking hereabouts as a hunted man in flight from the victorious Danes, there wasn't so much as a pump or a sluice in all the region. It was just as well for Alfred, and for posterity – if there had been a proper drainage system in place, if the Levels had not been a maze of tidal marshes and meres impenetrable to all but the web-footed locals, the Danes would surely have found, caught and killed the Wessex monarch, and Anglo-Saxon culture would have been snuffed out for ever.

At Burrowbridge I turned aside and pedalled down a back road, looking for Athelney and the Alfred Memorial. Athelney must be another Levels village more substantial in theory than in reality. I couldn't find the place, anyway. But I did stumble on the Alfred Memorial, a modest obelisk on a rise of ground behind a farmhouse, ringed by woolly brown bullocks with gently enquiring eyes and runny noses. It was upon this very spot that Alfred burned his hostess's cakes, according to legend, and got a smack round the ear for his pains. More historically, this tiny tump in the marshes – now an islet in a sea of grazing fields – was the place where the fugitive Alfred hid and knew despair early in AD878, and from where he somehow dredged up the will and courage to mount a counter-push against the Danes that culminated in victory at the Battle of Ethandun (maybe near Westbury in Wiltshire, though some Somerset romantics still like to think it was at Edington on the moors) in May that year. The Treaty of Wedmore and other subsequent pacts, and the baptising of the Danish leader Guthrum with Alfred as his Godfather, saw peace established – albeit shakily.

I found the inscription on the marble plaque of the obelisk weathered almost beyond reading. Copying it into my notebook, I wondered for how much longer visitors would be able to make out its noble sentiments.

> *King Alfred the Great in the Year of our Lord 879, having been defeated by the Danes, fled for refuge to the Forest of Athelney where he lay concealed from his enemies for the space of a whole year. He soon after regained possession of the throne, and in grateful remembrance of the protection he had received under the favour of Heaven, erected a monastery on this spot & endowed it with all the lands contained in the Isle of Athelney. To perpetuate the memorial of so remarkable an incident in the life of that illustrious prince, this edifice was founded by John Slade Esq of Mansel, the proprietor of Athelney Farm & Lord of the Manor of North Petherton, AD1801.*

Two hillocks in the Somerset Levels carry ruined church towers. One is the most celebrated and myth-laden hilltop in Somerset, if not in the whole of the West Country – Glastonbury Tor in far-famed Avalon, the prize at the end of this bicycle ride. The other is Burrow Mump. Who knows of St Michael's Church on Burrow Mump, other than those who live near enough to see its roofless walls and tower on their daily skyline? Yet it makes just as striking an impression on a Levels traveller as its more famous sister to the east. I hid the bike at the foot of the Mump and climbed the hill through drifts of scabious and buttercups. The church proved to be another grey and gold stone building, a hollow medieval tower and shell of walls commanding a most sensational view across the moors. Any mump, tump or tor in such a low-lying landscape is an obvious vantage point, and Burrow Mump has been used in this way since time out of mind. There's evidence of Roman occupation on the hilltop. It was one of the places fortified by King

Left **A classic Somerset Levels scene: flat grazing fields, a flooded river, and a line of pollarded willows beginning to sprout new sprigs of withy**

Above **'Have you let they cakes burn, you varmint?'** **'Oh, sorry, my good woman, I was miles away... ' Smack!**

Right **The ruin of St Michael's Church on Burrow Mump, a vantage point over the surrounding flat lands throughout history**

Alfred as a high point from which to get early warning of any movement of Danish shipping up the sluggish fen rivers of Parrett and Tone. The Normans refortified it with a castle before the monks built their chapel up here. From the empty arch of the chapel window I could see another tall tower rising in the north, my next aiming point in this long day of highs and lows.

Just before reaching St Mary's Church at Westonzoyland, I pulled up in the lane at the sign of L.A. Musgrove, Willow Makers. Those Levels willows are not pollarded for nothing. The long shoots, or withies, are famous materials for basket weaving, fence making, the construction of lobster pots and garden arbours, and all manner of other arty and crafty uses. I'd long wanted to see inside one of the dwindling number of Levels willow workshops, and here was young Jack Musgrove, son of Mike Musgrove the current owner, grandson of Arthur 'Les' Musgrove and great-grandson of founder Arthur 'Sam' Musgrove, all ready and willing to show me about, unexpected and uninvited as I had turned up. There are 60 different sorts of willow, I learned, from thick ones used for ornamental domes and sheep hurdles to thin, pliable ones handy for baskets and for arts and crafts. You plant them out in long beds and harvest them in the winter – 'used to be by hand,' said Jack. 'Yes,' struck in his Grandma, 'and what a hard job that was. That would make your arms ache!' Nowadays the withies are harvested by Mike Musgrove with a machine that cuts, binds and stacks them ready for collection. You dry them, steam them and skin them in a clattering stripping machine. Then you season them. Then after a time, you work with them.

The most celebrated piece of work to use Musgrove willow is Serena de la Hey's extraordinary Willow Man, 40ft (12m) tall, who runs athletically out of the Levels beside the M5 motorway near Bridgwater, startling and delighting north-bound drivers. Work at Musgrove's today, though, centred round the construction of a willow coffin, with foreman Dominic teaching Jack and his colleague James how to weave the whippy stems. 'We're the only willow makers still using a natural wood-fired boiler for the steaming,' said Jack's mother Ellen. 'That's what I like about this business – it's carbon-neutral, it's clean and it's useful.'

The Somerset Levels have always been odd ground. People here are disinclined to follow the herd. If more of the local farmers and small tradesmen had been disposed to listen to reason in the summer of 1685, the region might have been spared the horrors that were visited on it during and after the hopeless rebellion initiated and led by James Scott, Duke of Monmouth. The Duke, illegitimate son of King Charles II, landed from exile at Lyme Regis on 11 June of that year in an attempt to wrest the throne from his uncle James, who had occupied it since the death of Charles in February. But Monmouth was on a hiding to nothing. With a ragtag and bobtail army of some 3,000 poorly equipped peasants, small-time merchants and artisans gathered along the way, under the handicap of clumsy planning and poor communications, on 5 July he gambled everything in a night attack on his opponents just north of Westonzoyland. The two armies were fairly evenly balanced as to numbers, but the King's men, a force of foot, horse and dragoons, were far better trained and supplied. Forewarned by the premature explosion of clumsily handled pistols at dead of night as Monmouth's men tried to cross the 8ft (2.5m) ditch of Langmoor Rhyne, the loyalist army withstood the rebels' initial advance

Right **Many uses of the withy: a willow coffin is painstakingly constructed by hand in the weaving shed of L.A. Musgrove, Willow Makers of Westonzoyland**

Bottom left **Bunches of cut withy are propped upright with their butts in water to prevent them drying out and to keep the sap high**

Bottom right **Freshly pollarded willows lean together on the soft peat bank of a rhyne**

and then waited till first light on 6 July. They soon outflanked the peasant horde, and in a grim rehearsal for the Battle of Culloden 80 years later, they routed, rode down and brutally destroyed the fleeing rustics.

No-one has computed accurately the number of rebels captured and killed at the Battle of Sedgemoor, but it's pretty certain that the King's forces suffered about 50 dead and something over 200 wounded in all, while about a third of the rebels were slaughtered on the battlefield or in the surrounding countryside. Another 500 were captured, many of them being held for days in St Mary's Church with no food, water or medical attention. Monmouth himself fled, and was captured two days later. Nine days after the battle,

after pleading abjectly but unsuccessfully for his life before his uncle James, he was beheaded on Tower Hill in London, a grisly and badly botched execution in which it took eight axe blows to sever Monmouth's head. Eventually retribution came to the West Country, the notorious Bloody Assize under Judge Jeffreys, which resulted in mass hangings in towns all across the region that were deemed to have given the rebels help and comfort. On the wall of St Mary's I found a list like the tolling of a bell: a dozen men each at Lyme, Sherborne, Poole and Weymouth, 13 at Bridport, six at Wareham, one at Exeter, 14 at Taunton, and many, many more. Dorchester, the first town to feel the full weight of the King's desire for revenge, saw 74 men publicly executed, most by being hung, drawn and quartered – a barbaric death, and a salutary one,

as the victim's head and body parts were tarred and taken for display at corners and gates all over the area. Perhaps 200 rebels, or supposed rebels, or those who had helped the Monmouth cause, were executed, and nearly a thousand sentenced to transportation with hard labour for ten years or upwards.

The West Country never forgot the terrible events of 1685, and even on this still, sunny afternoon in Westonzoyland the stones and woodwork of St Mary's seemed to hold ghosts. I went out into the sunlight and rode away as quickly as I could. It was a good 6 miles by main road to the turn-off for Ashcott and the moor road to Meare, and all the way I rode with a head full of pities and horrors, while big lorries blew past with inches to spare. By the time I got to Meare I was saddle-sore, leg weary and bone tired. But the sight of the medieval manor house with its ecclesiastical buttresses and pointed windows revived my spirits. In the field nearby stood a rugged, bulgy building of rough grey stone, evidently of the same era as the manor, labelled 'Abbot's Fish Ho' on my Ordnance Survey map.

There was a tale here, and a roadside information board supplied it. The Fish House contained a hall, a bedroom and a garderobe, or long-drop latrine, on the first floor, a kitchen and storeroom below – a dignified and well-appointed residence in the early 14th century, when the head fisherman employed by the Abbot of Glastonbury lived here. Such a man was an important figure, responsible for supplying the great monastery at Glastonbury with one of its most useful and valued commodities. The Abbot might not have been the easiest of masters, it seems. The story of the ongoing row between successive Abbots of Glastonbury, Bishops of Bath and Wells and Deans of Wells over the ownership of the Isle of Meare is an extraordinary one. The isle was a plum possession, a source of meat, wool, hides, fish, timber, willow and peat. Everyone wanted it, and no-one would relent. The Abbot's men smashed up the Bishop's fish weir and piggery. The Bishop's men retaliated by destroying seven of the Abbot's weirs and uprooting his fruit trees. The Dean's men stole peat from the Abbot's moor. Then someone set the moor on fire. The bishop excommunicated the Abbot and his men. Eventually sanity prevailed. In 1327 the moor was divided up by a boundary bank, each claimant knew which side not to trespass onto, and an uneasy peace took hold.

At journey's end an hour later, looking out across the moors from a vantage point by the hollow-eyed tower on Glastonbury Tor, I thought of the conflicts great and petty that this flat and unemphatic landscape had witnessed down the centuries. Battles of wits between Danes and Saxons, battles of blood and savagery between rebels and King's men. Squabbles of cupidity and stupidity between powerful prelates and their oath-bound followers. Unremembered contests between forgotten British tribesmen for the hilltop lookouts. And interwoven all through these quarrels, the long battle without an end between man and the encroaching water. There was a gleam of floodwater from the old peat diggings at Ham Wall, a glint of ruler-straight rhynes running northwest towards the sea. I sat hugging my knees and watching the sun dip to the water. If King Arthur lies sleeping under Glastonbury Tor, as he's said to do, what better prospect could there be to greet the Once and Future King at his long-anticipated awakening hour?

The Oldest Road in Britain

Setting off at six on a hot summer's morning to tramp Britain's oldest road from end to end, I was rather smugly sure of my exclusive claim on the secret of the Harroway. Nobody had walked the route for a long time, I was certain of that. Nobody seemed even to know it was there.

Journey Planner

The Harroway from Surrey to the Devon coast

150 miles

Maps

OS 1:50,000 Landrangers 183–86, 192–94; 1:25,000 Explorers 145, 144, 131, 130, 143, 142, 129, 117, 116

Books

Ancient Trackways of Wessex by H. W. Timperley and Edith Brill (Nonsuch Publishing, 2005)

Websites

Weyhill Fair: www.southernlife.org.uk/weyhill_fair.htm

Cadbury Castle: www.britannia.com/history/arthur/cadcast. html

Following the Harroway: The course of the Harroway is sketched out in words and on a map in *Ancient Trackways of Wessex*. Explorers searching for the elusive old road today will find it disguised, in various stretches, as dual carriageway, A and B road, urban through-road, country lane and Byway Open to All Traffic (BOAT) more or less plagued by 4X4 drivers, as well as bridleway, footpath and faint scar in the landscape

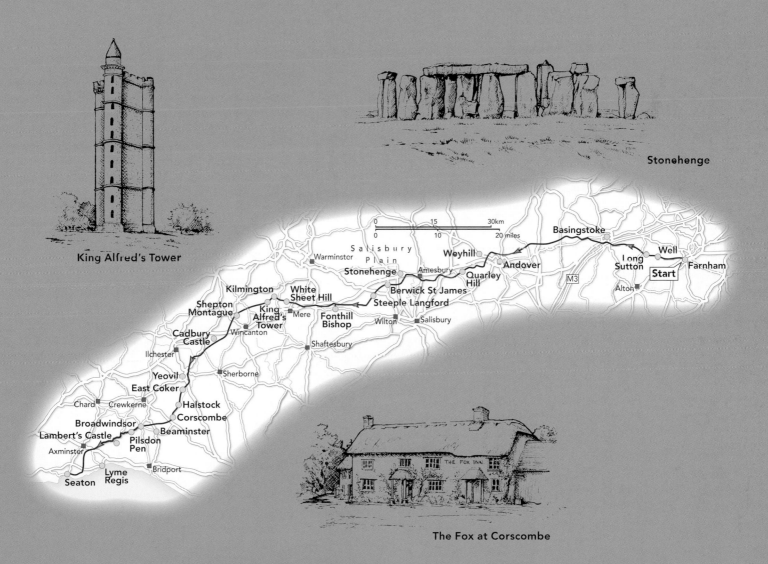

King Alfred's Tower

Stonehenge

The Fox at Corscombe

I had been searching for the old road, on maps and in books, ever since opening a map of the Hampshire downs and noticing the name 'Harroway' printed along a trackway in the Gothic script with which the Ordnance Survey marks something of historic interest. But no guidebook to the Harroway existed. I found only tantalising snippets: single lines or half-paragraphs, or a bare mention of its name. Then, at the back of a friend's bookshelf, I stumbled across *Ancient Trackways of Wessex*, written in the 1960s by H. W. Timperley and Edith Brill, a husband-and-wife team. There the whole course of the Harroway was discussed in scholarly fashion. Now I had some solid references to work with, I began to assemble a sketchy picture. Gradually the Harroway shook off its shadows and revealed itself as a great 150-mile highway, in use for at least 5,000 years, running clean across England from Seaton in Devon through Dorset, Somerset, Wiltshire and Hampshire into Surrey. At Farnham it joined the ancient trackway now called the North Downs Way, and ran for another 150 miles down to a terminus somewhere on the shores of the English Channel near Dover.

From short stretches of pathway between isolated settlements the old road had been cobbled together, piece by piece, through the late Stone Age and the Bronze Age, until it had become a constantly travelled, coherent route. It kept as much as possible to the high ground, away from the dangers of the forests and bogs in the valleys, up where travellers could see trouble approaching, and – equally important – spy out their route from landmark to landmark.

It was Cornish tin that turned the patchwork of local paths into a Bronze Age long-distance route, perhaps 3,000 years ago: tin that came by ship from the mines at Marazion to Seaton, to be dispersed up country through the bronze-smiths' skill among the communities all along the Harroway from Devon to Kent. The Harroway's fortunes fluctuated through local trade and war, with the passage of stone for Neolithic and Bronze Age monuments, labour for Iron Age forts, bricks and tiles for Roman villas. The Saxons named it Harroway, or Hoary Way – the Old Road. In medieval times it was a great packhorse road, and a drovers' greenway that saw the movement of millions upon millions of beasts; later, a celebrated coaching route between London and the West Country. Now, the maps told me, the old road still snaked across the hills and through the valleys, under tarmac in some places, under grass in others; here a roaring section of the A303 dual carriageway, there a country lane, there again a footpath in remote woodland. The itch in my feet became too much to bear.

A red-stockinged rambler with guidebook in hand was striding off eastwards from Farnham along the well-signposted North Downs Way as I prepared to set off along the Harroway on that first morning. For all the certainty of his route, I felt the luckier man as I set my face to the west and its unmarked, untried ground. The map showed a dozen miles of country lane, rising a little to the north and threading through a couple of tiny villages, Well and Long Sutton.

At Well, there was… a well. It stood at the crossroads on a little green, the gift of some philanthropic Victorian squire. But who knows for how many centuries the drovers on the Harroway – and on the ancient Maulthway, or Sheep Road, that joins it here – halted their flocks and herds to drink at Well? By Long Sutton village pond I had my breakfast biscuit pinched

Top right **The Harroway near Five Lanes End, a white groove hollowed in the soft chalk landscape by hooves, feet and wheels through 5,000 years**

Bottom right **In summer the hum of insects forms a constant background note along the wide verges of the Harroway, where umbellifers produce a soft foam of pungent white blooms**

from my fingers by a streetwise duck. He fled, chased by jealous rivals, and all but choked to death on the awkward beakful before swallowing it whole. A fine moral lesson that would have been appreciated by the pilgrims who passed through medieval Long Sutton on their way from Winchester to the shrine of St Thomas à Becket at Canterbury.

After 10 miles of tarmac it was a pleasure to strike off the road on a stretch of the Harroway not much changed in atmosphere from packhorse days. A rutted, chalky track, it climbed to the heights and stayed there. I swung along under a roasting sun and exuberant lark-song, trying to date, by rough rule of thumb, the hedges that flanked the Harroway – every major species in a measured hundred yards equalling a century of age. Hazel, holly, elm, elder, oak, sweet-scented may and ragged yew gave a planting date back in Plantagenet times. Yews were often planted, or preserved, along ancient trackways, both as shelter and landmarks and as good-luck totems for the traveller. They stood darkly in the hedges as I followed two girls clopping on horses up to Five Lanes End.

Hollowed many yards deep by the hooves, feet and wheels of the centuries, here the old road took on dignity and mystery under a canopy of enormous beech trees. The five lanes, chalk-white sunken tracks, came winding up from the valleys to their junction on this high saddle of ground. Under the branches were views over fields green with corn and yellow with oil-seed rape, out to horizons a dozen miles away. Five Lanes End represented an ideal meeting place for travellers in days when any journey was a dangerous one. Here they commanded a clear sight of the entire country around, while staying hidden themselves below the sunken lane banks under the trees. Five Lanes End is a triumphant shout of the Harroway as survivor in the landscape. The strangled groan of its passage through the southern outskirts of Basingstoke, though, makes a sad contrast.

The once pleasant market town has swelled, burst and engulfed its surroundings in the past few decades: a scapegoat and folk devil for all the cosy villages round about. 'At least it's not as bad as Basingstoke' has become a local saying. The town's nickname, born of a thousand new road roundabouts, is Doughnut City. Roads, roundabouts, a glimpse of raw

housing behind a blank-faced fence; more roads, another roundabout. Under the concrete and municipal grass, I trod the ancient Harroway as straight as a die. Clues to its course were thinly scattered – 'The Harrow Way' on a roadside nameplate, an old yew in a hedge, the name 'Pack Lane' where the old road shouldered a final burden of bungalows before shrugging them off at the western end of the town.

Out of Basingstoke and up onto the downs I trudged like a robot, broiling in the full sun, mesmerised by the Harroway's tricks with the landscape. Over a ridge a new view opened up, a tarmac lane winding past a duck pond and slatted wooden barns to a crossroads. Switch on the mental scanner, and the old road gradually revealed itself by centuries-old hollies and yews, a hollow groove in a hillside, a circle of grass lumpy with bricks where the roads met and a drovers' inn once stood. On and on I went, following the old road in a long sweep over the downs above Overton, a stretch unchanged since drovers used the route. Ancient yews, wild service trees and spindle lined the 30ft (12m) wide hedges – a lonely, silent trackway in deep country. Here, on the verge of the old road, a brace of skinny lurchers came snarling from the hedge as I passed. Beyond them a knot of leather-brown men sat smoking outside a caravan flashy with chrome trimming: the Harroway's contemporary long-distance travellers.

I covered 25 miles that first day, and my legs let me know I had been a fool the following morning as I winced out of Overton, trying to tread my blisters into numbness again. Back on the Harroway on a burning blue day I walked down a cool avenue of beech and yew where squirrels bounced from branch to branch. All too soon the old road left its green tunnel and ran in the open as a tarmac lane past Dirty Corner – named after the didicoys, or gypsies. At Chapmansford the chapmen, or pedlars, would hoist their packs to wade thigh-deep across the firm gravel shelf in the slippery bed of the Bourne Rivulet. The Harroway snaked about in the valley bottoms, straightening on each hill crest to align itself once more with the distant landmark of flat-topped Quarley Hill. Through the industrial sprawl of Andover's outskirts it stuttered, its line only to be guessed at, to meet the A303 road near Weyhill. And here I stopped, beaten to a standstill by the mid-afternoon heat.

Weyhill these days is a ghost of a place, a straggle of houses along a bypassed section of the A303. The lifeblood of passing trade now flows down the dual carriageway artery a mile to the south. There have been no fairs here for 60 years, but Michaelmas Fair at Weyhill was in its day the greatest sheep fair in the south of England. Half a million beasts would be driven along the Harroway and the half-dozen other old roads that meet here, to be sold along with cattle, cheese, hops and countless gallons of beer in ten October days of frantic moneymaking and merry-making.

My intention to press on down the Harroway towards Salisbury Plain and Stonehenge withered in the afternoon sun. Instead I got into a conversation with an old man in a farmyard by the road. It was a piece of good luck, for he had known Weyhill Fair in his youth, and carried memories of his father's descriptions of the fair before World War I when carters and shepherds would stand in line to be hired, holding their whips and crooks as badges of trade. Local farmers gave their workers 'Michaelmas money' in lieu of a harvest bonus and to make some amends for the rest of the underpaid year. The Weyhill farmer and his Dad had seen it all between them: the drunken brawls, the hop sacks piled in long roadside sheds, the funfair, the rigged fights in the boxing booths, the sheep jamming the Harroway solid and whitening the Weyhill fields. I idled away the rest of the day contentedly, mining his stack of stories. Stonehenge could wait.

Left Sheep farmers still use the Hampshire lanes to move their flocks from field to field with great efficiency

Right Hucksters, musicians, boxers and wrestlers, cheapjacks and playmongers all made their way to Wiltshire each October to shake a bob or two out of the credulous rustics gathered at Weyhill Fair

Next morning the Stonehenge monoliths looked at their best. Beyond them a pale sun was rising behind streamers of cloud, touching their edges with lines of steely light. Looming on the skyline the circle had looked large, a dominant thing in a subdued landscape. Close up it seemed both small and solid, surprisingly complete. Stonehenge stands where many ancient trackways meet; the Spaghetti Junction of Neolithic times. Some of these old roads were paths drawn to the magnetic attraction of the monument, so visible and powerful a focal point in the wide plain. But the Harroway was probably already thousands of years old when the chiefs of the Wessex culture, the high peak of Bronze Age development, ordered the completion of the outer ring of Stonehenge with its continuous lintel 'roof', and the erection of the five great trilithons, or doorways, at the heart of the structure, about 4,000 years ago.

The old road snaked away south over Normanton Down among those ancient aristocrats' burial mounds, a brave white zigzag of chalk dust on the smooth face of a rolling green landscape. I tramped it through a long day, hardly touching tarmac at all. The Harroway, here named Muddy Lane, dipped and rose across the valley-bottom village of Berwick St James and through Steeple Langford, where the wanderings of the River Wylye made a marshy bottom famed and feared among winter-travelling packmen and drovers.

Right **Bring the flower book when you explore the Harroway – dozens of beautiful species thrive in the overhung margins under the trees**

Far right **'Rapunzel, Rapunzel, let down your hair!' Alfred Tower is a great spot for children to give their fancies free rein**

Steeple Langford's 17th-century rector, Henry Collier, was thrown out of his living by Puritan zealots and forced to wander the old roads of the downs with his wife and 11 children. I wonder if the Colliers ever looked as bedraggled as the New Age travellers I came across, camped by the Harroway in their ramshackle old buses. One destination board read 'Don't Panic'. Dishevelled men with dreadlocks and in baggy, home-made sweaters came wandering up to stare gently, like mild-mannered cows at a gate. I set myself with anticipation for a round of tales about the mystical significance of the Harroway, but they had never even heard of it. 'Yeah, so this is an old trackway, right?' muttered one.

Magnificently hedged with may, its grass verges thick with yellow archangel and garlic-stinking jack-by-the-hedge, the Harroway swept grandly south and west for mile after mile, its final run on the high chalk downs. I slept that night just off the old road at Fonthill Bishop, and the next day made 20 miles along my favourite section of the Harroway. No great detective work was needed to decipher a route scored into the downland ridges through two centuries of use as a major coaching road between London and the West Country. Any Georgian coachman returning here with a ghostly four-in-hand would know his way at once. Over Charnage Down and Mere Down it ran, passing milestones put up when the route was turnpiked in 1750. Under their scabs of grey and yellow lichen, the mason's lettering was still sharp enough to read: XX miles from Sarum, XCIX from London.

Ticking off the miles by way of these old stones, I raced along, blown by a warm breeze, to the top of White Sheet Hill. On the summit the ramparts of an Iron Age hillfort stand alongside Bronze Age burial mounds and Stone Age enclosure banks. For at least 5,000 years men have been digging and mounding on White Sheet Hill. Today it was the engineers of Wessex Water, bedding in a new main. They sat drinking their tea and looking out on a landscape clothed differently but unaltered in shape since Neolithic labourers leaned on their digging sticks up here to rest and gaze. The chalk downs rose into their last rounded crests, and swept down to lose themselves in limestone country. Somerset lay spread out below, a network of close, intimate wooded valleys, warmer and less dramatic than the high downs.

Now called Long Lane, the Harroway sloped steeply off the brow of White Sheet Hill and made for the Red Lion at Kilmington, an old coaching and droving inn, where an elderly man once told me that his father drove cattle to market in London along 'that old Roman road'. In a deep green tunnel of oaks and holly trees the old road ran on, to come to Alfred Tower on the crest of Kingsettle Hill.

Built in 1772 by Henry Hoare – 'Henry the Magnificent' of nearby Stourhead House – to glorify both King Alfred and himself, the three-sided red-brick tower shoots skyward for 160ft (49m), window above window, topped with a candle-snuffer cone; a fairytale Rapunzel tower. I climbed the twisty

Anyone with a pure heart who bathes their eyes at Arthur's Well on Midsummer Eve will see the sides of the hill turn as clear as glass to reveal King Arthur and his knights sleeping within.

stair. At the top the wind shoved me sideways, blurring the view with tears. What a view, too: 80 miles, maybe, from Glastonbury Tor to the Dorset coast. To the east I looked my last on those smooth and airy chalk uplands that had already carried me nearly a hundred exhilarating miles.

The curator led me across the road and into the trees. He poked with his shoe at an ancient carved stone, half-buried in the undergrowth. 'Could be a plague stone,' he said. 'They swapped goods and money across it when the Black Death was on, keeping well away from each other. But some say it's the old boundary stone between Wiltshire, Somerset and Dorset. You stand on it, blow a kiss into your own county, fart towards another, and piss into the one you don't like.'

On Kingsettle Hill the Harroway changes name again and becomes the Hardway, with good reason. In spite of cobbles, this one-in-four haul up the hillside must always have been a struggle for man, beast and cart. In winter it became an ice slide, in summer a dust funnel. Cars still go down cautiously, in second gear. I skimmed down the Hardway under force of gravity, and on through the steepening, foreshortening valleys to Shepton Montague and the well-kept beer in the Montague Arms, another old droving inn.

By ten o'clock the following morning I was up on the Iron Age ramparts of Cadbury Castle, looking south towards the grey hills of Dorset as they marched ever closer. Arthurian legend lies thick

on the old fortifications of the hilltop and on the surrounding countryside. Anyone with a pure heart who bathes their eyes at Arthur's Well on Midsummer Eve will see the sides of the hill turn as clear as glass to reveal King Arthur and his knights sleeping within. The truth about Arthur is lost beyond unearthing, though archaeologists tried their best in a major excavation of Cadbury Castle in 1966–70. They found the remains of a great hall; perhaps the Camelot court of the 6th-century *dux bellorum,* or Romano-British battle leader, that Arthur may have been.

Stay high, stay safe and dry, had been the rule all along for route-finding on the Harroway. At Cadbury, seduced by that high-level view over flat and easy-looking lands to the south, I made a rash decision to try the low road. I paid for my poor judgement with a morning's floundering in trackless cornfields, followed by an afternoon's trudge on main roads in the face of heavy lorries, through Yeovil and out the other side, to fetch up, breathless and cross after 20 more or less unpleasant miles, in the dimity charm of East Coker.

The following day, though, was a delight. I drifted south by unfrequented, flowery side roads through Halstock and Corscombe. In the high-hedged, rutted lane above Corscombe I hung over a gate and idled away the best part of an hour on one of the Harroway's prize views – down beyond three old oaks and across a valley dotted with sheep to the village lying on its rise of ground under an immense green ridge hanging halfway up the sky.

I stopped at the Fox Inn at Corscombe for a quick glass of beer. The bar was as cool and still as well water, the bread, cheese and chutney all fresh and tangy, the pint drawn straight from the barrel as brown and rich as a nut. Then I climbed up over the ridge, sweating out the ale, and on along the edge of the down, looking over Beaminster and out to where the sea flashed in the dips of the cliffs. That night I slept beyond Broadwindsor, looking forward proudly to arriving at journey's end in Seaton the following day, the first traveller to pass the length of the Harroway since the Lord alone knew when. But at breakfast my host sprang a nasty surprise. A gentleman from Marlborough, a Mr Hearn, had stayed with her not six weeks before. What had he been up to? Walking an old road, he had said – the Harroway, as he had called it.

That took some of the gilt off the gingerbread. The shadow of Mr Hearn lay over the landscape all day, the spoilsport who had beaten me to it, Amundsen to my Scott. Compensation came in the stunning view from the top of Pilsdon Pen, another in the line of Iron Age forts along the Harroway, and at 909ft (277m) the highest point in Dorset. The Vale of Marshwood undulated away into the haze of distance, with the old road plain to be seen as it clung characteristically to a neck of high ground, through Marshwood village and on under the wooded crown of Lambert's Castle, yet another Iron Age camp.

Now the Harroway took on a purposeful stride again, forging west under great beech trees and swinging south over a dry heath to reach the coastal road just inland of the Lyme Regis Undercliff. At Seaton I went off to dip my feet ritually in the sea, thinking back over the 150 miles of long and winding road. Under all its disguises, the Harroway is still a road with a purpose and direction and almost all, from snaky lane to chalky track and green, grassy pathway, had been a delight to walk.

I soaked my battered feet, their Harroway itch well and truly scratched, and dredged up an inward salute to the mysterious Mr Hearn. All right, Mr H; good, wasn't it?

5

Mud, Marsh and Creek

Mile for mile, creek for creek, the moody and muddy Essex shore of the Thames estuary downriver of London is some of the least explored coastal country in Britain. The Thames of Dickens and Conan Doyle, the bleak romance of the region immortalised in the songs of Canvey Island songwriter Wilko Johnson, are for connoisseurs of unregarded treasure.

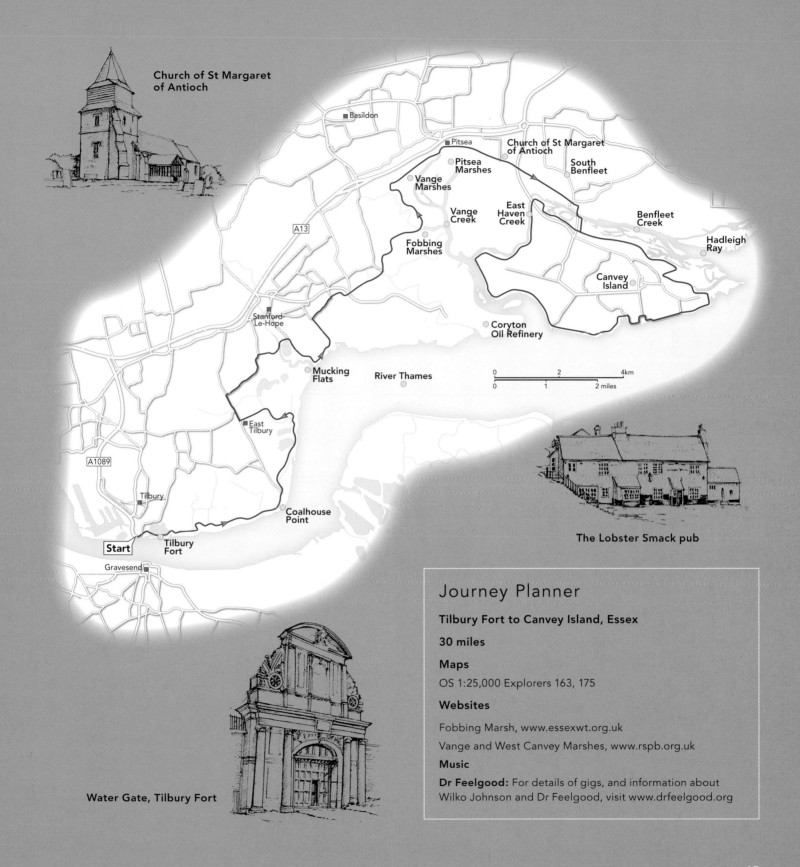

Church of St Margaret
of Antioch

Basildon

Pitsea

Church of St Margaret
of Antioch

South
Benfleet

Pitsea
Marshes

Vange
Marshes

Vange
Creek

East
Haven
Creek

Benfleet
Creek

Hadleigh
Ray

A13

Fobbing
Marshes

Canvey
Island

Stanford-
Le-Hope

Coryton
Oil Refinery

Mucking
Flats

River Thames

0   2   4km
0   1   2 miles

East
Tilbury

A1089

Tilbury

Coalhouse
Point

The Lobster Smack pub

Start

Tilbury
Fort

Gravesend

Water Gate, Tilbury Fort

Journey Planner

Tilbury Fort to Canvey Island, Essex

30 miles

Maps

OS 1:25,000 Explorers 163, 175

Websites

Fobbing Marsh, www.essexwt.org.uk

Vange and West Canvey Marshes, www.rspb.org.uk

Music

Dr Feelgood: For details of gigs, and information about
Wilko Johnson and Dr Feelgood, visit www.drfeelgood.org

The brent geese shouldn't have been on the mud flats by Tilbury docks this late into spring. By all the laws of nature they ought to have been long gone up north to the marshy Arctic coasts of northern Russia, on the lookout for sites to nest and breed in the two-month window of opportunity allowed them by the short, intense Siberian summer. Something must have delayed the northward imperative hard-wired into their DNA. There they were, at all events, making their hound-like clamour out on the Thames tideline as I walked off the Gravesend ferry and turned east along the river towards the great Water Gate of Tilbury Fort.

I paused on the sea wall to admire the slender-barrelled cannon, the stacks of classical armour and sheaves of spears all sculpted in the pale stone of the gateway in the time of King Charles II, when an upriver attack from the North Sea by the empire-building Dutch seemed all too likely. Inland of the Water Gate lay the star-shaped fort in its star-shaped moat, first constructed under King Henry VIII against a French invasion, re-founded after the Restoration to beat off the Hollanders. Built and dug at sharp angles against potential attackers, the proud stronghold of the Essex shore saw no military action for the best part of 400 years, until its guns brought down a Zeppelin during World War I. But it had known shots fired in anger. In 1776, while hosting a cricket match between an Essex and a Kentish team, the fort was the scene of a double murder. Things turned nasty after the qualification of one of the players was questioned, as the *London Chronicle* reported in November 1776:

> *A terrible affair happened this day at Tilbury Fort. A great match of cricket being to be played between Kent and Essex, the parties assembled on both sides. When they were met, a man appearing among the former, who should not have been there, the Essex men refused playing, on which a very bloody battle ensued, and the Kentish men being likely to be worsted, one of them ran into the guard-house and, getting a gun from one of the invalids, fired and killed one of the opposite party. On seeing this they all began running to the guard-house and, there being but four soldiers there, they took away the guns and fell to it, doing a great deal of mischief. An old invalid was run through the body with a bayonet; and a Serjeant who commands at the fort, in the absence of the officer, endeavouring*

Right **Ancient boats, awaiting the paintbrush and caulking iron when – or if – their owners get round to it, are a feature of the creeks and marsh waterways of the Essex shore**

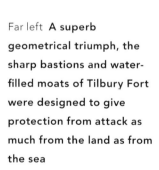

Far left **A superb geometrical triumph, the sharp bastions and water-filled moats of Tilbury Fort were designed to give protection from attack as much from the land as from the sea**

Left **Had Tilbury Fort ever been attacked in earnest, a couple of cannon balls would have put paid to the ornate Water Gate and its martial sculptures**

with his four men to quell them, was shot dead. At last the Essex men took to flight and, running over the drawbridge, made their escape. The Kentish men then made off in their boats, but search is making after them.

Typical Essex, the rest of the country might well have responded. There is something about the low-lying, creek-fringed county on London's eastern borders that has always generated a sort of puzzled amusement, bordering on contempt, mixed with a generous dollop of fear. Essex of the mysterious muds and marshes, lying like a ragged beggar at the back door of the capital, was a place where anything might happen. Essex folk were strange beings to such traveller observers as Daniel Defoe. In *A Tour through the Whole Island of Great Britain* (1724–26) he records a conversation with a 'merry fellow' from the River Blackwater country who claimed to have had 'about a dozen and a half of wives'. The pragmatic peasant told the London writer that as each wife in turn succumbed to the marsh ague, or malaria, in the noxious air of the marshes, he would hasten to collect a replacement, 'healthy, fresh and clear, and well', from the uplands nearby.

Downriver from London lay the prison hulks and the criminal classes, marginal land and marginal people, where sinister, amoral folk would rob you blind and slit your throat. Echoes of that prejudice have reached our day with the gold-dripping chancer Essex Man and his slapperish squeeze Essex Girl in her white stilettos. Essex Man and Essex Girl are still alive, and as well as can be expected. But they are not the only side to the story of this coastal county, much laughed at and much loved.

I turned my back on Tilbury Fort and the dockside cranes to the west, their jibs raised skywards like an anxious flock of skeleton geese. Ahead lay a great northward curve of the Thames from Coalhouse Point to Mucking Flats, down-to-earth names for swathes of tidal mud at the edge of the river. Beyond their dully gleaming banks rose a complex of geometrical shapes that had me standing and staring.

Coryton oil refinery is the last and the biggest of the Thames refineries, and it is a staggering spectacle by night or day, a giant's playground of pipework and chimneys, silos and tanks, fat-bellied retorts and flare stacks taller than skyscrapers belching incandescent orange flames so brilliant I could not rest my eyes on them.

Somewhere within the 500-acre (200-ha) plant lies the ghost of Kynochtown estate, home to the workers who processed gunpowder and cordite at the Kynoch explosives factory that was built on the empty marshes here at the end of the Victorian era. The factory was swallowed up in the 1920s when local coal merchants the Cory brothers built an oil storage depot on the site, renaming the workers' estate 'Coryton' to their own greater glory. Thirty years later the brothers themselves hit the chute of oblivion after selling their depot to Mobil. When did the refinery first come onstream? 'Dunno,' said Dave, lighting up outside the gate at the end of his shift. 'Yeah, dunno,' confirmed his colleague, puffing and coughing alongside. The flare behind the two men trailed a feathery black tail across half the sky, as heavy in the lungs as the high tar tobacco they were smoking.

Right **The view from the north sea wall on Canvey Island, looking across the mudflats and saltmarsh of Hadleigh Ray towards the distant sprawl of Southend-on-Sea**

Detouring inland, I followed winding footpaths through Fobbing Marshes and Vange Marshes, a curious no-man's-land of coarse grazing. Reedbeds sighed and bowed to the wind along the muddy creeks. A big dark bird of prey got up and went away in no sort of a hurry. I was too slow to get the binoculars onto it for an identification, but just to see it there in the desolate marshes against the backdrop of the oil flares and silos was extraordinary. On the far side of Vange Creek, the flooded pits out of which local brickmakers dug their clay a hundred years ago were loud with quacking. Mallard drakes in the iridescent glory of their springtime courting colours were chasing drab-coloured ducks about the ponds. The furious bursts of noise with which they warned off their rivals held exactly the quality of hysterical human laughter, so much so that I couldn't help giggling in sympathy. There really is no sound quite as infectiously silly.

Brickworks, explosives factories, oil refineries, chemical works. Prison hulks where good and bad men were left to rot to death together. Nightsoil wharves to land the capital's excrement for the fertilising of local fields which grew the food the capital ate. Long reaches of mudflats where London's dead dogs, potato peelings and murdered prostitutes, cast into the Thames, fetched up to lie and decompose. Such have been the indignities visited upon the lower Thames shore. Today it is the mountainous landfill sites that maintain this tradition of dumping on estuarine Essex. There was a proper corker over on the Pitsea marshes, a series of pale green whalebacks where the clay capping gleamed greyly through sparse, recently sown grass. The burial mounds of ancient kings must have looked much like this when newly raised, I thought as I followed the long curve of the Southend railway line east towards Canvey Island.

The path ran at the foot of a hill, passing right beside the door of the loneliest church in these south Essex marshes. The broad squat nave of the Church of St Margaret of Antioch was a riotous mishmash of ragstone, flints and shards of brick-red Roman tiles, the shadow of the stumpy tower – supported by a single, monstrous buttress out of all proportion to the rest of the church – falling along it in the late afternoon light. A home-going commuter train went

clattering past the churchyard, its occupants dimly seen as nose-to-paper silhouettes. Just west of the church a memorial slab stood alone in the foundations of a large building whose bricks sprouted a luxuriant miniature forest of lichens and mosses. The inscription announced it as the grave of Harold and Rose Howard – a very curious resting place, entirely peaceful save for the 30-second earthquake of a passing train every few minutes.

Antioch. What a name to stumble across in the sombre Essex flatlands – the place where the irresistible nymph Daphne transformed herself into a laurel tree to evade amorous Apollo; the beautiful city among the mountains of southeast Turkey, so fair that men called it the Crown of the Orient. Who was St Margaret of Antioch? I had no idea. Later I read how the Roman Governor of the East, wishing to marry this devout Christian shepherdess, ordered her to renounce her faith, and visited horrible tortures on her when she refused. Martyred in AD304, Margaret seems to have had a propensity for attracting trouble. On another occasion the Devil assumed the shape of a dragon and devoured the gentle shepherdess, but could not digest the crucifix she was carrying and was forced to spew her up again. It must have been this association with pains in the belly followed by a happy outcome that brought so many women during the Middle Ages to pray to St Margaret of Antioch for help and comfort in pregnancy and childbirth. But how did her name filter northwards to these marshes on the moody Thames? Perhaps a Crusader knight conceived a devotion to the shepherdess saint during the Siege of Antioch in 1097–98, and returned to Essex determined to share it. Or maybe a local minstrel got hold of the story and inspired his lord and master. Food for thought, at all events, as I walked on to Benfleet and over the bridge onto Canvey Island.

Imagination is a wonderful thing. The special place that the Haworth moors occupy in the heart of a Charlotte Brontë devotee, or the inspiration a lover of John Constable's landscapes imbibes in Dedham Vale – this kind of powerful magic is threaded for me, and for thousands of other music lovers all over the world, through the grey sea walls, the windy marshlands, the skeletal gas jetties and crowded pubs of Canvey Island. Where others see only a bleak Thames estuary shore seeded with chemical silos and cheek-by-jowl housing, I scent romance and adventure. The moment I cross East Haven Creek I enter a parallel universe – the chancy but captivating world of 'Oil City', where men are men and women are vixens, where devastating dames tap their scarlet nails on your wallet, and dodgy motors are forever about to screech up, driven by just the kind of hardboiled citizens you'd like to guzzle a shot of bourbon with.

It was Wilko Johnson, the Bard of Canvey, who created this fantasy island in my mind back in the early 1970s when he was Dr Feelgood's guitar-slinger supreme. Dr Feelgood, 'the greatest local band in the world', were Canvey to their boot-heels, a quartet of sharply dressed R&B belters who burst through the soft underbelly of the jaded post-Beatles music business like an uppercut from a private dick. Gruff-voiced Lee Brilleaux barked out the 100mph, three-minutes-maximum songs; John B. Sparks thwacked a bass impassively; the Big Figure thundered away on the drums. Wilko Johnson, meanwhile, played his red-and-black Telecaster like a stuttering machine-gun and jerked around the stage like a bug-eyed madman. But the guitarist was far more than simply a showman. Wilko was a rock'n'roll poet, a master craftsman of tales

Right **Dr Feelgood in their mean and moody pomp: (r to l) John B. Sparks, bass; Lee Brilleaux, vocals and harp; the Big Figure, drums; Wilko Johnson, guitarist, songwriter and expert weaver of Raymond Chandler-like fantasies**

Below **Looking as cool as a cucumber, St Margaret of Antioch overcomes the Devil, in the form of a rather camp-looking dragon, by the power of prayer alone**

Where others see only a bleak Thames estuary shore seeded with chemical silos and cheek-by-jowl housing, I scent romance and adventure. The moment I cross East Haven Creek I enter a parallel universe.

and tunes. The songs he wrote presented sharp cameos of cheerful chancers down on their luck, of cheating girls and hard men, citizens of a harsh yet lively town he called Oil City. Each miniature chronicle came across as pungently and economically as a Raymond Carver short story.

'Back when we were starting out,' Lee Brilleaux once told me, 'Canvey had an element of toughness, like most working-class places. Men were expected to be men. If you wanted to find a fight, you only had to spill another man's beer or look at his wife. But there was a warmth about it as well. People worked hard, and they played hard. The funny thing was, Canvey was really a rural community in lots of ways. Everyone on the island knew us kids, and they'd look out for us. I grew up playing on the creeks, building pirate dens out on the marshes – a country boy's background. We knew about tides, about birds and shellfish, alongside the bookies and the boozers.'

Wilko Johnson's songs did not exactly detail the real Canvey Island, but they played around with it as a setting and an atmosphere. In Wilko's Oil City, hard-boiled characters watch the refinery towers burning at the break of day as they wait for some red-eyed rendezvous; they go places and stay too long; they put their foot down on the boards with their headlights burning up the night; they jump up right out of a dream to find the front door wide open and the rain blowing in from the street. If a Wilko Johnson character is faced with an unfaithful girlfriend, he won't lose his cool or burst into tears: no, he'll just rasp, 'I'm gonna get some concrete mix and fill your back door up with bricks – and you'd better be there waiting when I get my business fixed.'

Wilko and his three Canvey Island bandmates parted company long ago. The guitarist tours with his own band these days. Dr Feelgood are still on the road, too, other musicians having slipped into the shoes of the original Feelgoods over the years. I go along to the gigs every so often for the sheer escapist pleasure of hearing those tight, razor-edged Oil City tales of drinking, cheating and losing the plot as their author always intended they should be heard – live and loud.

As for the 'real' Canvey Island: well, that's another story. All the east of the island is jam-rammed with housing; all the west lies open and green under empty grazing marshes, newly declared an RSPB bird reserve. For me the greatest Canvey

Island pleasure is the 14-mile (23-km) walk around the perimeter of the island, and that's what I did the next day. I strolled for hours with only oystercatchers and marsh horses for company. In front of me slowly expanded the nightmarish shape of a black oil jetty that rose out of the meadows like a demon and strode across the sea wall into the river. A grand plan in the 1970s to smother the West Canvey marshes with oil installations never came to anything; all that is left is the jetty, tarry black and gigantic in the flat landscape. One of Wilko Johnson's protagonists, having searched the streets of Oil City in vain for 'a man I know' with shady money burning a hole in his pocket, arranges a meet next morning down by the jetty. Canvey does not hold a more iconic place for the Feelgood fan. It was hereabouts that the photo for the band's first album cover was shot in gritty black and white – four young, hung-over hard men shivering and frowning in a bitter estuary wind.

Beyond the jetty I ducked into the Lobster Smack for plaice and chips and a pint. Charles Dickens, that supreme appreciator of lonely marsh country, used back-of-beyond Canvey Island and its lonely inn on the Thames shore in his masterpiece *Great Expectations*. Where better for Pip to hide out for a night than with the convict Magwitch, his unwelcome benefactor illegally returned from transportation, whom he was trying to smuggle out of England to safety on the Continent?

> *It was a dirty place enough, and I daresay not unknown to smuggling adventurers; but there was a good fire in the kitchen, and there were eggs and bacon to eat, and various liquors to drink. Also, there were two double-bedded rooms, 'such as they were,' the landlord said... We found the air as carefully excluded from both, as if air were fatal to life; and there were more dirty clothes and band-boxes under the beds than I should have thought the family possessed. But, we considered ourselves well off, notwithstanding, for a more solitary place we could not have found.*

Above left **A mallard drake takes off in a hurry from one of the marsh pools located at the western end of Canvey Island**

Above **Pleasure boats lie up along one of the muddy tidal creeks around Canvey Island, waiting for the next flood tide to set them afloat**

Right **Aftermath of a catastrophe: many folk on Canvey Island still recount the events of 31 January/ 1 February 1953, when 58 islanders died during the East Coast flood disaster**

The old pub in the shadow of the fuel silos under the sea wall still retains a strong individual flavour. From here the built-up half of the island trends away east along the Thames, its seawall path squeezed between oil and gas cylinders and the slimy pebbles of the foreshore. The path itself runs past funfairs and caravan sites, a beach of unexpectedly yellow sand and the Art Nouveau drum shape of the Labworth Café, all witness to Canvey's lasting appeal to London's East Enders as a holiday resort 30 miles (50km) seaward of home.

Back in medieval times, long before anyone thought of living here, there were six separate marsh islands along the north shore of the river, sloppy places liable to inundation at high water. The salt grass of the islets offered superb sheep grazing, though, and shepherds would drive their flocks to pasture between the tides. The graziers walked with tiny three-legged stools strapped to their backsides, sitting to milk each ewe before moving on to the next. Canvey cheese was a delicacy, Canvey mutton a treat.

In the 1620s Dutch engineer Joos van Croppenburgh constructed a sea wall all round the islands and pumped out the sea water. Canvey Island came into being as a single coherent piece of land, but it remained as remote as Dickens portrayed it until the railways began to bring adventurous folk east from London to see what might be down by the river there beyond the stepping stones in Benfleet Creek.

In mid-Victorian times barely a hundred people were living on Canvey; but the advent of the 20th century brought with it a population explosion. Once a swing bridge had been built across the creek, the island began to fill with ramshackle houses, clapboard shops and free-and-easy eateries, among which wriggled sandy unmade lanes. Eventually, more solid housing followed. The main body of the island lay below the high-water mark of the biggest spring tides, but everyone trusted the sea walls to keep the North Sea out. There were some 11,000 souls living on Canvey Island in the year of the island's flood disaster. Altogether 307 people lost their lives on the night of 31 January 1953 in the great floods that hit the east coast of Britain, and 58 of these died in little Canvey as the sea overtopped the inadequate sea wall and swept through the island.

After the disaster the sea wall was strengthened and raised. These days it forms a continuous grey concrete ribbon along which I sauntered on this brisk spring afternoon, slowing down now as I turned the corner at muddy Smallgains Creek and began to head back west into the wind once more. On my right hand, throwing a dun and olive barrier between island and mainland, the Canvey marshes and their tidal islets lay as nature intended them. The tide was making rapidly. Black-capped terns squeaked out their needly cries over Long Horse Island, and a seal put up its round gleaming head in the middle of Hadleigh Ray as the inflowing water carried it west up the channel. Here the ashes of Lee Brilleaux were scattered into the tide after his death in 1994.

As evening began to flush along the skyline ahead I looked out across the marshes and creeks where the Canvey bluesman rowed and played as a boy. You could hardly ask for anything better – to end up, indissolubly and for ever more, part of the place that shaped you.

Capital Ring

'Walking round London? What, you mean actually walking round the city itself – *for pleasure*? You must be out of your mind, mate. That's what the Home Counties are for, isn't it? No-one goes for a nice, leafy walk round London, do they?'

Harrow School coat of arms

St Mary's church, Stoke Newington

Journey Planner

Around London's Green Corridor

77-mile circuit; join at any point

Maps

Not necessary if you have the official guide or leaflets; but useful for a wide geographical perspective. OS 1:50,000 Landrangers 177, 178; 1:25,000 Explorers 161, 162, 173

Books

The Capital Ring by Colin Saunders (Aurum Press): Describes the whole route in great detail, with large-scale OS 1:25,000 maps

Transport

The Capital Ring lies in Transport Zones 2, 3 and 4; a Travelcard allows tube, bus and train travel throughout

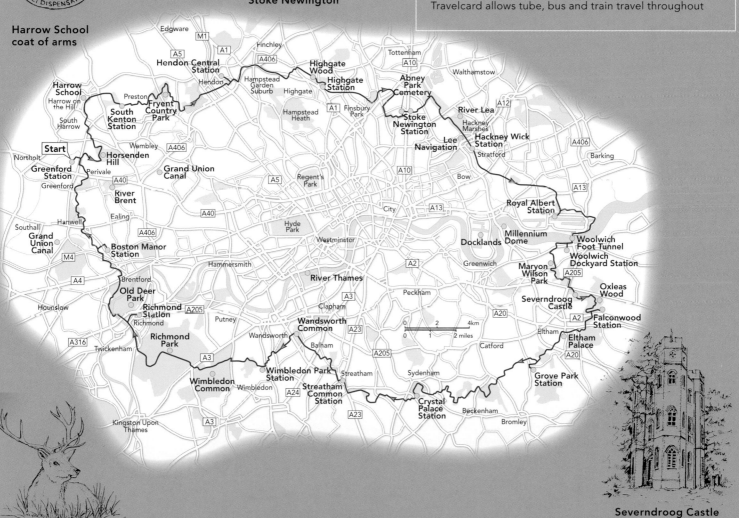

Red deer stag

Severndroog Castle

Urban ramblers are a very rare breed, and that is the sort of response generally forthcoming at any suggestion that London might be a pleasant, even a green place to go walking. Cities are cities, aren't they? Noisy, grimy places where everything's hard underfoot and the only greenery you're likely to see is the garnish with your tuna and mayo sandwich. Walking in the capital is for mugs, or those who have missed their bus.

That's the way I always thought of London. And I couldn't have been more wrong. To view London through such dark spectacles was to ignore the strange, piecemeal fashion in which the city developed. Central London is certainly as citified as can be, its green lungs provided solely by its famous, formal parks and gardens. But outside this inner core, in areas such as Eltham, Perivale, Highgate and Walthamstow – places that were rural villages only a couple of hundred years ago – open spaces full of fresh air and greenery abound. Round Eltham one can walk for miles through ancient woodland and wide meadows, seeing no-one else. The towpath of the River Lea leads through the broad marshlands of Walthamstow and Hackney, with immense views on every side. In the woods of Perivale and Highgate are wild flowers, rare butterflies and enough songbirds to deafen a stone fox.

These rich, unexpected treasures of London's wild places have been saved, one by one, as the city has expanded around and beyond them. Some have been preserved by enlightened local and county councils, some by dedicated individuals, others by pure luck. Patches of woodland, corners of heaths and parks, the linear corridors of old railways, green lanes nipped off at either end by new buildings – they lie dotted thickly over the map of London. Some have been adopted by local authorities and have their own name and identity: for example, The Greenway, a 5-mile path linking Bow to Beckton in east London, which has been developed along the line of a Victorian sewer, or the Parkland Walk in north London, along the tree-hung trackbed of a long disused branch railway from Finsbury Park to Alexandra Palace.

Local walkers always knew of London's green byways as wonderful places to enjoy a short stroll or take the dog for a run. But the city's wild places existed in isolation, each from its neighbour, until the formation of the London Walking Forum in the 1990s. Over more than a decade, these green dots on the map were joined up by linking routes to form a single, continuous circular footpath that threads its way through the outer parts of inner London like a well-kept, delightful secret.

Although you can commence the circuit anywhere you please, the Capital Ring starts officially at the southern end of the Woolwich Foot Tunnel under the Thames in east London. The route runs in a great clockwise circle for nearly 77 miles to its finishing point at the northern mouth of the Woolwich Tunnel. It makes a wonderful continuous walk in its own right. But most London walkers are likely to be looking for something a lot shorter and more manageable. For their sake, the Capital Ring has been divided into 15 stages, mostly between 4 and 8 miles long. Each stage is well served by public transport, and much of the path is wheelchair- and pushchair-friendly.

I found the Capital Ring still, to some extent, a work in progress. Short stretches were scruffy – notably the western end of The Greenway, and parts of the path beside the River Brent in northwest London. Some of the waymarks had gone missing, or had been scribbled over. And there were plenty of short stretches through suburban streets – inescapably, since this is after all a city walk.

But these minor imperfections paled in comparison with the beauty of the woodlands, the peace of the meadows and the open spaces of the great parks and commons that make up the Capital Ring. Whether one tackles it as I did, all in one sitting, or savours it as a well-spaced-out series of bite-sized chunks, the Ring is endlessly fascinating. From Eltham Palace to Severndroog Castle, from the Gothic thrills of overgrown Abney Park Cemetery to the hayfields of Horsenden Hill, I found surprises and delights round most corners. Above all, there were the pleasures of unearthing the hidden treasures of London, of exploring where I never dreamed I'd go, and of discovering for myself this secret byway round the city.

On a bitter winter morning I pushed a stick into the railings at Greenford Station, told myself I'd see if it was there when I got back in five days' time, and set out with tingling nose and fingers through the western outskirts of the capital to follow the green corridor wherever it might take me.

Day 1 – Greenford to Highgate (16½ miles)

The flight of redwings landed in the dew-soaked meadow beside Perivale Wood, the sudden flutter of their wings making me jump. At half-past seven on this cold, pearly winter's morning, no-one else was about on the canal towpath, and I had been idling along half asleep. The suburbs of west London – Perivale, Wembley, Greenford, South Harrow – lay all round, but from this rural stretch of the Capital Ring I could see only the occasional rooftop beyond the trees and meadows. The Ring dodged in and out of old bushy lanes and dived suddenly off suburban streets into belts of woodland, oases of birdsong. It wasn't until I had climbed the green back of Horsenden Hill and was looking out across the giant sprawl of the city that reality filtered in once more. Horsenden Hill is a snippet of ancient farming countryside, miraculously preserved from the encroaching city. Under its broad dome lies buried the Saxon warrior Horsa, slain while 'reminding' his boorish son-in-law to respect his daughter (the boor also died of the reminder).

I walked through the smart streets of Harrow-on-the-Hill in company with an army of gown-swishing masters and be-blazered boys in boaters on their way to lessons. In the High Street the mannequins in the old-fashioned plate glass windows of Billings & Edmonds, Gents Outfitters, sported white-tasselled school scarves, stripy blazers, fez-style caps and brogues with yellow socks, just as if the 20th – never mind the 21st – century had never dawned. Beyond the pristine town I trod the tussocky fields of North Wembley among cohorts of dog walkers. It was a day of contrasts: from the manicured neatness of suburban Preston Park to the rough open spaces of Fryent Country Park, the scruffy channel of the River Brent followed by the immaculately manicured banks of the winding Mutton Brook in Hampstead Garden Suburb. I dropped down through quiet Highgate Wood and the shadowy dells of Queen's Wood in the dusk, grey squirrels scampering everywhere with their puff-of-smoke tails trailing behind them as if their hindquarters were on fire, to find myself in a shock of noise and light on Archway Road among home-rushing city workers.

Above left Canal towpaths and riverside tracks form part of the network of green corridors that carry the Capital Ring round London

Above The Boaters and Blazers brigade: Harrow scholboys saunter to their lessons through the town

Top right The full Gothic glory of Victorian mourning enwrapped in trailing ivy in the depths of Abney Park Cemetery in Stoke Newington

Bottom right Hasidic Jews in sidelocks and sober hats form one of the many diverse ethnic and religious groups that co-exist along the route of the Capital Ring

Day 2 – Highgate to North Woolwich (16 miles)

In the tunnel of trees along the former Alexandra Palace branch railway's green footpath, the winter cold stung my ears and nose. Long-tailed tits went chinking through the leafless sycamores. It was a brisk walk to Stoke Newington, where I joined the curate of St Mary's Church at his lone morning devotions.

> *The hill of God is as the hill of Bashan; an high*
> * hill as the hill of Bashan.*
> *Why leap ye, ye high hills?*
> *this is the hill which God desireth to dwell in;*
> *yea, the LORD will dwell in it for ever.*

We shuttled Psalm 68 back and forth, all alone in the echoing magnificence of St Mary's, one of George Gilbert Scott's finest creations.

'Don't miss Abney Park cemetery,' urged the curate. I'm glad I didn't. Abney is a Gothic delight, utterly overgrown, its tangled paths threading a vast jumble of tombs and trees so closely intertwined they seem organically grown together. 'Went to Heaven, 20th August 1912,' was the confident inscription on the memorial to William Booth, founder of the Salvation Army. Further into the tangle stood a statue to Isaac Watts, the 'Father of Hymnody' – one of my favourite hymn writers. 'Jesus Shall Reign Where'er the Sun' and 'When I Survey the Wondrous Cross' were two of his, the former majestic in its triumphalist confidence, the latter redolent of bitter-sweet Good Friday ceremonies. Watts wrote other, lesser-known hymns, including (a cheap shot, but it made me smile as I stood there) 'Blest is the Man whose Bowels Move'.

Beyond the cemetery, sidelocked Jews and white-bearded Muslims strode the north London pavements. Down along the towpath of the River Lea through Walthamstow and Hackney Marshes I spotted pinkfoot geese and herons, tufted ducks and long-tailed tits, small life forms that somehow outfaced the giant tower of Canary Wharf that rose in the middle distance, its pyramidal roof jetting steam like a Victorian sweatshop. Skirting the East End among the filthy,

clangorous scrap-metal yards of Stratford was tedious, but once on The Greenway, a splendid cycleway laid out along the course of a Victorian sewer, I got up cruising speed all the way down to the River Thames.

Day 3 – Woolwich Free Ferry to Crystal Palace (18 miles)

Next morning I enjoyed a classic London view from the deck of the Woolwich Free Ferry – the tall hoods of the Thames Flood Barrier guarding the Millennium Dome's spiked crown and the enormo-blocks of Canary Wharf, all drifting in and out of the early morning mist as though waiting for Resurrection Day and the palette of Claude Monet. The Oz-like Emerald City shapes of Docklands were to be a recurring presence on the northern horizon during this long day's tramp south of the river. There were more surrealistic echoes in Maryon Park, too, where I passed the tennis courts that were the setting for the game of psychedelic tennis in Antonioni's *Blow-Up* film.

How I had loved that movie back in 1966, finding weighty significance in every frame. I'd never watched it since, being wary of what 40 years of cynicism and experience might have done to it – and me.

The main feature of this day, though, was a splendid string of ancient woods and commons – Eltham Common where crocuses were struggling up through the frosty grass, Castlewood with its triangular, turreted Severndroog Castle memorial and enormous hilltop views, Jack Wood and Oxleas Wood. Purchased by a farsighted London County Council between the world wars, they were saved from development. Now they form a line of precious jewels on a green necklace that stretches far across southeast London. Oxleas Wood and Jack Wood would have been torn apart in the 1990s by the projected East London River Crossing road, but a concerted campaign by protesters saved them. They shelter rare trees, including the wild service tree with its serrated, hand-shaped leaves, a sure indicator of ancient woodland.

Left **A classic composition incorporating three iconic east London structures: the Thames Flood Barrier, the Millennium Dome (now known as the O2), and the towering conglomerate of Canary Wharf**

Below **Insects laying their eggs inside the oak buds in Oxleas Wood cause the trees to produce these fantastically distorted acorns**

Below right **The landmark windmill on Wimbledon Common Is a favourite place for walkers to stop for a reviving cuppa**

No well-spread green fingers to help with identification on this February afternoon – just the scutter of squirrels in last year's fallen leaves that lay powdered with frost and too fragile to be picked up and straightened out.

At dusk I came by Crystal Palace, footsore, to find the sky-high transmitter mast lit by the evening sun like an etiolated Eiffel Tower of spun silver and gold: a memorable image.

Day 4 – Crystal Palace to Richmond (16½ miles)

Today I had my park-yomping, path-stomping sister Louisa for company, and the miles fairly flew by. We couldn't hang around: the wintry weather was colder than ever along the Capital Ring.

There were grand Victorian houses in the streets round Crystal Palace, and fine decorative Edwardian porches and window surrounds in the more modest side roads of Balham. Kids were skimming ice across the frozen ponds on Wandsworth Common. That was the first in another superb string of parks, commons and heaths that swung us away from traffic and houses in a great arc across central and southwest London, with occasional far views over the roofs to the smoky blue line of the downs and commons beyond Croydon – all intensely pressurised by developers over a century and a half, all saved for Londoners by philanthropic action.

On Wimbledon Common we marched along the scrubland paths to the Windmill Café for a cuppa and a sit-down, then plunged on through steep, densely wooded dells. In Richmond Park we saw and heard young stags clashing antlers, and ecstatic dogs barking and leaping

for joy across heather and grassland. At nightfall we came down the long slope into Petersham Meadows after a day of winter sun and frost-melt, finishing our walk beside a flooded, restless Thames.

Day 5 – Richmond to Greenford (9½ miles)

The final stretch of the Capital Ring, on another cold blue day. I crossed Richmond Green, a lone walker once more, overlooked by gorgeous Georgian and Victorian houses, and turned north along the Thames Path. Old fishing trawlers and swish yachts swung at their moorings flank to flank, and every mid-river buoy held a gull. 'It's been a pleasant trip,' ran the inscription on a memorial bench to John Young (1909–98), '...my thanks to Old Father Thames.'

Herons flew heavily over the flooded meadows of Old Deer Park, their umbrella wings reflected in the standing water. The pinnacles of Isleworth's church tower stood over their own shimmering image in the river. A lovely, peaceful waterside stretch; and so was the sinuous Grand Union Canal when I abandoned the Thames and took up with it. Rickety old industrial sheds gave way to gleaming ultra-modern office blocks at Brentford and, further north, trains went thundering across the great arches of the Arncliffe Viaduct over the River Brent – I'd last encountered the Brent five days ago when I set out along the Capital Ring, and now it accompanied me almost to the end of the walk. From Hanwell onwards it was a dirty old ditch, in all truth, but I didn't care. It was good to follow it up to Greenford, thinking back over the hugely varied and unexpectedly beautiful green circle I had been tracing round the hard grey heart of London. My stick was still there, too. Someone had capped it with a child's glove, in hopes of the owner returning to reclaim it. I left stick and glove where they were, and went off whistling.

Left **The bustling waterfront at Richmond is one of the most popular spots for a short stroll along the Thames**

Highlights of the Capital Ring

Eltham Common, Castlewood, Severndroog Castle, Jackwood, Oxleas Wood, Eltham Park North
An interconnecting string of southeast London commons and woodlands that are particularly rich in wildlife. Mercifully, the area was saved from major development in the 1920s and '30s by London County Council (Capital Ring Section 1, Woolwich to Falconwood: access via Falconwood Station).

Beckenham Place Park A big south London park, part grassland and part woods; once the grounds of Beckenham Place mansion (Capital Ring Section 3, Grove Park to Crystal Palace: Ravensbourne or Beckenham Hill stations).

Wimbledon Common Let yourself go wombling free through acres of deep woodland, scrub and open common on the borders of Putney Heath and Wimbledon Vale (Capital Ring Section 6, Wimbledon Park to Richmond: 15-minute walk from Southfields, Wimbledon Park or Wimbledon stations).

Richmond Park and Petersham Park Outer London's finest and grandest open space: miles of heath, ponds and woods, deer herds and songbirds (Capital Ring Section 6, Wimbledon Park to Richmond: North Sheen or Richmond stations).

Richmond and the Thames Path Sweet as honey, and plenty of money: handsome Richmond and the beautifully kept Thames Path National Trail to picturesque Isleworth (Capital Ring Section 7, Richmond to Osterley Lock: Richmond station).

Grand Union Canal towpath The surprisingly green and countrified windings of the London–Birmingham canal between Brentford and Hanwell (Capital Ring Section 7, Richmond to Osterley Lock, and 8, Osterley Lock to Greenford: Brentford or Hanwell stations).

Perivale Wood and Horsenden Hill Following the Grand Union Canal by Perivale Wood Local Nature Reserve, then climbing the traditionally managed meadows of Horsenden Hill to a stunning view over west London (Capital Ring Section 9, Greenford to South Kenton: Greenford or Sudbury Town stations).

Mutton Brook through Hampstead Garden Suburb
A short, delightful section through Northway Gardens, with the snaking Mutton Brook and its weeping willows beautifully kept (Capital Ring Section 11, Hendon Park to Highgate: East Finchley station).

Highgate Wood, Queen's Wood and Parkland Railway Walk Through neatly managed Highgate Wood and the tangly depths of Queen's Wood, then along the green corridor of the disused Ally Pally branch railway line (Capital Ring Section 11, Hendon Park to Highgate, and 12, Highgate to Stoke Newington: Highgate or Finsbury Park stations).

Abney Park Cemetery Weird and wonderful – thousands and thousands of graves of all shapes, sizes, eras and shades of eminence, half-smothered in a wood that's a carefully managed nature reserve (Capital Ring Section 12, Highgate to Stoke Newington: Stoke Newington station).

Lee Navigation towpath Waterside walking with a rural feel beside the Lee Navigation waterway from Walthamstow Marsh Nature Reserve to Hackney Marsh (Capital Ring Section 13, Stoke Newington to Hackney Wick: Clapton or Hackney Wick stations).

The Greenway Well-kept footpath/cycleway on an embankment, with grandstand views over east London – the best section is from Stratford High Street to Beckton (Capital Ring Section 14, Hackney Wick to Beckton District Park: Stratford West Ham or Plaistow stations).

7

Ancient Trackway of the Chiltern Hills

Ah, the Chilterns in summer! Red kites in blue skies, wild flowers spattering the hills with colour, and carefree walkers in shorts and T-shirts following the pale chalk ribbon of the Ridgeway path over the sunlit downs. And then there's winter, with the ancient trackway hard-frozen, a snowy blanket drawn across the hills, and the shades of warriors, packmen and cattle drovers at every turn of the way....

Journey Planner

Goring to Ivinghoe Beacon

44 miles

Maps

OS 1:25,000 Explorers 171, 181

Books

The Ridgeway National Trail Guide by Anthony
Burton (Aurum Press)

The Ridgeway National Trail Companion (National
Trails Office)

Websites

National Trails Office: www.nationaltrail.co.uk/
ridgeway

The Friends of the Ridgeway:
www.ridgewayfriends.org.uk

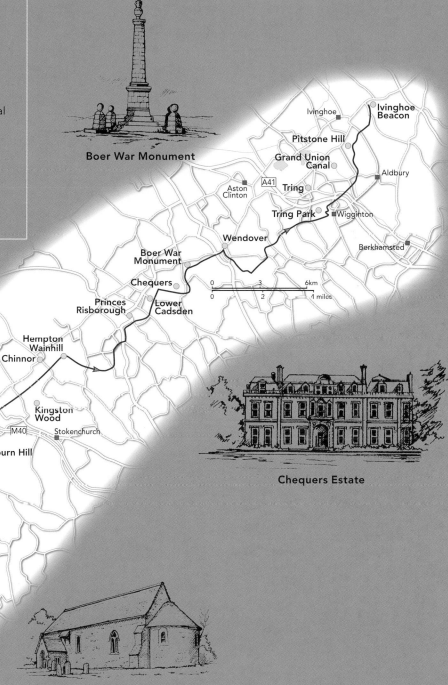

Boer War Monument

Ridgeway path

Chequers Estate

St Botolph's Church, Swyncombe

I came into Nuffield at nightfall well and truly shattered. There wasn't really any excuse for it. The day's walking had been easy, a 10-mile (16km) stretch that had started at lunchtime in Goring, followed the River Thames in flat, gentle floodplain country, and then forged eastwards along the old Iron Age boundary known as Grim's Ditch.

Maybe my leg-weariness was due to the heavy, clogging snow that had suddenly descended to fill the ditches, block the hedges and make a treacherous midwinter ice rink of every slight slope – conditions altogether familiar to our ancestors who followed the great upland track of the Ridgeway that I had set out to tackle in this frozen February. Whether my cosseted, Gore-Tex-clad, centrally heated 21st-century self could deal with all that snow and ice remained to be seen.

The ancient upland trackway known today as the Ridgeway runs east and then northeast for 85 miles (137km), leading from Overton Hill on the great Wiltshire Plain to Ivinghoe Beacon in the Chiltern Hills on the Buckinghamshire/Hertfordshire border. The Ridgeway is one of the oldest routes in Britain – perhaps the oldest. It has been in existence in one form or another for five or six thousand years, and probably half as long again. The alignment of Stone Age burial mounds along the course of the Ridgeway and the discovery of datable archaeological material makes a date of 4,000 or 5,000BC quite feasible as the earliest time that the Ridgeway might have been in more or less popular use. This was not some carefully surveyed route driven from A to B with a particular purpose in mind. The Ridgeway grew piecemeal. Salt-merchants, bronze traders, animals, men-at-arms, pilgrims, rogues and honest folk – all used different segments of the Ridgeway at need, a high and secure route that kept mostly to the sheltered slopes of the hills where strangers could be seen a long way off, whether friends or foes. The Ridgeway remained in fairly constant use until the late 18th century. Then canals were pushed through the hills, railways followed, and the old road became redundant.

The morning dawned freezing, clouded and thick with the promise of more snow. From Nuffield I followed the Ridgeway across a famous piece of sporting ground. Car manufacturer and philanthropist William Morris, Lord Nuffield, was such a golf nut that he bought Huntercombe Golf Course in 1926 to ensure that he could play there. He also purchased Nuffield Place because of its proximity to the course. However passionate a golf fiend though, Lord Nuffield's name was not the one that dominated my personal radar as I crunched the snowy fairways of Huntercombe. Thriller-writer Ian Fleming was a member at Huntercombe – and so was Fleming's creation, the invincible and irrepressible Secret Agent 007, James Bond. When off on exotic assignments to save the world and abolish baddies in far-flung parts of it, James Bond's game obviously had to go by the board. However, as Fleming reveals in the build-up to the famous needle match in *Goldfinger* between Bond and fiendish gold-obsessive Auric Goldfinger, our hero got in a good deal of weekend golf when he was at headquarters, including as many rounds as he could at Huntercombe. Bond's handicap was nine, 'a real nine – had to be, with the games he chose to play, the ten-pound Nassaus with the tough cheery men who were always so anxious to stand you a couple of double kümmels after lunch'.

A couple of double kümmels! How un-macho, yet how Sixties!

Top right **Crusaders, knights, packmen and walkers have all visited the 11th-century church of St Botolph, tucked away in its secret dell beside the Ridgeway at Swyncombe**

Bottom right **Ridgeway walkers are liable to get a nasty shock at any time, as a pheasant explodes out of the grass at their feet and clatters away with a loud *kok! kok!***

Now the Ridgeway forged north by Ewelme Park and made a steep and slippery descent to the gem-like church of St Botolph at Swyncombe. The whole look and feel of the church, from its eastern apse to the herringbone pattern of its flint walls, is Saxon, though St Botolph's dates from the early years of the Norman Conquest. Perhaps the Normans got their new subjects to build the church, and the locals did what they could in the style they knew best. Today St Botolph's resembled a sturdy little ship, afloat in a white foamy sea of half-unfolded snowdrops. Inside, faded blue Maltese crosses arched round the apse window where they were painted by crusader knights for good luck and God's protection 800 years ago. Behind the church lay the manor house of Swyncombe, a Victorian rebuild of a fine Elizabethan house. Manor, church and farm formed a harmonious picture, a medieval community clustered close in the secret valley.

The Ridgeway took a northern line, arrow-straight across the ridge of Swyncombe Downs, before settling in a decisive northeasterly course that it would follow with hardly a deviation for the next 30 miles (48km) to its terminus on Ivinghoe Beacon. The north-facing valley slopes of Swyncombe Downs still lay in unbroken white, sparkling and crystalline, while the southerly hillsides were already melted and green. The bare woods were full of the 'chakker' of rooks and jackdaws. The snow smothering the rutted track held the blurred prints of the boots of man and child, the paws of dog and rabbit, the three-pointed claw dints of pheasant and the delicate twin slots of deer hooves. In Westernend Shaw a full-grown roebuck, trotting down the path, came skidding to a halt in comical astonishment at the sight of me. For two or three minutes we stood motionless and at gaze, before he gave a dismissive sideways toss of the head and bounced off among the hazel saplings.

I crunched down out of the woods and along the track to North Farm, where an enormous bull stood phlegmatically chewing his cud among his wives in the straw-heaped stockyard. Here the Ridgeway changed not only direction, but character. Gone were the woodland track and the field path. In their place ran a proper old road, a deeply rutted trackway 30ft (9m) broad, curving between quickset hedges planted during the 18th century when the land all around was

enclosed and the ancient thoroughfare became constricted, disciplined and properly fixed and defined for the very first time in its six or seven millennia of existence.

The Enclosure episode of the 18th and 19th centuries represented an enormous land-grab by the moneyed and politically potent landowners of Britain. The nation was on a tremendous fiscal high back then. Fortunes were being made hand over fist from the expansion of trade brought about by the extension of Empire and the inexhaustible demands of the Industrial Revolution for goods, food, clothing, and minerals raw and refined. Rich men bought mansions and the parkland that went with them. They looked further afield for more land to have and to hold, and saw common land and open spaces, sheep walks and wild grazing – all land held in common or in disputed ownership, which for the expense and trouble of a suit at law and a Bill in Parliament could be theirs. They could afford the lawyers, and they could influence Parliament. So thousands of commoners were bought off, duped, fleeced or simply robbed.

In the century and a half following the first Enclosure Act of 1733, more than 5,000 such Acts of Parliament were passed, legalising the enclosure of almost 7 million acres (2.8 million ha) of open, common and waste land across England. The vast majority were claimed by local landowners, enclosed by hedges and put under sheep, cattle or the plough. One consequence of this legal ticketing and apportioning of the countryside, this tidying up and smoothing down of what had traditionally been a tangle of many ownerships and none, was the regularising of the courses of the old trackways across Britain – among them the Ridgeway.

Hitherto the ancient tracks used by traders and warriors, drovers and animals had tended to spread across the surrounding landscape as the vagaries of weather and the availability of grazing dictated. Cattle and sheep would stray hundreds of yards to either side to get at decent pasture as they were driven along. Merchants on their horses, packmen in charge of strings of pack ponies, other travellers great and small would naturally avoid the worst of the puddles and ruts

Beech and yew roots, hard cobbles of compacted chalk and soft patches of slippery chalk clay conspired to trip and trick my tiring legs.

left by those who had gone before. These gouges in the face of the countryside could become deadly in winter. Drovers and their beasts were frequently stuck in gluey, Flanders-like mud. Carts were engulfed above their axles. It was not unknown for beasts and men to drown on the worst routes, so deep and deadly were some of the mud lagoons. The Ridgeway and other similar highways became wider and wider, especially in the quagmire conditions of winter when the unsurfaced route could spread over more than a mile, splitting into multiple lesser tracks as travellers sought the drier and less slippery ground. This casual and informal situation, developed over many thousands of years, came quickly to an end with the Enclosures. Land was money. The new landowners would not tolerate incursions on their expensively acquired property. Fences and hedges were planted along the Ridgeway to mark exactly where the boundaries of the public highway were claimed to lie. The Ridgeway wriggled into a narrow, predictable and legally binding course, and stayed that way. Soon the scars of the broad winter thoroughfare faded from the newly planted or grazed land each side, and the chaotic spread of the ancient track was forgotten as if those many millennia had never even been.

Between the twin ribbons of hedges, always trending northeast towards the higher and drier escarpment of the Chiltern range, I walked as fast as the track surface would allow. The deep-frozen mud held iron-hard hoof pocks. Whole stretches of flooded rut had turned to skating rinks in the sub-zero temperatures. Every now and then my boots broke through the crust of ice with a splash and a shin-shocking gout of clay mud as cold and glutinous as batter straight from the fridge. Beyond a churned-up potato field packed with pig shelters like miniature Nissan huts and loud with the satisfied grunting of its residents, the Ridgeway had been sliced into impassable ruts by 4X4 drivers, the channels at least 2ft deep and filled with pale slush.

I detoured along the edge of a field where I put up a tiny muntjac deer, no bigger than a dog, that was sheltering in the hedge. It scampered away furtively, like a lurcher caught at the

Below The snug villages and wooded valleys imagined by Thomas Gainsborough (1727-88) represents every jaded Londoner's dream of bucolic bliss since before the Industrial Revolution

Below right Before the great 18th-century land enclosures, sections of the Ridgeway could spread more than a mile sideways in winter as travellers tried to bypass the worst parts. These days the route is demarcated by hedges, but it can still revert to a slushy morass after rain or snow

biscuit tin. Well scratched by bramble bushes, I went on past Leys Farm House with its frozen pond opaque and iron-bound, looking east at the long profiles of Watlington Hill and Shirburn Hill, great wooded downs that pushed their prow-like forefeet out above the Ridgeway like a pair of ships. To live properly up to its name, the Ridgeway ought to have been up there on the ridge, threading its way at the outer crest of the Chilterns through the beech hangers with a 40-mile (65km) westward view. Instead, it hugged the feet of the promontory hills, sheltered and orientated, always with a flank of ground and some kind of prospect to the west.

The advancing roar of the M40 motorway, registered subliminally over the last few miles, but not properly acknowledged in the forefront of the brain, now came up in the mix until it dominated everything, far and near. The ancient road burrowed under the modern one in a blur of high-sided lorries and a hellish rumble of accelerating engines. Then it was out the far side and undulating on, in a silence broken only by the crunching of my boots on hard-packed ice. A startled pheasant rocketed up from the grasses with a screech, leaving a shower of powdery snow flakes and a solitary downy feather to float to earth. A red kite flew out of the hedge and went flapping with slow wing beats 50ft (15m) above the fields, the deep russet of its flanks showing dramatically against the snow sheet. Beech and yew roots, hard cobbles of compacted chalk and soft patches of slippery chalk clay conspired to trip and trick my tiring legs. It was hard to spare a glance for the scenery, but a quick prospect of the Chiltern ridge on my right hand revealed the ground in Kingston Wood white with snow under the skeleton trees, a scene set for a posse of Breughel hunters to go tramping homeward with their greyhounds at heel, tails curled between meagrely muscled hind legs. How many years had it been since we'd had a winter like this, a proper frozen season to connect us to the winter joys and hardships of our forebears?

Now the Ridgeway entered a short but striking stretch of quarrying country on the outskirts of the hillfoot village of Chinnor. The old track had been left as a true ridgeway on a narrow spine of sticky chalk that plunged away either side to deep and vast quarries, flooded since they were abandoned – the works closed finally in 1999. The lagoons are possessed of a fabulous turquoise hue in sunshine, though today they glinted grey and ominous-looking under an afternoon sky beginning to draw in and thicken with snow clouds. I slipped and slid past Chinnor with a couple of pounds of glutinous clay on either foot, scrunched and crunched up through Hempton Wainhill in the skirts of Thickthorne Wood where the ice in the trackway ruts succeeded in cutting my boot burdens clean away.

The light began to drain away from the sky. I yomped along, out of the woods and on, following a Ridgeway sealed under tarmac into the outskirts of Princes Risborough. A last effort up the slippery steps of Brush Hill, past a Neolithic burial tump smothered in a coat of white and on down the long promontory nose of Giles Wood with a cold bright glare reflecting up from the snowy path to light my way through the dusk. The lights of the Plough Inn in the hamlet of Lower Cadsden drew me on down and in through the door, tired out and in need of a nice pint of never-mind-what, as the first flakes of yet another long night's snowfall began to twist and drive past the windows.

Right **There's a great view from Coombe Hill over the dignified Elizabethan manor of Chequers, the country residence of successive British prime ministers**

Next morning began cloudy and sharp, with gleams of sun spurring the blackbirds and warblers to bursts of ecstatic song in the gardens of Lower Cadsden. Blinking the sleep out of my eyes, I slogged up icy steps that climbed steeply to the wooded heights of Pulpit Hill. The open fields up there were crusted with patchy snow; others, a little further along, still lay under unbroken coats of white. I walked from one secret upland valley to the next as the Ridgeway rose and fell across their slopes, slippery and hazardous underfoot. Soon the sky cleared to a celestial blue, and a cold wind blowing from the north numbed my left cheek and set crystals of fog in each breath.

Down in its wide valley the great house of Chequers stood red and handsome among trees. No-one came and no-one went at the weekend retreat of successive prime ministers. I crunched across the drive and followed the Ridgeway as it curved through a horseshoe course to thread Goodmerhill Wood as a sodden track. Part deep-frozen, part melted and puddled, the boggy path lay so squashy with deep-packed leaf mulch that I found myself emulating the ancestors and treading ever more widely around the quagmires. Out on the flanks of Coombe Hill a huge view opened to the west – ploughland and pasture, village and town lying under a sky of pure, deep blue.

Above Wendover I came to the obelisk monument erected 'to the Men of Bucks who, at the Empire's call, laid down their lives during the War in South Africa, 1899–1902'. That noble line was followed by another: 'Dulce Et Decorum Est

Pro Patria Mori' – a sentiment to which the supreme Great War poet Wilfred Owen was to give the lie in 1918 with his stinging, desperate poem about a gas attack victim, 'Dulce Et Decorum Est'.

I inched my way down the frozen steps and gleaming slides of the ice-bound Ridgeway into the market town of Wendover, where a monstrous snowman around 10ft (3m) tall stood guard over a row of half-timbered, brick-nogged old cottages. Wendover is wholly charming, but it couldn't ensnare me today – not with the end of the walk close enough to taste, if not quite to see. I found the course of the Icknield Way, and followed it out of town as a narrow country lane running east as straight as an arrow.

How to disentangle Icknield Way and Ridgeway? Both names refer to much the same trackway in this part of the world, the great northeast-trending upland route that rides the bulges

of the chalk landscape on its way to… who knows where? Nowadays, for the convenience of walkers, the extremities of the path we call the Ridgeway have been fixed as Overton Hill in the west and Ivinghoe Beacon in the east. The Icknield Way is another very ancient name for this great ridgeway; but today we give that title to the walkers' and riders' route that runs on east from Ivinghoe Beacon for 100 miles (160km) into Suffolk. There it joins yet another ancient highway, styled Peddar's Way, that runs for 50 miles (80km) to the north Norfolk coast at Hunstanton. Did our ancestors really pursue such a course, 250 miles (400km) from Salisbury Plain to the bleak marshy shores of The Wash? More likely these tangles of paths, names and destinations exercise our over-classificatory modern minds far more than they ever did our Stone or Bronze Age forebears. They simply used the sections of upland track that they needed – and that was that.

Up in Hengrove Wood, Icknield Way met Ridgeway as a sunken holloway, and the reunited paths forged on northeast once more as a single broad track. Through Tring Park it rode a wooded ridge, with glimpses between the trees of the great Rothschild house of Tring Mansion. Down in the plains for the final time, I crossed the great cleft of the cutting opened in 1975 to let the A41 road through. Beyond on the outskirts of Tring lay two more giant cuttings, both spanned by the Ridgeway – the shadowy slit excavated in the 1790s to accommodate the Grand Junction Canal on a journey that would eventually take it the 150 miles (240km) from London to Birmingham, and a few hundred yards further on the huge delving dug in the 1830s to allow passage to the London & Birmingham Railway. Looking down from the three successive bridges over the three parallel gashes in the low landscape of the plain, I thought of the navvies who built canal and railway with pick and shovel. Each man was expected to shift daily, by the unaided power of his muscles, as much chalk as would fill two railway wagons. Exhaustion was part of the deal, injury commonplace, death a frequent visitor to the works. The canal and railway navvies randied and rioted, drank and fought, turned the air blue and scandalised every neighbourhood they descended upon. They built a transport system that became the envy of the world, yet lived and died in utter obscurity. They remain these islands' great unsung heroes.

Now came the final push to the crest and crown of the Ridgeway. The old track gave a last wriggle and settled itself into a northward course smack into the eye of the wind, hurdling the long backs of Aldbury Nowers and Pitstone Hill, then dipping for a final reunion with the Icknield Way. Now Ivinghoe Beacon was in clear view ahead, a snub nose of promontory streaked white with snow and green with grass. Up there at 755ft (230m) above sea level, after a last sharp upward climb, I stood in the oncoming dusk, lord of a 40-mile (65-km) prospect. Shadows were thickening below – mist, too, and the hint of more snow in the lemon-yellow sky away to the north. Very soon I would have to drop off the hill and look for lodgings before night and the gathering snowstorm could waylay me.

Not quite yet, though, not with a tawny owl heralding the oncoming night from the trees somewhere below, and a whole chapter of upland delights to think back on as I gazed east where the Icknield Way ran on and out of sight.

The Great Flats of Fenland

Thinking of Fenland, iconic images come thick and fast. Huge skies swirling with 50-mile blocks of cloud. A disc of rich black peat half a million acres broad, where lines of potato flowers, of carrot tops or beet sprouts spin by like the spokes of a bicycle wheel, running to a dead flat horizon and a vanishing point that shifts with every step a walker takes.

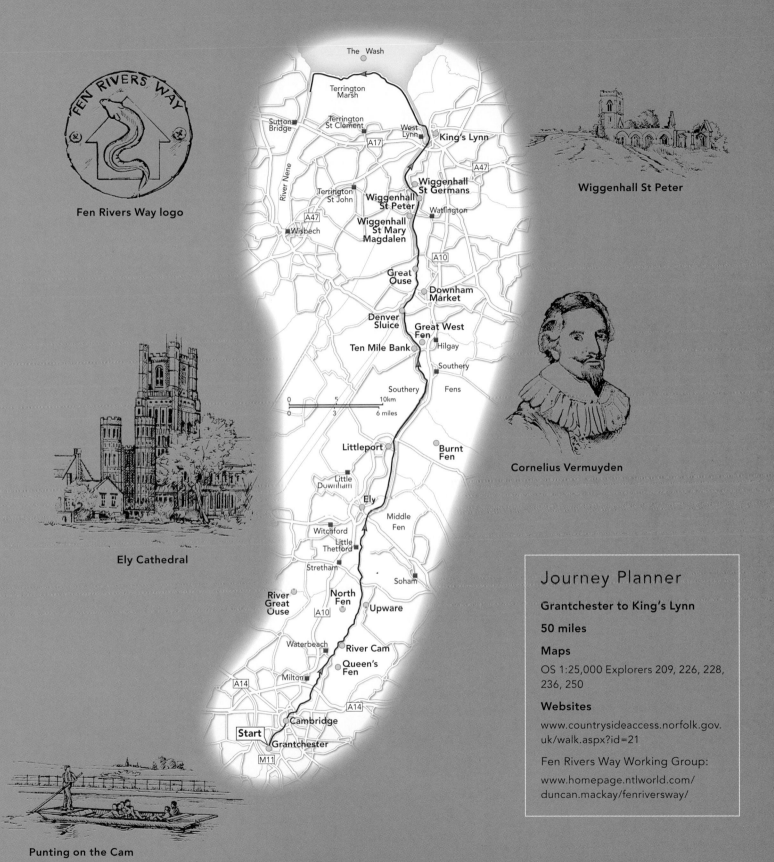

Fen Rivers Way logo

Ely Cathedral

Punting on the Cam

The Wash

Terrington Marsh

Sutton Bridge

Terrington St Clement

West Lynn

King's Lynn

A17

River Nene

Wiggenhall St Germans

A47

Terrington St John

Watlington

Wiggenhall St Peter

A47

Wiggenhall St Mary Magdalen

Wisbech

A10

Great Ouse

Downham Market

Denver Sluice

Great West Fen

Hilgay

Ten Mile Bank

Southery

Southery Fens

0   5   10km
0   3   6 miles

Littleport

Burnt Fen

Little Downham

Ely

Middle Fen

Witchford

Little Thetford

Stretham

Soham

River Great Ouse

North Fen

A10

Upware

Waterbeach

River Cam

Queen's Fen

Milton

A14

A14

Cambridge

Start

Grantchester

M11

Wiggenhall St Peter

Cornelius Vermuyden

Journey Planner

Grantchester to King's Lynn

50 miles

Maps

OS 1:25,000 Explorers 209, 226, 228, 236, 250

Websites

www.countrysideaccess.norfolk.gov.uk/walk.aspx?id=21

Fen Rivers Way Working Group:

www.homepage.ntlworld.com/duncan.mackay/fenriversway/

A hard, practical, no-nonsense land and people, imbued with deep eccentricities: wild men guarding their lonely farms with shotguns; barge dwellers; fen tigers; gumboots in the snug; wise women who have never been further than Wiggenhall St Germans; mastiffs raving in tumbledown barns worth a million pounds if the owner could ever be found and if he'd ever sell. Ruler-straight streams that flow higher than the highways, beeline roads running far above a shrinking land. Sluices, locks, outfalls, washes. Eaux, drains, cuts, lodes. And rivers, straight and broad, snaking and slender, cutting their way to the sea through a land the sea once had and will one day have again.

Could there be a more slumberous, soft-focus evocation of a river in an English summer setting than Rupert Brooke's *The Old Vicarage, Grantchester?* Brooke was recalling the lazy charm of the River Granta, which flows in long graceful curves through lush meadows near Grantchester, the rural Cambridgeshire village to which the young poet moved from rooms in King's College in June 1909 to immerse himself in a 'lovely and dim and rustic life'. That's where I started my walk to The Wash, Fenland's great square-sided drain of an estuary, about 50 miles north as the heron flies and a whole world away from the bicycling dons and idling undergraduates of Cambridge.

Oh! there the chestnuts, summer through,
Beside the river make for you
A tunnel of green gloom, and sleep
Deeply above; and green and deep
The stream mysterious glides beneath,
Green as a dream, and deep as death.

I only know that you may lie
Day long and watch the Cambridge sky,
And, flower-lulled in sleepy grass,
Hear the cool lapse of hours pass,
Until the centuries blend and blur
In Grantchester, in Grantchester…

Above **Punters cruising
by Queen's College glide
beneath Mathematical
Bridge as they pass the red
brick President's Lodge of
c1460, the oldest building
along the Backs**

Above right *And laughs
the immortal river still,
Under the mill, under
the mill?* **Rupert Brooke's
vision of Grantchester is
still alive and well**

Left **People still like to
laze, read and gossip in
Grantchester Meadows
on the banks of the River
Granta, just as they did in
Rupert Brooke's day**

The River Cam in Grantchester Meadows is a favourite bathing spot for undergraduates, now as in Rupert Brooke's pre-Great War idyll. I passed a party of them as soon as I got onto the footpath through the meadows – a dozen boys and girls on a couple of picnic rugs at the water's edge. Every minute or so someone would leap up and spring into the river with a tremendous splash, to the accompaniment of loud cheers. Beyond, other undergraduates were poling flat wooden punts under the willow branches. The polers' arms went slowly and rhythmically up and down, the punting poles flashed water droplets in the late afternoon sun, and the low murmur of conversation and laughter from the punt passengers underpinned the roistering of the bathing party.

The Fen Rivers Way long-distance footpath runs north from Cambridge, switching allegiance from Cam to Great Ouse as it carries a walker towards King's Lynn and The Wash. Next morning I set out early with a pale sun rising on my right hand. Empty champagne bottles littered the banks of the Cam, evidence of undergraduate boat club high jinks during the last week's Bumps races. Gonville & Caius Boat Club had somehow managed to paint the entire A45 road bridge across the river in their navy blue colours. 'Back Where We Belong' declared their victory inscription in huge wobbly letters.

Not a blade of grass, not a flowerbed petal was out of control in the gardens of the dimity thatched houses along the river as it snaked out of Cambridge. This was rich, peaceful, carefully manicured countryside. Sunlit water sparkled in bubbles and foam over the weirs at Baits Bite Lock. In a quiet backwater below the lock a pair of narrowboats lay moored beside the little flower garden their owners had created among the bankside weeds. Shirts and smalls flapped lazily in the breeze. The Cam curved on, flowing through a landscape that soon became harder, bleaker and more functional. The black peat soil of the fields was overlaid with green lines of potato plants, tangles of oilseed rape and smoothly stirring forests of pale green corn.

North Fen, said the map, naming these great squares of ground: Queen's Fen, Poor's Fen, Adventurer's Fen.

It was the Gentleman Adventurers, local venture capitalists, who risked their money and reaped their rewards in the 17th century when they invested in an epic scheme to drain the Fens. These sodden half-million acres of low-lying swampland, the flood basin of rivers and sea tides, had never been much good for anything. Fishers and fowlers lived among the miasmic fogs, eking a living, riddled with malaria, a race apart. Yet the peat soil, that part of it that lay unpolluted by salt, was potentially some of the most fertile in Britain. The Romans made a start on draining the Fens. Monks carried on the work a thousand years later; bishops paid for sections of drainage; other private individuals brought this patch and that corner under cultivation. But it took a daring widescreen vision to complete the job, a scheme initiated in

the 1630s by Francis Russell, 4th Earl of Bedford, and brought to fruition by the great Dutch water engineer Cornelius Vermuyden. Dutch know-how, English money and Scots prisoner-of-war muscle power saw it done in a few decades.

How the bloody-minded Fenmen hated the drainers! They saw their harsh, insular, self-sufficient way of life – wildfowling, reed-cutting, fishing – collapse as the black peat sprang into fertility. Sluices were blown up, lock gates smashed, drainage workers murdered. But the works went forward inexorably.

Something of the old lost-and-gone, lonely spirit of that older Fenland still hangs around isolated Upware, where I stopped for a bite to eat. 'Five Miles From Anywhere – No Hurry' is the apt name of the waterside pub. When the eccentric Richard Fielder proclaimed himself 'King of Upware' in the 1850s, he established his royal court in the pub. Fielder was an accomplished poet and a holy terror. He would fight with the Fen lightermen, dance with their daughters and distribute largesse in the form of rum punch from his seven-gallon gotch. The King of Upware had a high old time in his Fenland realm, until drink and the devil caught up with him.

Soon the River Great Ouse came sliding in to join the Cam and take me on up to my night stop at Ely. The little Fen town on its silty island of high ground was always a stronghold of local resistance to outsiders. When the Normans tried to get at the fugitive Hereward the Wake here, he set the fens on fire and roasted hundreds of enemy soldiers alive. But the Normans prevailed, and set their stamp on Ely by building one of Europe's great cathedrals to look down over the surrounding fenlands.

Left **Thousands of windpumps – nowadays often erroneously called windmills – were installed all over Fenland after the great drainage projects of the mid-17th century, in order to lift the water into the rivers and channels**

Right **Cutting reeds for use in thatching; an ancient craft, still very much alive, that forms an important part of the traditional management and economy of Fenland**

Next day the enormous twin-towered silhouette of the cathedral slowly diminished on the southern skyline as I moved north up the Great Ouse with a rainy wind at my back. Burnt Fen looked fully as dour as its name in this sinister half-light, with the stark shapes of black tarred barns and dark blocks of windbreak trees cutting into the bottom edge of an enormous sky of racing grey and silver clouds.

In *Poly-Olbion*, Michael Drayton's great topographical survey of England, the poet writes of the Fens as he saw them in the 1620s before Bedford and Vermuyden got to work. Drayton depicts the region as a prelapsarian Garden of Eden:

> The horse, or other beast, o'erweigh'd with his own mass,
> Lies wallowing in my fens, hid over head in grass;
> And in the place where grows rank fodder for my neat,
> The turf which bears the hay is wondrous needful peat;
> My full and batt'ning earth needs not the ploughman's pains,
> The rills which run in me are like the branchéd veins
> In human bodies seen; those ditches cut by hand,
> From the surrounding meres to win the measur'd land,
> To those choice waters I most fitly may compare,
> Wherewith nice women use to blanch their beauties rare.

Drainage changed everything in Fenland. The legacy of Bedford and Vermuyden was the conversion of Drayton's lush and pristine wilderness into half a million acres of the most productive farmland in Britain. The poet's Eden was lost. But the Serpent stayed behind. Nowadays the rivers run grossly polluted by pesticides and fertilisers, the wildlife is a sad shadow reduced by agrochemicals and loss of habitat, and the rich black peat has shrunk and sunk by as much as 30ft (9m) as the water that bulked it up has been drained away. As the precious soil dries, it breaks apart into its component shreds of ancient root, stalk and leaf. These elements, as light as gossamer, lie uncompounded on the surface of the fields, waiting for the next storm of wind over the flatlands to swirl them on high. The resultant phenomenon is known and feared as a Fen Blow, a dark fog of particles that shuts out light like an eclipse and can choke a passer-by caught out in the open.

I left the river bank just north of Littleport and struck out east across the black prairie of Burnt Fen. Ranks of lettuces, guarded from pigeon-raiding parties by bird-scaring streamers of yellow and white, ran to the horizon like a lesson in perspective painting. An enormous green spraying machine wobbled very slowly along the rows, its 100-ft (30-m) gantry hissing as it squirted a strong-smelling mist of chemicals across the vegetable plain. I halted on the embanked drove road high above the field to watch the work, and immediately the driver stopped, switched off and climbed down to walk across and inquire who I was and what I might be up to. There was a gun propped in the cab of the sprayer, and a motionless dog at its window. The farmer's questions were not exactly aggressive, but he wanted to know all about me before he'd let me move away.

Right **The Grade One, mineral-rich silt reclaimed from the sea at the margins of The Wash estuary is some of the finest agricultural land in Britain**

Far right **An early purple orchid, one of many beautiful species that thrive in the preserved Fenland habitat at Wicken Fen**

'Bloody pikeys,' was his attempt at explaining his suspicious demeanour. Travelling folk had robbed stuff out of his sheds, but they wouldn't get away with that again. Made him a bit quick to ask questions. Had he ever been caught in a Fen Blow? Yep. A bad one? Yep. Frightening? Yep. What was it like? Put it this way if I chopped a bag of turkey feathers up small and stuffed 'em in your eyes, up your nose and down your throat, what d'you reckon that would be like? He gave a small, sour laugh and turned away to his gun, dog and high seat over his black prairie.

I stopped for a cup of tea at a layby stall on the A10, then went on under slowly clearing skies by Ten Mile Bank and Great West Fen to Denver Sluice. Here at the heart and hub of Fenland, six great watercourses meet. Cornelius Vermuyden would hardly recognise the place where he built his first modest sluice in 1651. These days lock gates and guillotines, wheels and gantries, turbines and powerhouses control the bursting wetness of the region, sending hill floods harmlessly out into The Wash, keeping sea surges back, channelling water when it can work good and not harm.

A night in Downham Market, nursing sore feet blistered by the hard clay river banks, and then a final dozen miles up the Great Ouse towards the sea. The towers of Fen churches stood outlined against the sky: Wiggenhall St Mary Magdalen, Wiggenhall St Germans, the haunting riverbank ruin of Wiggenhall St Peter.

Black-capped terns and herring gulls were screaming over the Great Ouse as it made a final broad sweep past the churches, merchants' houses and quayside silos of King's Lynn. The old river port, glowing in afternoon sunshine, smelt of grain and sea salt. I took a last look at the brown tidal river as it swept on out into the mudbanks and marshes of The Wash, and then limped off down the narrow streets of Lynn.

... the Great Ouse made a final broad sweep past the churches, merchants' houses and quayside silos of King's Lynn. The old river port, glowing in afternoon sunshine, smelt of grain and sea salt.

The Rim of Gower

The long-horned cattle cropped the grass of West Cliff contentedly. Their dappled hides glittered in the late spring sunshine as if slivers of mirror had been sewn in among the hairs. I watched them for a long time, mesmerised by the slow blinking of their sleepy-looking eyes and the soft tearing noises they made as they pulled each mouthful free. If I were a stress doctor, I'd certainly prescribe cattle-watching in Gower as a sovereign remedy.

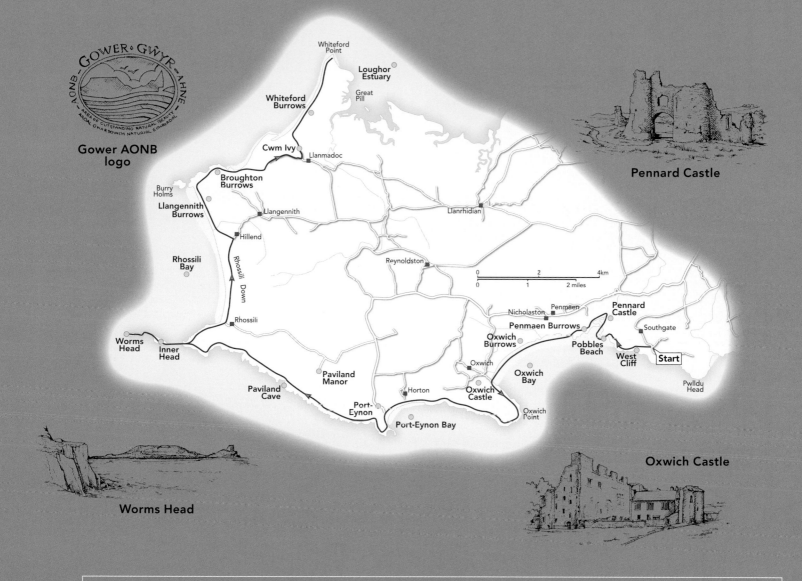

Gower AONB logo

Whiteford Point

Loughor Estuary

Whiteford Burrows

Great Pill

Cwm Ivy

Llanmadoc

Broughton Burrows

Burry Holms

Llangennith Burrows

Llangennith

Llanrhidian

Hillend

Rhossili Bay

Reynoldston

Rhossili Down

Nicholaston

Penmaen

Pennard Castle

Penmaen Burrows

Southgate

Oxwich Burrows

Pobbles Beach

West Cliff

Start

Rhossili

Worms Head

Inner Head

Oxwich

Oxwich Bay

Pwlldu Head

Paviland Manor

Horton

Oxwich Castle

Paviland Cave

Oxwich Point

Port-Eynon

Port-Eynon Bay

0   2   4km

0   1   2 miles

Pennard Castle

Worms Head

Oxwich Castle

Journey Planner

Three Cliffs Bay to Whiteford Sands

27 miles

Maps

OS 1:25,000 Explorer 164

Books

'Who Do You Wish Was With Us?' in *A Portrait of the Artist as a Young Dog* by Dylan Thomas (Phoenix)

Websites

The Gower Society: www.gowersociety.org.uk

www.explore-gower.co.uk

Worms Head: The causeway is accessible 2½ hours each side of low water; a total of 5 hours. Tide times are posted in the NT Visitor Centre below Rhossili car park (tel 01792 390707; www.nationaltrust.org.uk); or ring Coastwatch (01792 390512). It takes at least 15 minutes of rough scrambling to cross the causeway

Caves: Before attempting to explore Paviland and other caves, contact the NT Warden (tel 01792 390636)

The 18-mile-long peninsula on the South Wales coast is one of those places whose name brings nods of recognition and smiles of pleasure. 'Ah, Gower, yes, that's a special little corner, isn't it?' the Mumbles café owner had said over his shoulder that morning as he prepared my bacon sandwich. 'I go down to Gower when I want a bit of...well, *time out*, we'll call it.' And that's exactly it about Gower. The city of Swansea lies like a guard dog across the narrow threshold of the peninsula, keeping the outside world at bay. Gower is shaped like a huge-mouthed fish swimming west for the open Atlantic, trailing random fins and filaments. Its perimeter is all hollows, crevices and odd indentations. Bays and coves open suddenly; solid-looking headlands turn out to have arches eaten through them by the sea. There are hidden beaches and secret caves, promontory forts and ancient tombs. You can lose yourself along the shore and hide yourself in the cliff woods, or just stand and watch cows eat grass.

Down on Pobbles Beach three girls were towelling themselves off. The smiles they gave me were friendly enough, but there was a touch of *noli me tangere* too. I sympathised: when you're nice and early on a Gower beach, that beach is yours. I ducked out of their way through the wave-worn arch in the toe of the headland, and followed the winding course of Pennard Pill inland to its stepping stones under the stark ruin of Pennard Castle. A steep scramble up the dunes brought me level with the shell of the old fortification, established only a few decades after the Norman Conquest and rebuilt in stone (not too cleverly, according to expert opinion) a couple of centuries later. The architects seem to have tried to build the stronghold in accordance with contemporary military fashions, but didn't really understand what they were up to. As finished, the castle had insufficient and badly sited arrow slits, an ill-fitting portcullis and poorly crafted masonry.

In its high and mighty position on the sandhills the castle might have been able to withstand a siege by mortal men, but a combination of natural and supernatural forces proved too much for it. History suggests it was gradually smothered, along with its village and church, by the blown sand of the coast. Legend, as ever, has a better tale to tell... During the Dark Ages a mighty warrior chief, a rough and tough winner of battles, lived in Pennard Castle with his men, a drunken band of savage fighters. Hearing of the chief's reputation, a king who was prosecuting a war with a neighbouring prince sent word to the castle, offering whatever reward the warrior cared to name in exchange for his help. The ferocious men of the garrison marched forthwith behind their leader, routed the prince and his followers in a terrible bloodbath somewhere on the borders of Gwynedd, and returned to Pennard Castle with the prize the warrior chief had claimed for himself – the king's own beloved and beautiful daughter.

This innocent maiden, a great favourite with the fairies for her gentle ways and generosity, found herself in the midst of a full-scale orgy. The castle was foul with vomit and curses, and filled with drunken men fornicating and fighting. Horrified, the princess ran to hide. Just then a cheer was heard outside. It was her friends the fairies, arriving in high spirits for the wedding feast. Thinking they were being attacked by an enemy army, the warrior chief and his befuddled men seized their weapons, ran out and set about the newcomers. When their sword cuts fell on empty air, they realised that they were dealing with no mortal foes. But it was too late to retract the blows. So offended were the fairies that they summoned up the mother of all sandstorms. It blew for three days, and when calm finally returned to the bay the castle was seen no more. It had been buried fathoms deep, along with its brutal guardians. As for the gentle princess, she may lie among her oafish oppressors in the heart of Pennard Burrows. Or perhaps, as some stories tell, she was rescued by the fairies and lived happily ever after in their delightful company.

Left **The Pennard Pill river comes snaking down through the sands of Three Cliffs Bay, skirting the promontory at Pobbles Beach to make its way to the sea**

Right **Overlooking the Pennard Pill are the ruins of Pennard Castle, never the most secure of strongholds, but a great focus for wild tales**

There is something about the act of crossing a river from stone to stone that never quite loses its childhood magic. On the headland of Penmaen Burrows beyond, my notes assured me that I'd find the motte of another early Norman castle, the ruin of a limekiln, a stone-walled depression holding fragments of a medieval church (an incense burner in the shape of Jerusalem had been unearthed from its ruins, a nice touch), and the Neolithic chambered tomb of Pen-y-Crug, the 'top of the tump'. It sounded amazing. But in the event only the tomb seemed to be there. Perhaps the fairies had made off with the other sites, or hidden them under the sand?

In Nicholaston Woods all was very still under the heat of midday. Hints of salt and tar came up through the trees from the direction of Oxwich Burrows, and when I had descended to the beach the same smells came more strongly from a tideline heaped with twisted remnants of old sea-bleached timbers. Sandhoppers leaped among the empty limpet and mussel shells, each hop productive of a just-audible 'ping'. I could have idled there all afternoon among the pyramidal orchids and the big blue blooms of sea holly, watching the turnstones and sandpipers examining the pickings at the edge of the sea. But I wanted to renew my acquaintance with Oxwich Castle, really a fortified house of the Tudor era, a wonderful jumble of a ruin with dozens of tiny blank windows, bushy fireplaces and a gatehouse complete with a murder slit and the crumbling coat of arms of Sir Rice Mansel, builder of the castle. It was in the gateway that Sir Rice's young son Edward, in the absence of his father, confronted a gang led by Sir George Herbert of Swansea at the end of December 1557, a few days after a French vessel had been wrecked in Oxwich Bay.

The Mansels had salvaged the ship's cargo and stashed it away in various houses on their estate, and now Herbert's men were out to steal as much of it as they could while Rice Mansel was from home. Sir George taunted young Edward at his own front door, threatening to 'bynde him like a boy, and send him to his father like a coke'. Then someone smacked the lad with a sword, causing him to draw his own weapon and begin laying about him. The fight that erupted ended with Edward's aunt Anne Mansel lying dead in the archway, her brain pierced with a sharp stone thrown by one of the trespassers. At the ensuing trial, Herbert was heavily fined and imprisoned.

Far left **An oystercatcher probes the tideline in Oxwich Bay**

Left **Oxwich Castle, scene of murder and mayhem in Tudor times, possesses a very fine dovecot that contains eleven layers of nesting holes – enough to keep a besieged garrison in meat for many a day**

Right **Sunset over the rugged promontories of Gower, the 'secret peninsula' beyond the gateway city of Swansea**

If you were looking for a stretch of coast to entice you round the next headland and over the one after that, this run of tilted strata along the southern rim of Gower with their square cave mouths and tiny crescent inserts of sand would be hard to better.

Aggression and boorish behaviour, headstrong brutality leading to catastrophe and fierce punishment: Gower's castles seemed destined to form the backdrop to these dark and primitive morality plays.

The sun slipped behind a bank of cloud driving up from the west, and I felt like moving on and getting some more clean salt air in my lungs. I hadn't really bargained on walking 20 miles that day, but somehow that's what happened. If you were looking for a stretch of coast to entice you round the next headland and over the one after that, this run of tilted strata along the southern rim of Gower with their square cave mouths and tiny crescent inserts of sand would be hard to better. There were stunning views from the long blunt headland of Oxwich Burrows, back over the beach and dunes, forward to the distant sands in Port-Eynon Bay with the red-roofed village tucked hard down on the far side in the shelter of its own rocky promontory point. Beyond Port-Eynon I walked like a man in a dream, drugged with the exercise and the up-and-down of the path, in and out of gorse patches as thick as a sheep's fleece, head down and collar up into the wind, while a bell buoy clanged dolorously and the sea thumped into the cliffs and flew up in foam that sparkled like a shower of brilliants in the low evening sunlight.

On the path below Paviland Manor three beautiful milk-white horses came trotting up to look me over. A stony path led steeply down towards the sea below a great pointed shark's tooth of cliff. I scrambled out along the rocks as far as I could in the failing light, but a turn in the cliff concealed the entrance to Paviland Cave. I had to content myself with sending my imagination back to 1823, and setting it to follow the tweedy back and hobnailed soles of the Reverend William Buckley, Oxford University's first Professor of Geology, into what was then known as Goat Hole. The human remains that Rev. Buckley dug out of the cave floor were to turn the fledgling science of archaeology on its head. He excavated a headless skeleton stained red with ochre, along with some seashell beads and artefacts of bone, antler and ivory. He thought he'd unearthed the 2,000-year-old remains of a prostitute – inevitably soon dubbed the Red Lady – who had served the soldiers of the nearby Roman camp. But another examination nearly a century later by anthropologist Professor William Sollas, using more advanced scientific technology, determined that what the Rev. Buckley had actually discovered was a Red Gentleman, a hunter-gatherer chieftain, tall and well nourished, fond of shellfish and hunted game, who had been buried with much ceremony in Paviland Cave at the height of the last Ice Age some 25,000 years before. The red ochre dressing of his bones suggests a powerful person, perhaps a shaman. The enormously tall wall of the southern face of the great ice shelf would have been less than a day's journey north, the sea half-frozen, the land white, the air a knife in the throat. It would be hard to envisage a wilder, weirder or more resonant place to be laid to rest.

Next day I had another rocky scramble, a familiar one. The 2-mile promontory of Worms Head snakes out into the sea from the southwest corner of Gower, its central and outer segments rearing out of the water like the humped back and upthrust head of a monster. In vigorous weather the head spouts a jet of water from a blowhole with the hissing sigh of a venting whale. Norsemen came to raid Gower in the 9th century, and stayed to farm and fish. They dubbed

Right **From the craggy rock floor of Paviland Cave, high in the cliffs of Gower, pioneer archaeologist Rev. William Buckley excavated in 1823 the remains of the 'Red Lady of Paviland' – actually a priest or nobleman who died some 25,000 years ago**

Worms Head snakes out into the sea from the southwest corner of Gower, its central and outer segments rearing out of the water like the humped back and upthrust head of a monster.

the promontory *wurm*, or 'dragon', a name so apt it stuck fast. You have to watch the tides when you venture out along the promontory: the pooled and pitted causeway between the mainland and the Inner Head, as rough as sandpaper with barnacles and awkwardly canted blades of rock, is a tougher proposition than it looks from the mainland, and the crossing between Inner and Outer Heads is an ankle-twister, too. Dylan Thomas got himself stuck out there and had to wait till midnight, in terror of 'rats, and of things I am ashamed to be frightened of', before the tide turned far enough for the young poet to creep ashore. Out on the Outer Head today it was kittiwake heaven, smack in the middle of the breeding season for the seabirds with the black-tipped wings. *Ee-WAKE! Ee-WAKE!* they shrieked, thousands of voices with just the one comment for sorrow or joy, hunger or alarm. *Ee-WAKE! Ee-WAKE!* Dylan Thomas may have run on rather a lot, but at least he had a bit of vocabulary to his name.

Back across the causeway I walked the 3-mile curve of Rhossili Beach, the 3-mile sandhills of Llangennith and Broughton Burrows, with hardly a thought in my head. This, the open mouth of the great westward-swimming fish of Gower, was pure reaction country, a luxurious saunter for the senses: the acupuncture pricks of wind-blown sand against the ankles and arms, the piercing pip!-pip!-pip! of startled oystercatchers, the velvet nap of the dune grasses rippling like a muscled body under a pelt, the iodine smell of the open sea giving way to the sun-warmed algal stink of the mudflats in the Loughor Estuary. Towards evening I dropped down the bank from Cwm Ivy and headed out along the dune path of Whiteford Burrows under a threatening slaty sky. The path switched left and right through birch and willow scrub, through black shadow patches under stands of pine trees planted here for some harvest that never happened.

Out at the north point the view suddenly opened through the sandhills to the wide half-tide muds and sands of the estuary, blearily gleaming as a rainstorm pocked them. I took off my boots and went down to cool my feet in the mud, then climbed the nearest dune and sat with chocolate feet and wet limbs to watch the sun ditch in the cloud banks over Pembrokeshire, shooting out a last gleam as it sank. If melancholy and beauty ever truly harmonised, it was exactly here and now.

Mystery and Magic in the Berwyn Hills

On the road to the fall, the grass banks under the neatly laid hedges were brilliant with primrose clumps, white star-bursts of stitchwort and individual violets with pendulous nether lips and velvety leaves. Every flower, every grass blade and hawthorn spray held a weight of trembling rain globules, the legacy of last night's rainstorms that had marched across North Wales. 'It'll clear,' said the farmer at Tyn-y-ddol, glancing west up the valley towards the mist-shrouded Berwyn Hills. The confidence in his tone convinced me that he knew what he was talking about.

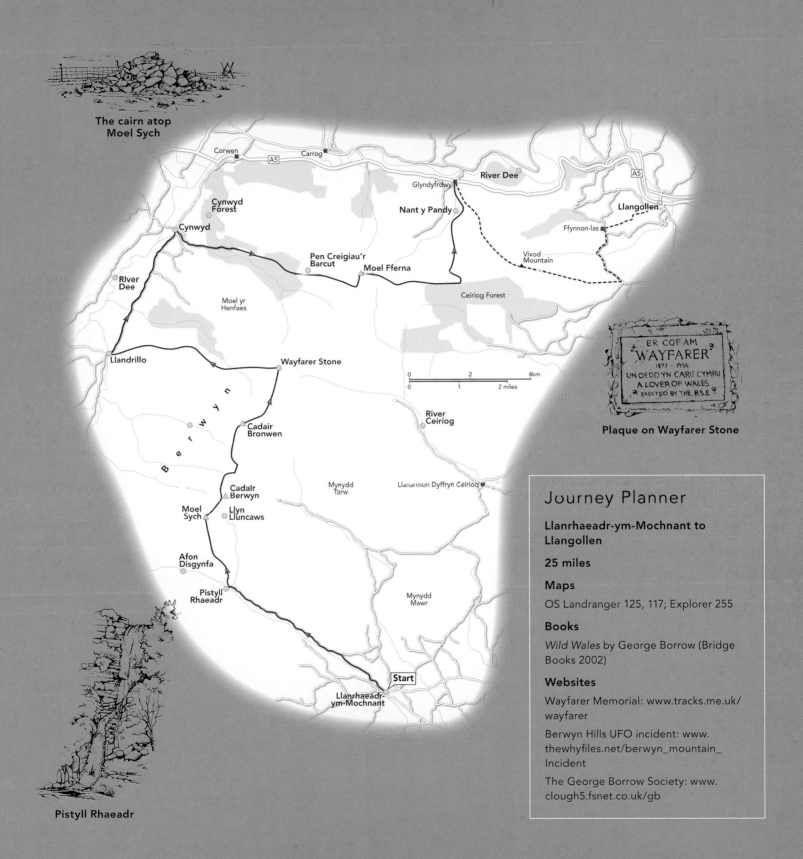

The cairn atop
Moel Sych

Corwen
A5
Carrog
River Dee
Glyndyfrdwy
Nant y Pandy
Llangollen
Cynwyd
Forest
Ffynnon-las
Cynwyd
Pen Creigiau'r
Barcut
Moel Fferna
Vivod
Mountain
River
Dee
Moel yr
Henfaes
Ceiriog Forest
Llandrillo
Wayfarer Stone
B e r w y n
River
Ceiriog
Cadair
Bronwen
Cadair
Berwyn
Mynydd
Tarw
Llanarmon Dyffryn Ceiriog
Moel
Sych
Llyn
Lluncaws
Afon
Disgynfa
Pistyll
Rhaeadr
Mynydd
Mawr
Start
Llanrhaeadr-
ym-Mochnant

ER COF AM
"WAYFARER"
1877 – 1956
UN OEDD YN CARU CYMRU
A LOVER OF WALES
ERECTED BY THE R.S.F

Plaque on Wayfarer Stone

0   2   4km
0   1   2 miles

Journey Planner

Llanrhaeadr-ym-Mochnant to Llangollen

25 miles

Maps

OS Landranger 125, 117; Explorer 255

Books

Wild Wales by George Borrow (Bridge Books 2002)

Websites

Wayfarer Memorial: www.tracks.me.uk/ wayfarer

Berwyn Hills UFO incident: www. thewhyfiles.net/berwyn_mountain_ Incident

The George Borrow Society: www. clough5.fsnet.co.uk/gb

Pistyll Rhaeadr

Up at the end of the road a muffled hissing filled the air. The last time I was here, two years before, the valley head had been filled with a deep-throated thunder. Rain had been falling for five days solid over the Berwyns, and the grossly engorged Afon Disgynfa had hurled itself over the lip of its 200-ft (60-m) cliff as brown, thick and creamy as a vat burst in a Guinness brewery. Today Pistyll Rhaeadr, the highest waterfall in Wales, was a muted presence, as I saw when I turned the corner and stood in full view of the great wall of iron-hard felsite down which it was sluicing. The Disgynfa fell in heavy folds like the ruches in a thick lace curtain, a double fall that stunned the mind, a straight initial plunge of 100ft (30m) into a pool, then a smoking jet that funnelled out through the black hole of a natural rock bridge and on down to smash into a lower pool. Standing on the footbridge at the bottom of Pistyll Rhaeadr I stared up, mesmerised by the weight and energy of the falling water.

'What shall I liken it to?' apostrophised George Borrow when he came to inspect the fall in 1854. 'I scarcely know, unless to an immense skein of silk agitated and disturbed by tempestuous blasts, or to the long tail of a courser at furious speed.' The horse's tail was a superb analogy, Borrow at his best. Born a Saxon of East Anglian origin, there was nothing in this world that Borrow longed for more passionately than to be accepted in the land of the Celts. He taught himself Welsh, he boned up on every Welsh poet, hymner and obscure writer he came across. He crammed his head with Welsh history, and his heart and soul with Welsh customs and manners. In 1854 he brought his wife and step-daughter to Llangollen for a change of air, and left them there to twiddle their thumbs while he went charging off on foot across his beloved adopted land, striding across Anglesey, bounding up Snowdon, hustling and hurrying the length of the country in search of Wales and the Welsh. Also – very important to the supreme egotist Borrow – he took every opportunity to show off in front of the country people he met, causing astonishment as a Saesneg who could speak Cymric, confounding innkeepers and rural doctors with his expertise in Welsh poetry, dazzling hedgers and ditchers with his intimate knowledge of their native geography and folklore. Reading *Wild Wales*, his breathlessly boastful account of these wanderings, it's clear that among the country folk Borrow encountered, he provoked as much mirth as admiration with his clever-dickery. But the sheer force and self-belief of the man, even when he is being mocked by rustics or deliberately led astray by cunning guides, never fail to sweep this reader like a whirlwind through the pages of *Wild Wales*.

As for Pistyll Rhaeadr: Borrow thought it exceeded all the waterfalls of Britain for altitude and beauty. But like a true egotist, he couldn't allow himself to surrender completely to the majesty of the cataract. The black rock bridge halfway down offended him by getting in the way. 'What beautiful object has not something which more or less mars its loveliness?' he complained. 'This unsightly object has stood where it now stands since the day of creation, and will probably remain there to the day of judgement. It would be a desecration of nature to remove it by art, but no one could regret if nature in one of her floods were to sweep it away.'

Borrow fell into conversation with the woman of the house at the foot of the fall, and heard from her of a Russian visitor whom she had watched wriggling up one side of the rock bridge like

Right **Rippling like 'the long tail of a courser at furious speed', the waterfall of Pistyll Rhaeadr – the highest in Wales at 240ft (74m) – plunges down a cliff of dark felsite at the head of the lower Disgynfa valley**

an eel. The man had stood upright at the apex for a minute, and then slithered down the other side. Borrow drank a bowl of buttermilk with the woman, and took a look at her guest book. True to form, he rose to the challenge of a rival:

'I took up the book which contained a number of names mingled here and there with pieces of poetry. Amongst these compositions was a Welsh englyn on the Rhyadr, which though incorrect in its prosody I thought stirring and grand. I copied it, and subjoin it with a translation which I made on the spot.'

"Crychiawg, ewynawg anian-yw y Rhyadr
Yn rhuo mal taran;
Colofn o dwr, gloyw-dwr glan,
Gorwyllt, un lliw ag arian."

"Foaming and frothing from mountainous
  height,
Roaring like thunder the Rhyadr falls;
Though its silvery splendour the eye may
  delight,
Its fury the heart of the bravest appals."

After I'd gazed my fill at Pistyll Rhaeadr I shouldered my pack and set off up the steep rocky path to the top of the fall. Up there I found a silent land, devoid of people, the metallic *chip-chip* of pipits and the phlegmy bleating of ewes forming a counterpoint to the hiss and rustle of the cataract. Ferny pastures, lichen-speckled gates and mossy fingerposts attested to the dampness and purity of the air of these hills, and of the omnipresent influence of Pistyll Rhaeadr and its moist exhalations. At the brink of the fall I inched out onto an arrow-shaped spur of rock, its grass rubbed bare and its earth beaten flat by centuries of intimate contact with the bellies and knees of heart-in-mouth visitors creeping forward in the prone position to peep over the lip of the cataract. The Rhaeadr dropped into space quite modestly, its smooth 90 degree curve of molten glass giving no hint of the crashing and concussion of lawless water 200ft (60m) below.

From close to, the mist blanketing the Berwyns looked thicker than ever. I tightened the pack and struck off up the path, a green quarryman's trod that led steeply and purposefully up towards the gathering murk. Ten minutes later, scratching my head, I lugged out the Satmap satellite navigation device. GPS, let me say, is a gizmo I have always mistrusted. What if it goes wrong, or you press one of the array of fiddly little buttons by mistake and find you are now in Kyrgyzstan? Or if it just gets lost – falls off the lanyard when you are climbing a stile, or can't be found when you get up from your picnic? Today Satmap's little blue dot agreed that I was where I thought I was: quite a long way off the path.

The Berwyns are well placed for mystery and magic – not to say mistiness. These lumpy, remote hills of shale, sandstone and mudstone boast few paths and many mires. They are knapsack-and-boots, map-and-compass country, rising in humps and billows to a height of 2,713ft (827m) between the valleys of Afon Dyfrdwy (River Dee) and Afon Ceiriog. In times past they represented a formidable obstacle for the shepherds, packmen and farmers who had to cross them. Everyone respected them for their sudden mists and moods of ill weather. Wayfarers with active imaginations feared them for the ghosts and lake monsters that haunted them. More solidly founded are the stories of aircraft wrecks on the Berwyns. Most extraordinary of all is the tale of the UFO that crashed on the hills one January night, sparking a full-scale top secret alert.

What actually happened on 23 January 1974 is still a matter of hot debate locally. Everyone agrees that a huge explosion was heard from Cadair Berwyn, the summit of the range, just after 8.30pm, followed by a prolonged, earthquake-like rumbling. A white glow was seen on the mountain. Strong beams of light appeared to be searching the sky. Next day, crazy tales began to do the rounds. They spoke of would-be rescuers being turned brusquely away by tight-lipped policemen and soldiers; of planes and helicopters criss-crossing the mountain; of mysterious men in black hurrying down the hills with large boxes containing the remains of beings never born of mortal woman. When all was said and done, the likeliest scenario seems to have been an earth tremor along the Berwyn fault that follows the mountain ridge, coupled by chance with sightings, magnified by the prevailing atmospheric conditions, of light beams from the powerful lamps and torches wielded by a gang of poachers who were out on the mountain that night. That has by no means satisfied local gossips, nor the ever-avid online community of conspiracy theorists.

I got back on the path again and recommenced plodding by zigs and zags up the steep breast of Moel Felen towards the peaks. The path grew soft and floody, with sloppy black patches where walkers had trodden wider and wider afield to avoid the peaty morass. A surge of thick white vapour advanced downhill and engulfed me. Tricks of acoustics brought up the rushing of the Afon Disgynfa from 600ft

(180m) below and far behind. Invisible larks sang ecstatically overhead, perhaps in blue sky. Down here there was nothing whatsoever to see. The map told me I should come to a boundary line, a fence or wall, which would be my guide along the high ridge. By keeping the unseen cliffs of Moel Sych close on my right hand, as near as I could judge, I came to the boundary, a wire fence leading north, and followed it up into ever thicker mist.

The summit of Moel Sych, when I'd sweated up to it, revealed a cairn of stones in the gloom. I couldn't see 20 yards ahead. Everything was utterly quiet. Even the pipits had stopped cheeping. Somewhere far below, so the map told me, lay the lonely lake of Llyn Lluncaws, lair of the Gwybr of Llanrhaeadr, a fearsome man-eating dragon whom the local folk had defeated by their quick wits and bravery in the dim and mythic past. Beyond the peak, walking on towards Cadair Berwyn, I began to sense great precipices on my right hand, plunging into invisibility – 600ft (180m) of fall, said the map, but all the majesty of these tremendous mountain walls was robbed by the thick curtain of the mist. Only the fence stood between me and the edge. Then the path crossed the wires and began to run right at the rim of the cliffs through a slough of boot-churned bog. Halfway across I slipped over and landed with a thud. I got up gingerly and considered. Don't be a wimp. Yes, and don't be a bloody fool either. Where's the problem with a bit of mist? It's dangerous on these wet clifftops, and I'm walking alone. Oh, come on – you've got that nice helpful Satmap telling you exactly where you are. Oh, aye – and if it packs up? It's not going to pack up. Well, I'm not going to risk it. Well, *I'm* going on, anyway. What's the point, when you can't see anything? Huh, what are you, man or mouse?

Mouse, evidently. I turned round with a sigh. The gluey path back to the waterfall seemed to take for ever, and it was raining when I got down there. The 4 miles along the lane into Llanrhaeadr-ym-Mochnant weren't much fun. By the time I'd driven round the foot of the hills to Llandrillo on the western side of the range, though, things were looking up. A watery sun tried to look through the clouds, and the lower slopes of the Berwyns were coming into focus as the mist slowly moved up and away from them. The feeling of defeat, sour in my stomach, lifted with the weather. I looked up at the steadily rising mistline. There was plenty of daylight left. Why not do the second half of the crossing in reverse? The thought was father to the deed. I left the heavy pack behind and hurried up the Wayfarer's road into the hills with the internal supercharger on thrust once more.

The old drove road leads over the mountains between the Dee and Ceiriog valleys, a peaceful track these days, winding up and along the hill sides, twisting in and out of hazel dells where it fords streams coming tumbling off the hills. Silver birch and rowan shade it, stone walls shape and guard it. These walls are lovely things, curvilinear and full of bulges, made up of countless million thin blades of stone whose native grey has been softened by centuries of weathering and lichen growth to a muted olive green. Here and there the builders have inserted blocks of quartz as big as a man's head, maybe intended to guide drovers and beasts with their gleam at night or in mist or perhaps following Celtic traditions of investing quartz with magical properties of healing and good luck. Whatever the purpose, these dully shining inserts look beautiful in their multi-layered setting.

I walked up past the barking dogs at Tyn-y-cae-mawr, and on across hillsides where lambs went jumping away on spring heels. Their plaintive high-pitched bleating pushed the same sympathy buttons in my guts as a baby's crying. Far wilder were the bubbly, tremulous calls that floated up from the valley beyond. I looked over the wall and caught a glimpse of a brown bird planing close over the slopes, wings held in a tight, sabre-shaped curve as it braked and fluttered before landing in a series of light bounces in the boggy ground by the Afon Llynon. The unselfconscious grace of the curlew's movement and the haunting quality of its call held me spell-bound. It was as if the hills had found a springtime voice.

At Bwlch Nant Rhyd Wilym, the head of the pass, I found a shiny steel plaque held between twin boulders of white quartzite, commemorating the writer Walter Robinson – 'Wayfarer' to his readers and admirers. Robinson inspired a whole generation of young cyclists in the 1920s with his example, and specifically with an article entitled 'Over The Top' in which he celebrated the delights of bicycling off-piste. In 1957, the year after Wayfarer's death, the Rough Stuff Fellowship of off-road cyclists placed a memorial stone to their guru at the pass. The metal slab is a recent replacement, I was told by a passing Lancastrian cyclist who stopped to wipe the sweat from his neck and face. 'And not bad neither,' he said with a crisp nod of approval as he remounted and pelted off downhill.

A lead box sunk in the ground in front of the memorial held diaries and notebooks dating back decades. 'Fine day, clear sky, marvellous views,' enthused older entries from a politer era. 'The Redditch Massive!' bragged a contemporary scrawl from an off-road driver. 'Rippin' up the Valleys!' The deep ruts scored in the old drove road running over the pass authenticated the boast. Off-road driving was evidently a source of aggressive glee for the perpetrators, of bitter angst for walkers and cyclists. 'Anyone who brings a 4X4 to this beautiful, lonely place,' an indignant hiker had written in a thick, exasperated scribble, 'must surely be an insensitive, selfish idiot!' I was to find out the truth of that myself the following day.

I turned south up the spine of the Berwyns as the last curl of mist unstuck itself and drifted up into the sky. The late sun lit up the peak of Cadair Bronwen, with Cadair Berwyn looking over its shoulder. It was sublime on the ridge with the late-afternoon sun pouring like thick honey across the slopes, picking up the nap of the creamy moorgrass like a millionaire's billiard table. I hurried on up the rising ground until I could look along the first of the four great bowls of the eastern face, a steely blue in profound shadow. Along there and out of sight stood Moel Sych and the dip where I had nearly gone over the edge. I wasn't sorry now that I'd turned back. If I hadn't, apart from the fair chance of breaking my neck, I'd never have known the range from its other end as I knew it now, stretched out like a big sleeping cat in the sunshine.

I got down to Y Llwyn guesthouse in Llandrillo at nightfall, and was welcomed with a floury handshake by Eilys Jones. The joint of lamb was sizzling in the carving dish, the wine was open on the table. The morning of doubts and disappointments on misty Moel Sych seemed a long way off in this hospitable Welsh-speaking house. Under the tutelage of Eilys and her husband Aeron I learned the Welsh for bacon, *bacwn*; eggs, *wyau*; porridge, *huwd*; tea, *te* – a curiously

I turned south up the spine of the Berwyns as the last curl of mist unstuck itself and drifted up into the sky. The late sun lit up the peak of Cadair Bronwen, with Cadair Berwyn looking over its shoulder.

Right **Beware the Gwybr of Llanrhaeadr when you venture near Llyn Lluncaws! Legendary lair of the man-eating dragon, the mountain lake lies like a glittering jewel below the craggy summit of Cadair Berwyn**

culinary list, cribbed from the bilingual breakfast menu lying on the table. As for Welsh in the Dee Valley, Eilys and Aeron reckoned it was in decline. 'People move here from a non-Welsh speaking area,' said Aeron, 'and often enough they won't try and learn a word of Welsh.' Eilys nodded. 'Yes, when I went to primary school in Llandrillo, everyone spoke Welsh, in and out of school, in and out of the house. That was it. But now people who have moved here and don't see the need to speak Welsh will send their children to an English-speaking school down the valley, in order to *stop* them speaking Welsh. Perhaps they see it as a disadvantage – but we don't,' she added mildly.

So why speak Welsh at all? Why bother to keep a minority language alive? 'It's not a minority hereabouts, you see,' Aeron said. 'And what you can express in Welsh is something you won't ever achieve in English, powerful though that language might be.'

George Borrow, the Welsh-spouting Saesneg, would have applauded – in fact he'd probably have composed an englyn about roast lamb upon the spot. I remembered a Scots Gaelic speaker in the Western Isles telling me, 'If you don't understand any Gaelic, then you'll be walking through the islands as a deaf, dumb and blind man.' In my room at Y Llwyn later that night, full of good food, red wine and warm talk, I spread out the OS Explorer map of the day's walk on my bed, opened my little paperback dictionary of Welsh/English place names, and went exploring anew.

The southern sector of the Berwyn Hills pivots on the high south–north ridge from Pistyll Rhaeadr via Moel Sych and Cadairs Berwyn and Bronwen to the Wayfarer's Pass. The northern half is entirely different in character, a rolling succession of east–west waves of ground with few dramatic features. Notwithstanding the absence of cliffs and crags, this is still wild and lonely country. I was lucky indeed that

Ron Williams, the Ramblers' Association's regional footpaths officer, had declared himself free and willing to be my companion. Next morning Ron was waiting for me in the bus shelter at Cynwyd, just up the road from Llandrillo – a calm, droll North Walian, very active in the politics and practicalities of Welsh walking for the past 50 years; also a priceless optimist. 'The cloud? Oh, that'll lift by the time we get up there. Thunder and lightning? No chance. Rain? It'll ease off, you'll see.' It poured down as we set off. Thunder cracked directly overhead. Lightning flashed. The mist clung to the hilltops like a satisfied lover. 'Lovely weather,' said Ron. 'Soon be behind us.' The tracks ran and wept with water as we gained height and left Cynwyd Forest. There were no problems with way-finding; we simply followed the silver thread of the flooded track below Pen Creigiau'r Barcut, the 'top of the red kite's crags'. If there was a red kite up there, he would have been grounded today. 'Wonderful view from the top of Moel Fferna,' prophesied Ron. 'A hundred miles – you'll see.'

If wishes were isobars, we'd have seen that jaw-dropping prospect. Maybe Merlin was asserting sovereignty over his native land. Whatever the truth of it, we ate our sandwiches in the stone shelter at the 2,000-ft (610-m) summit of Moel Fferna in a low cloudbase grey-out. Ron rehearsed the view beyond the walls of mist for me: Berwyns and Arans close at hand, the peak of Snowdon to the west, Cadair Idris down south, Liverpool Bay to the north.

The boundary fence between the neighbouring regions of Denbigh and Wrexham had guided us up to Moel Fferna, and the same fence led us off the peak and on east along the ridge. It was just as well we had the firm ground by the fence to tread; the path wasn't much use to us. Off-road 4X4 drivers and motorbikers had reduced it to a squashy, shapeless quagmire. Far worse than anything I'd squelched through yesterday was this deep, seeping scar across the mountain. The skin of heather and moor grass had been flayed away by the heavy-duty

Right *'Gone, gone are thy
gates, Dinas Bran on the
height!*

*Thy warders are blood-
crows and ravens, I trow;
Now no one will wend from
the field of the fight
To the fortress on high,
save the raven and crow.'*

tyres; the black flesh of the peat was laid painfully bare to the white stones beneath. 'It's the off-roaders' *right* to use the byways, we all know that,' snorted Ron, 'but don't any of them consider not exercising that right? They just shouldn't be up here spoiling it for everybody else. Where is safe for walkers, for God's sake?'

In times past, the Berwyns were never seen as particularly safe for anyone venturing through them. Demonic hounds haunted their high places. Big cats were seen skulking in hollows. There are plenty of tales about people waylaid by the 'little people' and danced off their feet, transported through the air or shown great stores of gold underground. Often these episodes end with the victim sinking into a swoon and waking older, colder and wiser on the mountainside. The fact that almost all the protagonists are depicted returning home over the hills by night, after a wild dancing or drinking session, might contain a clue or two. But what could account for the bizarre adventure of the two otter hunters of Llandrillo? They were out in a field when they saw something red-coloured run into a burrow at the roots of a tree. Thinking it was an otter, they poked it out with a stick, trapped it in a bag and started home in high glee. They hadn't gone far before a voice cried out, 'My mother is calling for me!' Terrified, the two rustics threw the bag onto the ground. A little man all

dressed in red scrambled out, gave them a glare, and rushed away into the woods.

Ron and I strode the ridge for several miles, splashing in and out of the ruts. The hills of Clwyd began to materialise, dreamy castles outlined against a dark sky. We dropped into the steep little valley of the Nant y Pandy, and followed an old quarry track down towards the River Dee. Llangollen lay just to the east, the town where George Borrow, his wife and step-daughter put up in 1854. I would make my way there shortly, to climb the high eminence of Castell Dinas Bran and look down on the little town in the low light of this murky spring evening. Just now, though, I was content to follow Ron Williams down the mountainside, imagining Borrow as he ascended the knoll of Dinas Bran.

Noble Welshmen and their glorious deeds had filled that eccentric Saxon mind. No matter that he trailed a line of cheeky little children from Llangollen, or that the locals he met were quite evidently laughing at the Saesneg and his shaky Welsh and pretentious prosody. Wales never had a more passionate advocate than the Norfolk-born author of *Wild Wales* – snob, savant and ultra-romantic, whose greatest memorial remains that masterpiece of fact, fiction and all stations in between.

11

A Midlands Odyssey

A rainy grey sky threatening from the direction of Wales was hanging heavy over the Venice of the North as I stood on the Worcester Bar in Gas Street Basin, trying to recall John Freeth's immortal 'Ode to Inland Navigation'. Not really a habitual activity for me, poetry before breakfast, but a fragment of Freeth's hymn to the lifeblood of 18th-century Birmingham kept stirring in the dusty chambers of my memory. Something about the Tagus, the Ganges and the Patagonian Strand…

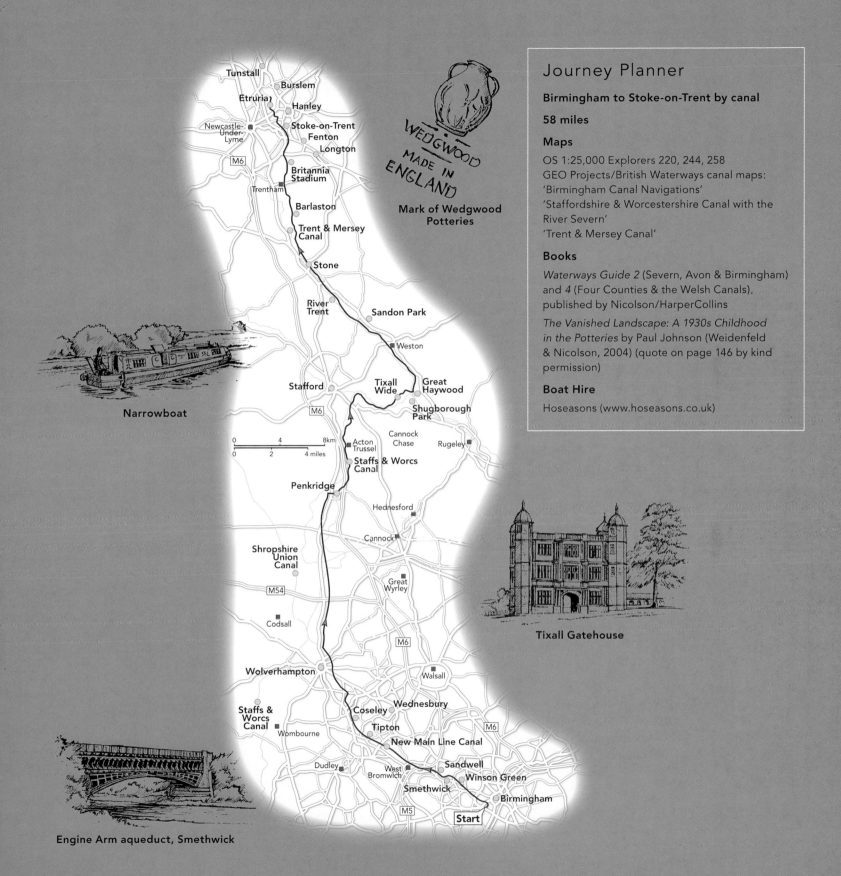

Tunstall

Burslem

Etruria

Hanley

Newcastle-Under-Lyme

Stoke-on-Trent
Fenton
Longton

M6

Britannia Stadium

Trentham

Barlaston

Trent & Mersey Canal

Stone

River Trent

Sandon Park

Weston

Stafford

Tixall Wide

Great Haywood

Shugborough Park

M6

Cannock Chase

Rugeley

Acton Trussel

Staffs & Worcs Canal

Penkridge

Hednesford

Shropshire Union Canal

Cannock

M54

Great Wyrley

Codsall

Wolverhampton

Walsall

Staffs & Worcs Canal

Wednesbury

Coseley

Tipton

Wombourne

M6

New Main Line Canal

Dudley

West Bromwich

Sandwell

Winson Green

Smethwick

M5

Birmingham

Start

0   4   8km
0   2   4 miles

Narrowboat

Mark of Wedgwood Potteries

WEDGWOOD MADE IN ENGLAND

Tixall Gatehouse

Engine Arm aqueduct, Smethwick

Journey Planner

Birmingham to Stoke-on-Trent by canal

58 miles

Maps

OS 1:25,000 Explorers 220, 244, 258
GEO Projects/British Waterways canal maps:
'Birmingham Canal Navigations'
'Staffordshire & Worcestershire Canal with the River Severn'
'Trent & Mersey Canal'

Books

Waterways Guide 2 (Severn, Avon & Birmingham) and *4* (Four Counties & the Welsh Canals), published by Nicolson/HarperCollins

The Vanished Landscape: A 1930s Childhood in the Potteries by Paul Johnson (Weidenfeld & Nicolson, 2004) (quote on page 146 by kind permission)

Boat Hire

Hoseasons (www.hoseasons.co.uk)

After I'd completed this three-day journey by foot, train and narrowboat through the industrial Midlands, I went back to an old notebook and found the verse, scrawled down 15 years before:

Birmingham, for arts renowned
O'er the globe shall foremost stand:
Nor its vast increase be found
To be equall'd in the land.
If the will of fancy ranges
From the Tagus to the Ganges,
Or from Lapland cliffs extend
To the Patagonian Strand,
For Mechanic skill and pow'r,
In what Kingdom, on what shore,
Lies the place that can supply
The world with such variety?

It's a certain bet that John Freeth, a native of Birmingham, never clapped eyes on Tagus, Ganges, Lapland cliffs or Patagonian Strand. But his sense of wonder and civic pride shine through the poetic curlicues. 'More canals than Venice' is Birmingham's tongue-in-cheek brag today, but in Freeth's time it was variety of 'Mechanic skill and pow'r' that made every Birmingham man and woman proud of their native city. The Industrial Revolution was already well in gear by 1769, the year the illiterate engineering genius James Brindley completed the city's first canal from the coal mines at Wednesbury in the Black Country to Birmingham city centre. At a stroke the price of coal tumbled – the stimulus for John Freeth's muse, rather than anything more high-falutin:

Then revel in gladness, let harmony flow,
From the district of Bordesley to Paradise Row;
For true feeling joy in each breast must be wrought,
When coals under Five-pence per hundred are
brought.

It didn't stop at cheap coal. Within a century Birmingham and the Black Country could boast well over a hundred miles of canal – yes, a greater mileage than Venice! The watery spokes had extended enormously from their West Midlands hub, too – south to London, southwest to the River Severn, north to Liverpool, Manchester and Leeds. And the railways had not only followed in their tracks; they had vastly outstripped them in speed, in convenience, in cheapness and in passenger accessibility. The transport revolution had burst out all over the land, and things would never be the same again.

The view from the Worcester Bar's thick barrier of brick encapsulates the great and gross upheaval that has overtaken Birmingham since Brindley opened his pioneering canal and Freeth hymned it. Up to 30ft (9m) above water level, all is 18th-century human scale – humpy-back bridges, three-storey canal offices, moored narrowboats, little waterside pubs. Such is their attraction to the eye, their modesty of size and homely brick-built appeal, that it takes some time to assimilate the enormity of the monsters that rear late 20th-century heads into the sky immediately beyond: vast plate-glass edifices 25 storeys tall, office blocks and hotels with polaroid windows that scrape the clouds.

A pony-tailed man stood engulfing a bacon sandwich at the cabin door of the narrowboat *Aquamara*. 'Cold one, mate?' he stated laconically, with the characteristic West Midlands uplift at the end of the sentence that makes the most emphatic pronouncement sound like a question. New canalside bars and eateries – the Blue Mango Indian Brasserie & Bar, the Pitcher & Piano, the Handmade Burger Company – had proliferated around Gas Street Basin since the early 1980s when I had lived in Birmingham. But the same mat of scum, goose feathers, plastic bottles and crisp packets still floated familiarly at the wharfside. Deep Cutting Junction had changed a long way, too. The hub of the entire English inland waterways system, the central point around which its huge figure of eight revolves, lies dominated these days by the hulking shapes of the National Indoor Arena and the Sealife Centre (about as far from the sea as it's possible to be in England).

Three canals meet at Deep Cutting Junction: the Birmingham Canal Navigation's rump from Gas Street Basin, the Birmingham & Fazeley heading off northeast, and the New Main Line making northwest in an arrow-straight line for Sandwell, Tipton, Coseley and the heart of the Black Country. 'Wolverhampton', said the fingerpost that pointed up the New Main Line from its island in the middle of Deep Cutting Junction. I braced my top-gallant, sheeted home and squared away for that distant destination.

People were bicycling and walking to work, using the New Main Line as a traffic-free short cut to the city centre. Two office girls went clickety-clacking by, six-inch heels beating a tattoo on the cobbled quay, newly styled hair flicking in the wind, right hands cocked at identical angles with a fag held between the tips of index and middle fingers, each trailer of smoke whipped by the wind into invisibility a yard behind their immaculate heads. The canal environs, at first lined with desirable residences and slick developments, quickly assumed a grittier aspect as I passed out of the city centre's aura. Around Rotton Park and Winson Green there were no

smart new apartments. I found myself among bricked-up bridges, overgrown wharves, acres of barren land plagued by derelict factories with broken windows and empty plains of rubble or dead ground. Tall industrial chimneys spewed buddleia bushes from their mouths in lieu of toxic smoke. Sheets of corrugated tin, unsecured since the factories closed, clanged dolorously in the wind. Only a mile from central Birmingham, but what a contrast. The late 20th-century collapse of British heavy industry had hit this inner city waterfront hard, it seemed.

Loops of canal ran away from the New Main Line, exotically signposted: 'Soho Loop, Hockley Port'. When Thomas Telford, the premier industrial engineer of his day, surveyed the Birmingham Canal Navigation's new route to Wolverhampton in 1820, he found James Brindley's work sadly decayed after half a century of constant over-use. Telford reported the parlous state of 'a canal little better than a crooked ditch, the horses frequently sliding and staggering into the water… and the entanglement at the meeting of boats incessant; while at the locks, crowds of boatmen were always quarrelling, or offering premiums for a preference of passage, and the mine owners, injured by the delay, were loud in their complaint'. The great engineer cut decisively through this muddle with his New Main Line, a canal of long straight stretches with passing places and improved locks, at either side of which Brindley's original loops now curved to more obscure local destinations, or decayed away to worm-like curves in the ground.

I threaded the cuttings through Winson Green and Smethwick, walking in a green cocoon shut away from the police sirens, lorry fumes and shopping bustle of the workaday world above. There was a feeling of being already out in the countryside, and a sense of time having slipped its moorings. The diesel stink of a passing train was cut across by a waft of sweet coconut scent

Left **Constructed of functional mid-20th-century concrete, a motorway bridge on a Brobdingnagian scale sweeps the M5 high over the modest brick arches of Stewart Aqueduct – which itself carries James Brindley's pioneering 18th-century canal across Thomas Telford's much-improved New Main Line of the 1820s**

Right **Beans Foundry at Tipton, once the proud producer of Bean cars, including the one-off, hand-built 'Thunderbolt' in which George Eyston set a new world land speed record of 312mph on 19 November 1937. Now the foundry lies silent, empty and awaiting redevelopment**

from the canal-side gorse bushes; then diesel stole back into the air as the first working boat I'd seen, the diminutive blue British Waterways tug *Growler*, came up the canal pushing a rusty old barge full of black dredged mud. A little further along I came across her sister tug *Prowler* similarly engaged, both craft helmed by solid men with serious, responsible expressions, just the look I remembered seeing as a child on the faces of steam locomotive drivers.

Northwest from Birmingham stretches the congeries of manufacturing towns and villages collectively known as the Black Country – a name entirely apt in the past, when chain makers, wire spinners, panel beaters, bar forgers and locksmiths kept the furnaces roaring and the skies black with smoke 24 hours a day. The Black Country made things; the canals brought the raw materials and took away the finished products. Before Brindley built his canal, for example, Birmingham manufacturers of brassware had to import brass sheets from Bristol, laboriously, by road. By 1865, the canals and the railways had wrought such a change that Birmingham

and the Black Country had over 200 brass manufacturers and 400 brassworks – and a substantial population of men and women with green hair, the toxic distinguishing sign of a brassworker.

The corner brickwork and the cast-iron handrails of bridges showed deeply scored grooves where canal boat ropes had been dragged through the centuries by straining barge horses. I walked on through Soho, Sandwell and Tipton, Black Country places where manufacturing still seemed to be limping on beside the canals. Yellow cranes dug into mountains of scrap metal, their buckets dipping like sea monsters' heads, producing a faint oceanic roaring as metal shards slid down the slopes in their millions. Nicholls Steel, Caparo Precision Strip, and – next to a canalside mosque complete with dome and miniature minaret – The Bolt & Nut Company (Tipton), Ltd. Clangs, steam hisses, hoarse shouts. I passed under Thomas Telford's beautiful brown-and-white Engine Arm Aqueduct, stamped 1825, then beneath the sky-high M5 motorway bridge, plain and strong, a humorous

graffitist's work on its piers – a huge scarlet tongue emblazoned 'Kiss Moi'. The successive bridges over the New Main Line formed a graph of the rise and fall of industry and empire: delicate Georgian brick- and latticework on an intimate scale, elaborate stone and iron monuments to Victorian self-confidence all pillar'd and portico'd, mighty steel girders of the early 20th century, functional and ugly concrete of our modern age. Against this variegated manmade backdrop the natural world pursued its timeless purposes; moorhens tiptoed to the water with furtive haste, coots hooted from the reedbeds, a pair of Canada geese flew along a black factory wall, and a long red fox stole through the heathland and scrub of Puppy Green.

Beyond the 360-yd (330-m) Coseley Tunnel the canal began to wriggle around as it followed the contours and dived under a succession of bridges. Wanting to rinse the dust out of my throat, I left the waterside in search of the bridge where my excellent canal map assured me I'd find the Boat Inn. I rounded the corner of the street in high anticipation of old canal photographs, barge horse brasses and salty stories of lockside smackdowns. But the Boat Inn had been reduced to a heap of bricks. 'Redevelopment,' said a passing Coseleyite, with all the gnomic sarcasm in the world.

A sudden increase in property values and maintenance around Spring Vale: a couple of 'artworks' of galvanised security fencing, raised beds planted with cotoneaster, new apartments well built in red brick. A sharpening of canal-side graffitists' humour, too. 'Meat Kills!' preached one of the slogans under Rough Hall railway bridge. Someone had added with much calligraphic skill: 'But gravy's nice!'

The New Main Line ran past the coal stacks at Minerva Wharf to reach the heart of Wolverhampton by Little Lane Bridge at another set of neat locks and canal offices. Evening was setting in. My feet hurt. I'd had enough for the day. I hobbled off to find Wolverhampton station, a train to Penkridge and a rendezvous with my wife Jane.

If you're going to follow the canals through the heart of England, you can't just ponce around on the towpath. Those who haven't steered a 40-ft (12-m) narrowboat into a slippery lock, negotiated her between a line of boats parked either side, or tried to coax her through a just-wide-enough aqueduct in a blustery side wind – well, they haven't really drunk that canal cup to the bottom. How on earth are clumsy fools permitted to take charge of such a potentially lethal weapon – lethal to themselves as much as others – after half an hour's perfunctory explanation of the basics? 'Push the tiller left and she'll go right, right and she'll go left – push this lever forward and she'll go forward, back and she'll go back – here's the lump hammer and there are the mooring pins – here's how you work in and out of a lock – first, middle and last rule of the canals is *save water* – yonder's the weed hatch, and *don't put your fingers down there*. All right? Off you go, then!'

Big Dave of Napton Boats, large and calm, was the man, if anyone, to show us how to handle the narrowboat *Emma*. Jane and I had not been on the canals for 30 years. I thought I vaguely remembered one or two things. After ramming Park Gate lock with a sickening crunch, then

Right **Passing scene: a beautifully restored and painted working boat, encountered on the Staffordshire & Worcestershire Canal near Penkridge**

Far right **One of the most characteristic sounds of the Staffordshire & Worcestershire Canal is the sharp, echoing croak of a moorhen**

steering for the bank beyond to pick Jane up and ramming that, too, I remembered how tricky it had all actually been. The problem was the slowness of *Emma's* bows to respond to the suggestions of her rudder. She was subject to the same difficulties as those inherent in the design of the brontosaurus – her head was so far from her tail that messages from one to the other took fatally long to arrive and be acted upon. In the case of a brontosaurus this meant that a tyrannosaurus rex could pounce and chew up a considerable length of the victim's rear end before the head had begun to wonder what that unpleasant sensation back there might be. In the case of *Emma*, it meant that a tug to starboard on the tiller produced no answering swing to port of the bows – not for several seconds, by which time I would have overcompensated, yanked again to starboard, then suddenly doubted my own senses and pushed as hard as I could to port, by which time the bows would have started their movement to port, shuddered in protest and nosed over to starboard, where I absolutely didn't want them to go, because the steersman of the narrowboat that had suddenly appeared round the bend had ported *his* helm and put himself on a good solid collision course, and was beginning to round eyes and mouth in an unctuous expression of injured righteousness and pantomime disbelief…

After an hour or so Jane and I thought we had some kind of a grasp on matters. We stopped banging around the locks and

banks of Penkridge, and set off gingerly up the Staffordshire and Worcestershire Canal in the general direction of Great Haywood Junction.

The Staffs & Worcs formed one of the key components in a grandiose waterways scheme hatched by James Brindley, the gifted if under-educated engineering genius who had connected Birmingham and Wolverhampton by water. The great canal pioneer was nothing if not a blue-sky thinker. Why not link up Middle England's four great tidal rivers of Thames, Severn, Humber and Mersey with a network of canals, and set flowing an uninterrupted commerce between east and west coasts, between the capital and the great land-bound manufacturing cities, and between those cities and the broad mercantile highway of the sea? A preposterous notion, many thought. Dig up all that countryside, build all those bridges and aqueducts, square all those recalcitrant landowners, trap and retain all that water? Impossible. But that's what Brindley and those who came after him achieved, with pick, shovel and immense determination – not to mention the wealth of Empire and Industry behind them.

The Staffs & Worcs was inaugurated in 1766, and its 46½-mile (75-km) course between the River Severn at Stourport-on-Severn and the Trent & Mersey Canal at Great Haywood Junction took only six years to complete. Carrying products and raw materials of all sorts from the mines and quarries

and manufactories of the Midlands, the two canals, Staffs & Worcs and Trent & Mersey, flourished in tandem for more than 60 years, despite the looping eastward diversion to Great Haywood Junction that caused the Staffs & Worcs to bulge a long way out of true. Then in 1835 the Shropshire Union was cut northwest between Wolverhampton and the River Mersey complex of waterways, a much more direct route to Liverpool and the Atlantic coast which attracted most of the trade that had been the Staffs & Worcs's alone. That drew the confidence out of the old stager. Wars of tariffs developed, inflated tolls and much backbiting. The coming of the railways sapped most of the remaining lifeblood from the Staffs & Worcs, though the canal limped on as a coal carrier until the mid-20th century. Then the conservationists of the Staffordshire and Worcestershire Canal Society stepped in to lobby successfully for a reprieve from total abandonment.

Nowadays the canal is a leisure cruiser's dream, passing stately houses and quiet old villages on its way through the broad acres of backwater Staffordshire, dimpling under the weeping willows just as if the Industrial Revolution had never brought it into being in the first place.

I learned eventually that it was better to coax Emma than to fight her. The advent of a bridge, a lock or an oncoming craft, at first conducive to pounding heart and sweaty palms as inches of clearance were calculated and throttle and tiller nervously juggled, soon became merely the occasion for a casual duck of the head, a bankside swoop or a hand raised in comradely salute. We were getting on famously. Stafford town hove up on the port bow. 'Lunch?' 'Yes, for sure – how

about that pub by the bridge?' 'The Radford Bank Inn – mmm, lovely.'

We were halfway through our ploughman's lunches (giant doorsteps more solid than a ploughboy's hobnails, enough cheese to choke a plough horse, a lake of Branston pickle big enough to drown a jolly farmer in, typical overflow-the-plate Midlands style) when a cheerful voice cut through the row in the crowded bar. 'Anyone own a boat?' We looked up. 'Narrowboat, a blue one?' We looked at each other. 'Name of Emma?' We groaned. 'Aye, well, she's dragged her lines. She's across the canal.'

We ran out and down to the towpath. Emma's bows were buried in the opposite bank, her head rope trailing in the water. One of my nautical knots, a classic half-granny-with-two-clove-buns, still just held her stern to its mooring pin. But even as I watched, the pin slipped out of the bank and plopped into the canal, and the rest of Emma slid sideways across the waterway to cleave to the far bank. I said a bad word or six. 'Ne'er mind,' chuckled our chum, 'I've been living on the canals four year – that yellow boat there – and I'm still mekking it up as I go along. Here, chuck us that hook,' and he calmly and quietly snared the trailing stern rope, drew the renegade back to our side of the canal and made all fast. Then he showed us what we should have done with the mooring pin. 'Don't bother banging it into the bank with the hammer they'll give you – bloody useless. Slip it down between the bank and the metal fender, like this – then loop the line round top and bottom, pull tight, and Bob's your uncle. It'd tek an elephant to shift that.'

Chastened, we re-embarked and burbled on slowly through the green and pleasant land. A man stood in his front garden, squeezing the water out of a chamois leather with the help of an old-fashioned mangle. A moorhen skittered across the canal on long green toes, outlining her passage in thick water drops. Geese hooted from marshy ground. The countryside got hillier, wilder, less primped and manicured. A most magnificent edifice appeared beyond trees to the north, a structure almost as tall as the surrounding trees, with the appearance of a classical mansion house sporting pepperpot towers at each shoulder. 'Tixall Gatehouse', the map suggested. Here the Staffs and Worcs bulged like a python after a good meal. 'Tixall Wide', said the map. Just the spot to pull in for the night. We got *Emma* thoroughly subdued against the canal side as our Radford Bank chum had shown us, Jane took a bath (Huh! A bath in a boat! World going to hell in a handbasket, harrumph!), and I lay on the bed and rummaged out a book. Tixall Gatehouse – built 1580s – two Tixall Halls been and gone – gatehouse survived – now a holiday place to rent. I might have searched out a footpath and walked over to take a closer look. But it was so peaceful here under our willow, with the canal chuckling softly under the bows and a glass of wine on the bedside table...

I woke with a jerk. Pitch black, and a wind howling outside. Water crashing against the hull an inch away from my nose, and a snubbing, jerking motion as *Emma* tugged at her moorings. I slid back the curtain, half expecting to see the canal bank receding. But the tree outside hadn't moved a muscle. The Radford Bank fastening seemed to be doing its job. I put my head down again and let the patter and whistle of the rainstorm and the rhythmical slosh-slosh of the water in Tixall Wide lull me back to sleep.

Next day it wept and sighed. We ended our little cruise early, leaving the Staffs & Worcs and rounding the corner into the Trent & Mersey Canal where Big Dave was waiting by the bank to relieve us of *Emma*. We confessed our sins and a couple of scrapes, Big Dave had a look and laughed them off, and we patted our now docile narrowboat goodbye. Jane headed for

Left **Classic Midlands view – Acton Bridge (no. 93), on the outskirts of Acton Trussell between Penkridge and Stafford, contemplates its own reflection in the calm waters of the Staffordshire & Worcestershire Canal**

Right **Canalside workers' cottages near Barlaston, as pretty as a picture – and highly desirable residences these days**

Stafford and a southward train, while I greased the boots, got out all my waterproofs, girded my loins for the third and final act of this little Midlands comedy (I hoped it was going to turn out that way), and set out along the towpath of the Trent & Mersey for Stoke-on-Trent and the Potteries, some 20 miles (32km) away.

The morning was all grey and green. It started with prospects of the wide slopes and specimen trees of Shugborough Park and Sandon Park, dotted with fat sheep, their new-born lambs at foot. Now I had the River Trent and the Stoke–Rugby railway line for company. The former snaked under graceful old bridges in a wide flood plain of meadows and willows. The latter ran through wooded cuttings out of which the red and silver trains came rushing like dragons with snarling yellow snouts and headlights glaring, roaring past to streak back into the cover of the trees once more. The canal itself lay overhung with trees, a dark river pocked with raindrops and lank with last winter's weeds.

A proper rainstorm had been building away in the north, and as I reached Stone it came whirling down. I looked around for a refuge, and found it in the Talbot. Rain slashed at the windows and spat down the chimney of the little corner pub, but inside all was snug. A bright coal fire was burning,

the fire irons were polished, the carpet was clean, and four real ales were waiting in the pumps. The one I chose, brewed in the town, was as sharp as a cider apple, and not in a good way. The tattooed barman ran water through the system and pulled off half a dozen pints. He tasted anew, grimaced and poured the jug away. His colleague came anxiously to his side. 'Aye – that's wrong!' Together they pored over the ill-tasting brew as assiduously as any pair of doctors might puzzle over a patient. After sipping, sniffing, holding the jug up to the light – everything but listening to its chest – they pronounce the ale's life extinct, turned the pump label ceremoniously back-to-front, and pulled me another brew with gruff apologies. I nursed it by the fire, sitting the rainstorm out until it pattered off down the Trent valley and a gleam of better weather showed in the north.

The narrowboat *Cahoon*, moored up near Stone Locks, bore the motto 'Gubernate Navem Deus' – 'The Lord is my Steersman'. Next to her, *Elwood* trailed pungent, tarry-smelling smoke from her blackened chimney. Everyone seemed battened down this blustery afternoon. I walked on fast along the Trent & Mersey Canal, past old villages hugely swollen with new building developments. At Barlaston, the familiar name of Wedgwood stood proud and tall in bold blue letters along a factory roofline. But the pride concealed

a recent fall. In 1936, after two centuries of production up the valley in its famous old works at Etruria in the smoky heart of the Potteries, the celebrated ceramics firm bought up the Barlaston Estate and moved out here into leafy rural Staffordshire. Now it was on the brink of going bust. Unable to cope with cheap foreign competition, a passer-by told me, Wedgwood had gone into administration and was waiting for a buyer.

The news saddened me. If it hadn't been for Josiah Wedgwood, the Trent & Mersey would probably never have been built. Wedgwood's pottery had grown into an enormously successful business by the 1760s, and it was he who urged forward plans to connect the two river systems with the nerve centre of his operation. The Trent & Mersey's Act was passed by Parliament in 1766, and the canal was fully open 11 years later. It cost £300,000 to drive its course almost a hundred miles through Cheshire, the Potteries and the East Midlands – and once again it was James Brindley, commissioned by the master potter Wedgwood, who engineered and oversaw the work.

The sad state of the Wedgwood firm was the first of many such examples of industrial decline I saw as I followed the Trent & Mersey Canal into the Potteries. The canal became dirtier, with a side order of plastic bags, bottle tops and tin foil. There were more walkers around now, more dogs, more runners, and they moved through a landscape half-rural, half-ravaged. I passed the site of Hem Heath colliery, the last of the Potteries' deep pits to close in 1996. The great colliery had been distinguishable for many miles around by its huge A-frame that carried the winding gear for No. 2 shaft, more than half a mile deep. Neither its iconic status nor its remarkable presence in the landscape had saved the 'Big A' from the demolition men. Now the colliery site is all open scrubby fields, grazed by horses and flanked by the enormo-architecture of the late 20th century – an absolutely monstrous supermarket distribution centre as stark and square as a prison block, a cloud-scraping incinerator chimney right beside the canal.

Across the water sailed the huge, futuristic spaceship of Stoke City Football Club's Britannia Stadium, gleaming white and red against the scudding grey clouds. What would Stanley Matthews have made of that? The Hanley-born 'Wizard of the Dribble', counted by many the greatest English footballer of all time, played professionally for Stoke from 1932 until 1947 (with a break for wartime service in the RAF), and then again from 1961 until his retirement in 1965 at the hard-to-credit age of 50. There were near-riots in Stoke when he first threatened to leave the club in 1938. He won the European Footballer of the Year title; he was awarded the CBE; he was knighted in 1965 for his services to the game. Most people loved him; everyone admired him. After his death in 2000, Matthews's ashes were buried under the centre spot at the Britannia Stadium, the best of whose contemporary heroes earn a thousand times what their incomparable forerunner took home each week.

Graffiti on the bridges ranged from the sublime to the subliminal: 'Think Green! The World is Your's!' 'Create…Destruction!' 'Fat Ryan is Gay!' The railway pressed in close on the waterway. Here the North Staffordshire Railway Company built nearly 200 shunting engines at its locomotive, carriage and wagon repair workshop. A plaque near Whieldon Road told how

Above **Josiah Wedgwood (1730–95), the one-legged pottery designer from Burslem who created the world's greatest ceramics empire in his native town, and funded the building of the Trent & Mersey Canal**

Left **Historic Shugborough Hall overlooks the junction of the Staffordshire & Worcestershire and the Trent & Mersey Canals at Great Haywood** potteries employing 500 men or more lined these canal banks – the Colonial Pottery, Winkle & Wood, Opaque Porcelain Manufacturers. Small-scale production boomed, too. The tall, bottle-shaped pottery kilns rose from back yards and waste ground in their thousands, each trailing a snail track of dark smoke and fumes to join the heavy grey pall that hung permanently over the Six Towns. Few of the bottle kilns survived the collapse of the pottery industry; almost all were demolished. But a splendid specimen still stood over the canal near the premises of Jones and Shufflebottom, its chimney cap sprouting a bush of mayweed.

The building of the Trent & Mersey Canal encouraged coal and iron mining, clay digging and pottery making all across the region, widespread and uncontrolled, so that the Six Towns of the Potteries – Longton, Fenton, Stoke, Hanley, Burslem and Tunstall – grew both fabulously rich and hellishly poor, depending on which side of the shop floor you stood, while nature suffered a slow and disgusting trial by fumes, fires, polluted outfalls, torn land and ash heaps. Burslem was reckoned the worst of the lot. In Burslem lay The Sytch, 'the dark heart of the Potteries', a region of bare ground, industrial detritus, waste tips, poisoned rivers and flaring furnaces, vehemently and unforgettably described by Paul Johnson in *The Vanished Landscape*, his account of growing up in the area in the 1930s:

When my father first showed me The Sytch, dusk was gathering and the place was lighting up. Some of its furnaces were never extinguished. They glowed ominously as the shadows fell and leapt into intense activity as fresh loads of slack coal were thrust through the oven doors. Sparks rocketed fifty feet into the air, huge puffs of livid orange smoke came shooting out of the banks and the countless chimneys, short and tall, which punctuated the horizon every few yards. In the light of the furnace glow, black figures could be seen in frenzied activity, feeding the gluttonous flames with long fire shovels, or raking out the grids beneath, which sent fresh fiery clouds of cinder on to the ground and into the air. Reflected from one cloud to another, the glow reached hundreds – perhaps thousands – of feet into the atmosphere and turned the buildings at the top of Tunstall Square into pink shapes. The dark waters of river, canal and pools doubled the illuminations, and gave to everything a glitter and a mirage of stern beauty. It was not fairyland but devil-land, a desperate romantic hell in which flibbertigibbets and other imps, demons and trolls could dwell in delight.

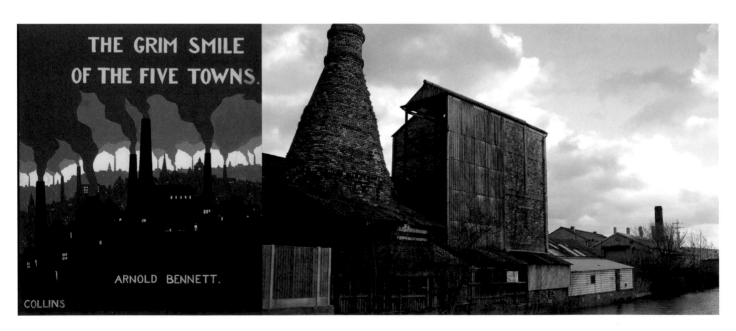

THE GRIM SMILE OF THE FIVE TOWNS.

ARNOLD BENNETT.

COLLINS

Far left **Where there was muck, there was brass; Arnold Bennett's writings expertly portrayed the grimmer aspects of life in the smoky, fiery atmosphere of the Potteries**

Left **Preserved bottle kiln beside the Trent & Mersey Canal in Stoke-on-Trent, one survivor of the many thousand such backyard kilns that proliferated in the 19th-century heyday of pottery-making in the Five Towns**

I walked on and on, tired but unable to tear myself away from this shadowy route through the bowels of the Potteries. Under a girder railway bridge packed with heavy-bellied china clay wagons from Cornwall; through creepy, Dickensian cobbled tunnels roofed with rusty iron bristling with bolts; beside a mountain of bricks marking the grave of yet another pottery; up by spurting lock gates, past a sprawling cemetery and the dark offices of the Etruscan Bone and Flint Mill – another eerily Dickensian touch – and on into Etruria. Here Josiah Wedgwood set up his pottery in 1769, grandly renaming the district in honour of the Etruscan potters of classical Latium. Ranks of smart new homes were creeping over the ground where the potbanks once fumed and roared. The front entrance to the Wedgwood works stood in elegant obscurity, waiting to be turned into desirable apartments. Of the great ceramic revolution that galvanised the Midlands and spread money, muck and misery in equal proportions, there was no sign of life.

I stood on the canal bridge, easing my feet and chatting to an ex-pottery worker who was leaning over the parapet with all the time in the world to study the water. How dirty had the Potteries really been, back in the bad old days?

'I'll tell you, mate. They brought some cows into the city from the countryside for slaughter one day,' he said with slow humour, 'but they could only do half 'cos City were playing and all the slaughtermen took half a day off. So they put all them's they couldn't do out on the town fields overnight, and did 'em next morning. Now them's they did straight off had lungs and guts as pink and juicy as you like. But them's they did in the morning, after a night in the Potteries – their innards came out completely black!'

Under a girder railway bridge packed with heavy-bellied china clay wagons from Cornwall; through creepy, Dickensian cobbled tunnels roofed with rusty iron bristling with bolts.

12

Mighty Tideway

The Humber is a curious river. At under 40 miles it is certainly not remarkable for its length. No picturesque mountain ranges flank it, no dramatic gorges constrict it in whitewater fury. The Humber glides smoothly through its flat eastern landscape, inland or seaward according to the tide; it fills and empties obediently twice each 24 hours, keeping politely within its bed. Yet it fascinates with its breadth, its power and its purpose.

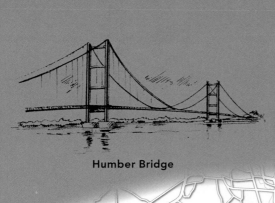

Humber Bridge

St Patrick's Church, Patrington

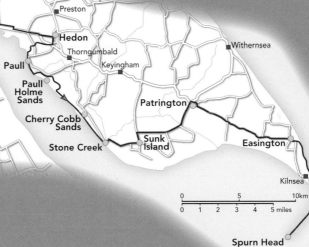

Maze at Julian's Bower

Spurn Head lighthouse

Journey Planner

River Humber from its source near Alkborough to its mouth at Spurn Head

40 miles

Maps

OS 1:25,000 Explorers 281, 284, 291, 292, 293

Websites

Far Ings Nature Reserve: www.lincstrust.org.uk/reserves/far_ings/index.php

Spurn Point National Nature Reserve: www.spurnpoint.com/

I was hoping to find a bit of magic up at Julian's Bower, and I wasn't disappointed. The ancient turf maze looked as beautiful and enigmatic as I had imagined, its tightly packed pathways in their cradling circle lying canted westward at the crest of the Lincolnshire escarpment known simply as The Cliff. How did Julian's Bower come by its odd name? Was it cut by monks in medieval times, or fashioned a thousand years earlier by druids? What were those May Eve 'games' that the villagers of Alkborough indulged in around their maze until mid-Victorian prudery put an end to them? I could only stand, speculate and stare.

There was plenty to gaze at this late winter morning. The Cliff rises only 140ft (43m) above sea level, but in the immense flatlands of northernmost Lincolnshire that gives a mountain-top perspective. The westward view stretched from the green whalebacks of the Yorkshire Wolds to the Pennine hills hidden in a gold horizon haze. Shimmering in the late afternoon sun of winter, two broad rivers came winding through the plains – the Trent at the end of its 170-mile journey from Staffordshire, and the Ouse completing its wanderings from Wensleydale away in west Yorkshire. Below me they joined in a confusion of sand banks, backwaters and mud islets to engender the River Humber, the great eastern tideway that I was setting out to follow to the sea.

This powerful tideway drains one-fifth of England. Huge ships negotiate its treacherous shifting sands and mud-banks, seeming to sail through the fields to the ports, docks and industrial plants that lie scattered downstream of Hull, the river's one big town. Yet the Humber flows through some of the loneliest country you'll find in lowland Britain. Many millions of wildfowl cavort and clamour along its food-rich banks and shallows. Even at its birthplace it is half a mile wide; by the time it has reached the sea some 40 miles to the east, the Humber measures a mighty 5 miles from shore to shore. It is a truly great estuarine river, and one under constant threat from the rising level of the sea.

When I first discovered Julian's Bower, several years ago, the flat lands between the foot of the Cliff and the mouth of the River Trent were all green cornfields. Now they glinted and gleamed in chocolate and fawn, purple and ochre, with straight-edged panes of ice blue inset like panels of glass. Following the puddled lane down the face of the Cliff, I found the 1,100-acre (445-ha) swathe of ground had been transformed. In 2005 the decision was taken to breach the flood banks that kept the tidal river out of the farmland. The subsequent flooding had created new mud banks, on which saltmarsh was establishing itself astonishingly quickly. It was a striking example of the practice of 'managed realignment' (the previously used term, 'managed retreat', was felt to be too defeatist), a policy of meeting nature halfway in her impulse – unstoppable in the case of the North Sea tides – to recapture land she once had. Sea levels are rising, the whole of Britain's eastern seaboard is sinking, flooding is an ever more pressing problem, the cost of defending every inch of coast is simply prohibitive... go figure. At selected low-lying agricultural sites on the Humber, and elsewhere along the East Coast, too, the sea is being allowed to creep back across the land, creating as it does so a better buffer against its own power than man could ever devise – the gradually rising, smoothly water-repellent mudflats, and the mazily channelled, wonderfully absorbent saltmarsh.

If I saw one goose feeding on Alkborough Flats and the surrounding grasslands and tidelines, I saw five thousand. Curlews probed the mud with those characteristic slender down-curved bills that look so flimsy but are built to

Above **The transformed scene at Alkborough Flats, where 1,100 acres (445ha) of farmland have been released back into the control of the tides that sweep up the River Humber, creating new saltmarshes and mudflats**

Left **How old is the ancient maze of Julian's Bower? What is it for? Who made it? Questions to ponder as you look out over the maze to the tidal landscape of Alkborough Flats**

withstand their never-ending stabbing and suction of the mud. Golden plovers picked the shores and swirled over the rivers, their massed voices as shrill and bell-like as a forest full of cicadas. Above the shrilling rose the *cleek-curleek* of a solitary curlew flying inland, a sound so mournful and poignant it raised the hair on the back of my neck.

> *At Whitton's town end, brave boys, brave boys,*
> *At Whitton's town end, brave boys,*
> *At every door there sits a whore,*
> *At Whitton's town end, brave boys.*

So shantied Lincolnshire's jolly jack-tars, once upon a time. It was a great walk through Whitton, anyway, and on round the Humber's southern shore. There were more lapwings along the river than one could shake a stick at, and very many more around the flooded delvings of Barton Clay Pits. During their 19th-century heyday locals named the line of pits 'Dawson City' after the US gold-rush mecca, so many fortunes were made from their clay. The brick- and tile-makers feeding the building frenzy of Britain's Industrial Revolution found their requirements completely satisfied by the Humberside deposits – so much so that they established more than 20 manufactories and dug a string of clay pits 5 miles long. Now almost all the tile-makers have shut up shop, and the pits have flooded to become the freshwater lagoons of the Far Ings Nature Reserve. I sauntered their high walkways with binoculars, seeing shoveler and teal, along with snipe, grebe and a whole fleet of tufted duck. I didn't spot the famously shy and scarce bittern, though, the solitary skulker in the reeds that is making a slow comeback after a century of extinction in Britain.

Barton, in the shadow of the giant suspension bridge that crosses the Humber to Hull, is a handsome little town of Georgian brick houses. St Peter's Church boasted a fine Saxon tower with narrow windows, some round-topped and others arrow-shaped; St Mary's a couple of hundred yards away had beautiful medieval stone carving, including some remarkable Green Men sprouting thickets of leaves. I walked on and on by New Holland and Goxhill Haven in a cold rising wind, looking across a tideway now 2 miles wide to the cranes and big white ferries along the Humber downriver of Hull. A freighter the size of a city block came rumbling upriver. Beyond the industrial stretch, the north bank ran away towards a wafer-thin sliver of horizon. Time to hop across the bridge, spend the night in Hull, and follow the skyline to vanishing point.

Walking the Humber Bridge is a tricky art. It takes nerve, I found, to venture out onto that 4,720-yd (4,330-m) span, with the strong tides pushing and coiling hypnotically 100ft (30m) below. The side wind didn't help. Halfway across, I caught a proper glimpse of the town of Hull. No fancies or fears assailed me after that. I was mesmerised.

Hull is one of those towns the stranger probably doesn't expect too much of. There's something about its isolation, stuck way out east where the motorways peter out in the great flatlands of southeast Yorkshire; something about its otherness, connected to foreign shores and looking more to them than to the country at whose outer margin it stands. History took no notice of Hull until the early Middle Ages, when 'Wyke-upon-Hull' began to be mentioned as a portal through which men and materials departed for other lands – wool from the East Yorkshire wolds for France, for example, to help ransom King Richard I in 1193; men-at-arms en route to smash the termagant Scots a century later at the behest of King Edward Longshanks, seeking a speedier passage to the north than they could possibly have managed on the roads of the day. By that time only London and Boston outdid Wyke-upon-Hull in importance, though it was foreign merchants who controlled nine-tenths of the trade in lead pigs, hides, wool and wine.

The merchants who settled in Hull grew rich over the centuries, and they developed an independent, not to say bloody-minded streak. Hull became strongly anti-Royalist and anti-Catholic. It refused entry to King Charles during the Civil War, and endured two sieges – the second came to an end when Governor Fairfax deliberately broke the tide defences along the Humber, flooded the countryside where the besiegers were encamped, and then sallied forth and chased them away. Hull welcomed King William of Orange when he landed in 1688 to accept the throne in lieu of the discredited Stuarts. In the 19th century the town was strongly Puritan, strongly anti-Tory and anti-establishment. Its ordinary fisherfolk were very much their own men, too. By the 17th century they were already ranging far afield, engaged in the extraordinarily dangerous whaling business. Two centuries later the town was sending as many as 2,000 men and 50 whaling ships as far as Greenland and the south Atlantic, pursuing a desperately hazardous occupation with an attrition rate equivalent to Bomber Command

Right **The vast sweep of the Humber Bridge – a span nearly 3 miles long, which you can cross on foot, provided you have a good head for heights...**

during World War II. Whalers worked hard; they lived hard, too, and generally died that way. Anyone who survived five trips was actuarially dead. Anyone who couldn't take it went deep-sea fishing instead, a calling only marginally less brutal and demanding. Such tough occupations, such isolation and self-reliance, have lent Hull a bluff and cheery air which it prides itself on retaining, a palpable flavour of 'Nobody likes us, and we don't care!'

Those who come to Hull ought in fact to expect something special of the place. Any town with a river as wide and mighty as the Humber washing its flanks is bound to have a tang of salt and a spit of excitement about it. Walking with the last light of day towards the river down Humber Dock Street, passing the tar-black hull of the Spurn lightship in stately

retirement next to impudent, halyard-chinking yachts in the marina, I remembered strolling here with my chum Ian Middleton, Hull born and bred, a few years before. Ian could remember the town in the 1950s when the fishing fleet was still hunting as far afield as Iceland and the northern waters of Russia. Riding on the top deck of a bus in the company of 'patty-slappers' or fishcake factory workers going home at the end of their shift meant being knocked sideways by the stink of fish and smouldering Woodbines. 'When the wind was in the wrong direction,' Ian had mused as he leaned on the riverfront railings, 'the whole town used to be full of this incredible smell of fish. My Dad worked for the Customs, and when he was on a Saturday shift he'd take me with him on his bike, first for a haircut and then down to take a look at the ships in the docks. We *had* ships in the docks then.'

tall, of fragile oolitic limestone studded with seashells, had to be moved further inland on more than one occasion over the centuries to save it from the ever-advancing sea. Its survival was improbable; but here it stood, unremarked in the quiet little garden of the retirement home, its heraldic beasts and inscriptions smoothed into indecipherability by wind and weather, witness to a defining moment in these islands' history.

Magdalen Fair on 2 August was the day to be in Hedon in jollier and simpler times past, provided you kept your wits about you:

> *Here's wrestling and vaulting and dancing on wire,*
> *With fiddling and juggling and men eating fire;*
> *Bold Sergeants recruiting, lads 'listing for life,*
> *And family lessons from Punch and his wife.*

How many unthinking village boys at fairs all over the land were treated to a drink of beer by spry and jolly sergeants, only to find the King's shilling staring up at them from the bottom of the mug?

Down beyond the seawall tavern at Paull I set out along the river path, staring out at a Humber suddenly grown 4 miles wide, with a far shore invisible in haze kicked up by a rising sea wind. I walked into that wind all day, 20 miles or more, the great tideway still widening imperceptibly at my right hand, vast cornfields running inland on my left with never a contour to break their fertiliser-green flatness. Seals lay plump and glistening like drowned slugs on Paull Holme Sands. In the fields beyond, unaccustomed water gleamed. Managed realignment was taking place here, too. New mudflats, fresh young saltmarsh and clouds of plover and creaky-voiced lapwing had replaced the corn prairies tended with such care and pain over the years by the farmers of this purely agricultural place.

The sea wall path led on east by Cherry Cobb Sands and Stone Creek House. Here, beside the loneliest house in all this outland steppe, I took to the narrow lanes through Sunk Island. These 10,000 acres (4,000ha) of ruler-flat land were reclaimed from the estuary by Cornelius Vermuyden

What about over there, I'd asked, pointing out across the Humber to the low dark line of the Lincolnshire shore. 'Foreign country,' snorted Ian, a staunch East Riding Yorkshireman, with maximum dismissiveness. 'Two of us went across on the paddle-steamer for a camping trip when we were about 14. Got a couple of miles inland' – he paused for full effect – 'and decided we'd seen enough of Lincolnshire.'

In the morning I was down by the river at first light. The Humber, brown with silt, swept seawards past the town. No giant flexing an arm, no army of 10,000 pulling on ropes could rival the power of that 2-mile-wide tideway surging irresistibly out to sea. I caught the first bus out to Hedon, and was in Baxtergate knocking on the door of Holyrood House before many of the elderly residents had had their breakfasts. I felt a bit shamefaced about it, but the nice woman who answered the door was not in the slightest bit fazed. 'Oh, the Kilnsea Cross? Through the door there and you'll find it outside in the garden.'

The Kilnsea Cross stood ragged and weather-eaten. Mossy and half-crumbled, it looked much reduced over the centuries from the nobly carved monument first erected upon Spurn Point 15 miles to the east to commemorate the return from exile of Henry Bolingbroke, Duke of Lancaster, on 30 June 1399. That landing 'upon the naked shore at Ravenspurg', as William Shakespeare immortalised it in *King Henry the Fourth Part 1*, saw the reigning King Richard II swiftly supplanted and then murdered, while Bolingbroke himself assumed lands, titles, riches and the crown. The great cross, 15ft (5m)

three centuries ago. A strange land with no outsiders; a country of sunken horizons where the farmhouses stood up stark, square and functional, isolated in seas of corn seethed by a continuous wind. Life was precarious here in former times among the marsh agues and fevers. John Spilman of Creek Farm outlived his wife, Emma, and all three of his children, and provided each in turn with a grim headstone under the gloomy trees of Sunk Island churchyard, carved with withered flowers and memorial verses long on 'death and darkness and the tomb'.

That night I slept at Patrington, too tired to visit the Queen of Holderness. But I called in on her the following morning – a magnificent church under a soaring spire. Patrington was a port on the Humber until the reclamation of Sunk Island and the silting of the channels. The village had been prosperous enough in medieval times through exporting corn and wool to build a church as splendid as the graceful pale stone 'Queen'. Now the old granary, where the boats would load up with grain and sail away, stands on its quay some 3 miles from the sea.

I caught the morning bus to Easington on the coast 6 miles away, a village crowded by its North Sea gas terminal. Then I walked south along the most eroded coast in Britain, past the point where Henry Bolingbroke set foot on shore that historic summer's day, past the spot where the Kilnsea Cross had once faced the waves and been bitten into by the salty North Sea winds. Out along the anteater snout of the 3-mile-long sand and shingle spit of Spurn that curves down across the mouth of the Humber and would grow to close it off altogether were it not for the tremendous scouring power of the tides. The seaward side of Spurn lay littered with timber baulks, concrete blocks, hoops and angles of iron, all installed at one time or another as defences against erosion, all washed away or burst apart or eased aside by the unstoppable power of the sea. Out to Spurn Head where the most isolated community of lifeboatmen in Britain live, work and raise their families; out beyond the lighthouse and down onto the shore, to throw myself down at last in the dunes and stare to my heart's content across the 5-mile mouth of the Humber, and further east into unfathomed sea and unlimited sky.

13

The Great Sands of Lakeland

I'll never forget my barefoot crossing of Morecambe Sands under Cedric Robinson's command. The official Sands Guide to the Duchy of Lancaster has been doing the job nearly 50 years, earning £15 a year with a rent-free house and a field or two as payment for shepherding thousands of people across the most treacherous piece of not-quite-land, not-quite-sea in Britain.

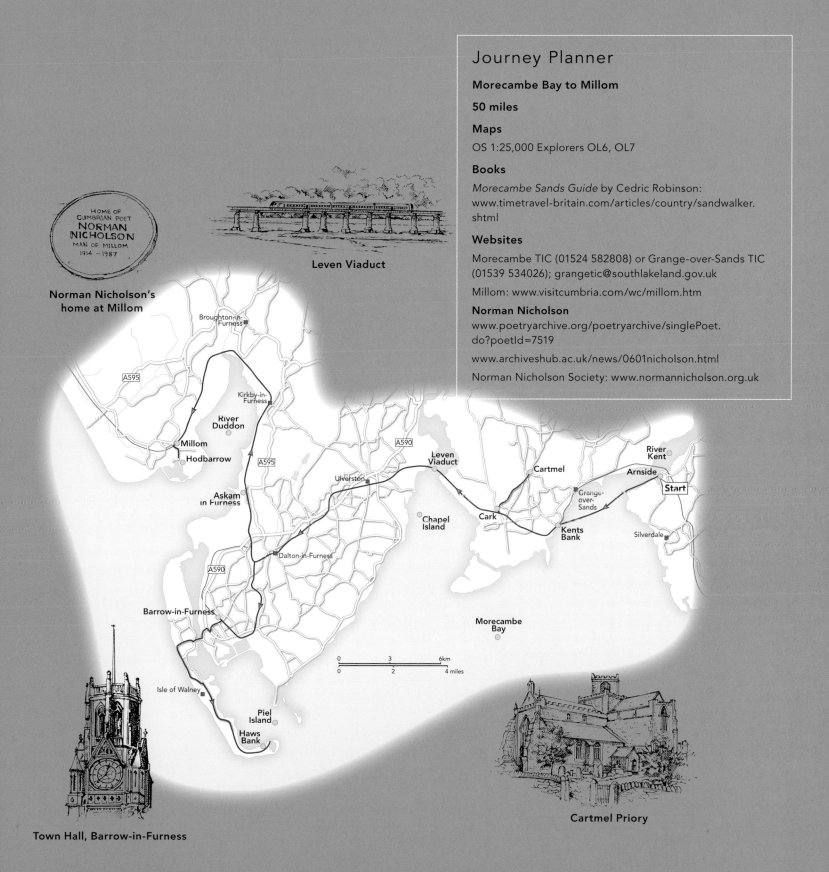

Norman Nicholson's
home at Millom

Leven Viaduct

Journey Planner

Morecambe Bay to Millom

50 miles

Maps

OS 1:25,000 Explorers OL6, OL7

Books

Morecambe Sands Guide by Cedric Robinson:
www.timetravel-britain.com/articles/country/sandwalker.
shtml

Websites

Morecambe TIC (01524 582808) or Grange-over-Sands TIC
(01539 534026); grangetic@southlakeland.gov.uk

Millom: www.visitcumbria.com/wc/millom.htm

Norman Nicholson

www.poetryarchive.org/poetryarchive/singlePoet.
do?poetId=7519

www.archiveshub.ac.uk/news/0601nicholson.html

Norman Nicholson Society: www.normannicholson.org.uk

Broughton-in-Furness

Kirkby-in-Furness

River Duddon

A595

Millom

Hodbarrow

A595

Askam in Furness

Ulverston

A590

Leven Viaduct

Cartmel

Arnside

Start

River Kent

Grange-over-Sands

Cark

Chapel Island

Kents Bank

Silverdale

Dalton-in-Furness

A590

Barrow-in-Furness

Morecambe Bay

| 0 | 3 | 6km |
| 0 | 2 | 4 miles |

Isle of Walney

Piel Island

Haws Bank

Town Hall, Barrow-in-Furness

Cartmel Priory

A careless or unlucky traveller can get into very serious trouble out in the middle of the vast saucer of sands and mudbanks that separates the two halves of Lancashire, upper and lower. The River Kent lies in an uneasy bed, switching from one side of the bay to the other as the mood takes it. Morecambe Bay at low tide is a place of treacheries, of unexpected waterways, of hidden gullies and sinking sands and wind-rippled pools. Before the Furness Railway was built across the narrows of the Kent Estuary, the routes across the sands were heavily used by coach-borne travellers and folk on foot, despite the dangers from quicksands and galloping tides. Hundreds paid with their lives for navigational errors or miscalculation of the state of the tide. Cockle pickers, fluke fishermen and mussel collectors still work the bay. These locals know the hazards, but strangers may not properly appreciate them. The 21 Chinese cockle pickers trapped by the tide and drowned on the night of 5 February 2004 were immigrant workers, cruelly exploited and neglected, whose awful story made headlines around the world. That was the worst of the bay's recorded tragedies; but Morecambe Sands have claimed numberless unremembered victims down the centuries.

Cedric Robinson knows every inch of Morecambe Bay. He checks the tides, the rivers and the shifting banks each day, and marks his safe routes with traditional 'brobs', or sprigs, of laurel. When I joined a group of walkers crossing the bay with Mr Robinson, I was aware of a curious atmosphere, part celebration, part apprehension, with a deal of healthy respect and a dash of pop star adulation for the broad-chested and barefoot figure of the Sands Guide as he strode ahead with his tall thumbstick through streams and tides like Moses parting the Red Sea. I've never seen a man put out so much energy, growling like a genial sheepdog at stragglers, racing to and fro to keep his flock together. Deserts of sand swallowed us up at Silverdale. They disgorged us hours later, full of exhilaration at having made the crossing, tired out and wet to the waist, at Kent's Bank on the shore of the Cartmel peninsula. Here I subsided onto a platform bench and waited for the train to Cark & Cartmel station.

Cartmel is one of three broad peninsulas, separated by the three sister rivers of Kent, Leven and Duddon, that push into the tidal sands from the southernmost tip of the Lake District. Together they resemble a diving sea eagle, its wings folded back as it plummets from the mountains of Lakeland into the Irish Sea. Ten miles to the north the great fells begin to rise – Scafell, Bow Fell, Great Gable, majestic in their height and rocky nakedness. The great sands of South Lakeland, by contrast, take their grandeur from their breadth and emptiness. Between the three peninsulas the eye roams undistracted across huge expanses of wind-scoured sand, flat deltas of dun and grey through which rivers that have sprung among mountains come snaking and widening to the sea. Tiny islands lie humped like seals in the sands. Along the coast arc villages that still operate a few fishing and cockling businesses to supplement the tourism, and one or two small industrial towns whose long-defunct slag banks poke scabby fingers out into the sands from ranks of terraced housing, reminders of the iron-working past that lend the region a character far removed from the poetic purity of the Lakes.

Left **As the tide recedes from the shores of Morecambe Bay, vast expanses of sand are exposed; not only sand, but mudflats, pools, hidden creeks and large, deadly areas of quicksand**

Right **Traditional methods of fishing the bay are still used around the region of the Great Sands – hard, physically demanding and potentially dangerous**

Iron ore mining and iron-making are finished now; but the Furness Railway, opened in 1846 to bring the ore from the hills to the coastal foundries, still runs its looping course across the peninsulas and bays, carried on the skeleton legs of viaducts sunk in the sands. It's a rattling, old-fashioned railway adventure, one you can punctuate at many wayside stations. I got down from the two-car train at Cark & Cartmel station and followed a lane beside the exotically named River Eea into Cartmel village. Above the slate roofs of this entirely charming tangle of whitewashed and grey stone houses rose the bulk of a Norman priory church. The churchyard was being neatly mown by a flock of sheep. 'Unfortunately drowned' was the cause of death recorded on many of the tombstones. Inside the church the dusky light of late afternoon filtered down, striping the roof-high pillars. A stone memorial sunk in the floor mourned a double drowning – Robert Harrison in 1782 at the age of 24, and his mother Margaret the following year in the self-same spot. A photograph mounted on one of the pillars showed a locket retrieved from the body of another young man who drowned more than two centuries ago while crossing the sands to visit his sweetheart, Isobel Crosfield. The darkly beautiful eyes of Isobel still glance from the miniature, while a braid of her glossy brown hair fills the back compartment of the locket. It was a poignant image to take with me out of the church and across the fields to my night's lodging.

In the morning I caught the Carlisle train and went clattering west over the Leven Viaduct into the Furness peninsula. Chapel Island lay marooned in a tan desert of low-tide sands, across which a solitary pilgrim figure was making its way towards the lonely islet. The Furness Railway dipped south through the 'Vale of Deadly Nightshade' towards Barrow-in-Furness at the tip of the peninsula, passing so close to the dark red sandstone ruin of Furness Abbey that I thought I could have tossed a pebble into the sacristy. The Abbot of Furness with his far-flung fellsides of sheep and cattle, his shipping and smuggling, farms and furnaces, was one of the richest prelates in medieval Britain, and some of that power and consequence still clings to the great roofless church in its shadowy vale.

Below left **Badge of the Furness Railway Company (prudent motto: 'Safety Through Caution'), whose snaking line takes railway enthusiasts on a fascinating journey across the estuaries and peninsulas of the Great Sands country**

Below **Many tombstones in the graveyard of Cartmel's priory church carry brief, poignant accounts of death by drowning while attempting to cross the treacherous sands**

Right **Superb in decay: the sandstone ruins of Furness Abbey rise beside the railway line in the Vale of Deadly Nightshade**

Barrow-in-Furness was a powerhouse of late Victorian industry, and it shows all over the town. The former fishing village of a couple of hundred inhabitants grew phenomenally quickly to become, in its heyday of the late 19th and early 20th centuries, an enormously busy shipbuilding centre and the biggest producer of iron and steel in the world, a roaring and smoking town of over 70,000 people. Barrow had everything the processes needed – iron in the hills behind, coal in the cliffs just up the coast, plenty of water, plenty of room to expand, a good local workforce, and the transport system to import raw materials and export the finished products – docks at its front door, the Furness Railway behind. Blast furnaces proliferated along the shore. The Barrow shipyards clanged night and day. And the town itself, far from following the general north of England pattern of developing in an uncontrolled and meanly built sprawl, was meticulously planned by the Furness Railway's superintendent James Ramsden. I wandered through Barrow for most of the morning, admiring the ambitious breadth of the tree-shaded streets lined with dignified houses, the width of the town's squares, and the fabulous red wedding-cake of a Town Hall under its solid rocket of a clock tower. 'Aye, no need for a policeman in Barra,' said a man who pulled up next to me. 'We can allus tell the time.'

Down on the tip of the peninsula lie the big dock basins, their water preserved from ebb tides by mighty walls and gates. Here are the giant hump-backed sheds of BAE Systems, the submarine builders who underpin employment in isolated, out-on-a-limb Barrow. And beyond, across the bridge that spans the 200yd (183m) narrows of Walney Channel, lies the hammerhead island of Walney with its hooked ends and slender, deeply indented waist. By the time I'd walked out to the shingly banks and old gravel pits of South End Haws, the tide was pushing in and the sands were flooding over. I settled down on the point of Haws Bank under clouds of ill-tempered lesser black-backed gulls and contented myself with a good stare across the rapidly disappearing sand flats to Piel Island. I'd been across there once before for a pint in the Ship Inn and a chat with the King of Piel – and once visited, never forgotten. Out on the tiny teardrop-shaped isle I could make out the row of former coastguard cottages still keeping a weather eye on the craggy ruin of the castle built by the monks of Furness Abbey to defend this smuggling stronghold of theirs. Standing between cottages and castle as if keeping the peace between these opposing interests was the white-painted Ship Inn. Each successive resident landlord of this most isolated pub is entitled to rejoice in the title of 'King of Piel'. I'd often dreamed of revisiting the

Ship and receiving my second knighthood by the simple process of sitting once more in the ceremonial chair which confers that honour. 'Twice a knight, at your age!' – what a splendid opportunity for all my dear friends. But I had happened upon an interregnum. The former landlord had gone ashore, and the new one had yet to assume the throne of Piel. I could only gaze across the tide at the white-walled Ship, and resign myself to savouring that treat some other day.

Next morning dawned fiery and beautiful, with storms forecast from the west. The Furness Railway rattled me on around the long sandy rake of the Duddon Estuary, up past Askam-in-Furness where the ashen bank of 'Askam Pier', a great rampart of ironworks slag, poked its grey finger half a mile out into the bay. In his River Duddon sonnets William Wordsworth expressed his dread at such an eyesore attaching itself to his beloved river:

> Child of the clouds! remote from every taint
> Of sordid industry thy lot is cast;
> Thine are the honours of the lofty waste...

That was all very true upstream among the mountains, but down here beside the Furness railway on the polluted shores of the Duddon Estuary, the river once ran orange and black and its banks lay grey and brown with haematite and iron slag. No longer, though. These days the Duddon flows fresh and clear, and nature is recapturing the badlands where the ironworks used to stand.

Above left and right **Pretty girls turn a cyclist's head in Barrow-in-Furness in the pre-motorcar era; nowadays the fashions may be different, but wide streets and fine sandstone architecture still characterise the town**

Right **In the heyday of shipbuilding in Barrow-in-Furness, the whole dock region of the town would ring with the chatter and roar of riveting**

Round the inner curve of the estuary ran the train, clacking beside the marshes fringing Duddon Sands. Down there lies Millom, forgotten on its going-nowhere loop of road, a town whose ironworks closed. I left the train and went to find 14 St George's Terrace, a modest house with a blue plaque on the front wall announcing it as the 'home of the Cumbrian poet Norman Nicholson, Man of Millom (1914–1987)'. What would have become of Norman Nicholson's reputation if he had lived in Grasmere and extolled the beauties of the Lakes? As it is, few seem to know of the man who wrote about a real Cumberland of slag banks and sinter dust, of 'black-scum shadows stagnating between backyard walls', of the poetry of the nicknames of weeds ('Fat hen, rat's tail, cat's ear, old men's baccy'), and of what a man of Millom saw and felt as the ironworks, the social and economic backbone of the town, were dismantled:

> ...the Duddon rediscovers
> Its former channel almost unencumbered – mines
> Drowned under stagnant waters, chimneys felled and uprooted,
> Slagbanks ploughed down to half their height, all cragginess,

Below **Norman Nicholson, this coast's master poet, was born in the ironworking town of Millom and wrote magnificently of grime and smoke, fiery skies, furnace roar and the grinding of wheeled machinery**

Right **When Hodbarrow iron ore mine expanded seaward in the early 20th century, a new sea wall was built along with the handsome cast-iron Hodbarrow Lighthouse**

*Scrag-end and scree ironed out, and re-soiled
  and greened over
To long sulky drumlins, dumped there by the
  look of them
An ice-age ago. They cut up the carcass of the
  old ironworks
Like a fat beast in a slaughter-house; they
  shovelled my childhood
On to a rubbish heap…*

I went down to the big lake on the shore where the Hodbarrow haematite mines and blast furnaces once flared and clattered. Norman Nicholson's uncle Jack was killed in an industrial accident here, and Hodbarrow always loomed large in the poet's psyche with its 'proud battery of chimneys, the hell-mouth roar of the furnace/The midnight sunsets ladled across a cloudy sky…'

Beside the lake middle-aged men idled, hands in pockets, smoking and yawning. A young tearaway drove an old home-painted Ford Capri recklessly fast up Devonshire Road; he couldn't have been more than 13, and was hardly able to see over the steering wheel. No more midnight sunsets or hell-mouth roars around Millom for a young poet to cut his teeth on; but maybe, I thought as I walked back towards the railway station, some youngster was even now on his hand and knees among the weeds of the slag banks, the fat hen and old men's baccy, tasting the potency of words, of his parents' names for things, and trying out a few of his own devising.

An ice-age ago. They cut up the carcass of the old ironworks
Like a fat beast in a slaughter-house; they shovelled my childhood
On to a rubbish heap…

(Quotation from 'On the Dismantling of Millom Ironworks', in *Sea to the West* by Norman Nicholson (Faber 1981)

14

Spring in Upper Teesdale

The valley of the River Tees runs east for the best part of 100 miles from its high springs on the spongy moors of the North Pennines to the sprawling estuary of Teesmouth with its chemical works, iron foundry and ship-breaking yards; and nowhere along its length are river and surroundings more perfectly in harmony than in the glacier-gouged limestone hollow of Upper Teesdale.

High Force waterfall

Journey Planner

Cauldron Snout to Middleton-in-Teesdale

15 miles

Maps

OS 1:25,000 Explorer OL31

Books

Journey Through Britain by John Hillaby
(Constable 1995)

Websites

Moor House National Nature Reserve: Guided
walks, volunteer days, information etc.
01833 622374; www.ecn.ac.uk/sites/moorh.
html; www.naturalengland.org.uk

Cow Green Reservoir

Langdon Beck

Widdybank Fell

River Tees

Forest-in-Teesdale

Ettersgill

Cronkley Footbridge

Cauldron Snout

Start

Moor House & Upper Teesdale NNR

Cronkley Farm

High Force

White Force

Cronkley Fell

Bowlees

Newbiggin

Holwick Fell

Holwick

Pennine Way

High Dyke

Middleton-in-Teesdale

Crossthwaite Common

Laithkirk

Mickleton

Lapwing

Pennine Way signpost

It is a springtime walker's good fortune

that the Pennine Way takes advantage of the easy navigating beside the River Tees in the broad, snaking valley bottom; for here under the limestone cliffs, and in the grassy ledges of the dale sides, a fabulous treasury of tiny and delicate survivors from the post-Ice Age tundra still lies open for the delight of anyone passing by with a pair of sharp eyes.

John Hillaby's sublime recounting of his 1965 Land's End to John O'Groats walk in spring, *Journey Through Britain*, first infused my imagination with the magic of this unique flora. 'No botanical name-dropping,' he wrote, 'can give an adequate impression of the botanical jewels sprinkled on the ground above High Force… In this valley a tundra has been marvellously preserved; the glint of colour, the reds, deep purples, and blues have the quality of Chartres glass.' I longed to hunt for those jewels for myself. But that would have to wait until tomorrow. Just now, on a rainy spring evening after 20 miles of battle with the Pennine Way, I had energy only to scramble down the dark rocks beside the tumbling fall of Cauldron Snout.

The 200-ft (60-m) dolerite staircase that forms Cauldron Snout is just one of a series of remarkable landscape features in Teesdale caused by the long, slow cooling of a tongue of molten rock that thrust its way in amongst the limestone of the region some 300 million years ago. One can picture it as a horizontal volcano, squeezing its lava like toothpaste between two bedding planes of carboniferous limestone. The great glob of hot magma gradually solidified into a wedge of dark basalt of a kind known as dolerite.

This intrusive band of hard rock formed the giant shelf of the Whin Sill, whose chain of exposed outcrops stretches all across the north of England – most notably along Hadrian's Wall, 50 miles north of Cauldron Snout, where a great petrified tsunami of rock rears towards Scotland with the Roman wall clinging to its back like a determined surfer. Here in Upper Teesdale the sombre dolerite makes an equally dramatic statement, forming a succession of sharp steps in the bed of the River Tees. These are no mere shelves for white-water rafters to bounce down; they are serious cliffs, over which the rain-swollen river crashes in splendour.

Above **The River Tees tumbles down the dolerite 'staircase' of Cauldron Snout**

Top right **Snipe in the meadows of Upper Teesdale**

Bottom right **Looking down over the farms and meadows of Upper Teesdale**

It was a piece of good fortune to find that Chris McCarty had discovered a free day in his normally jam-packed diary to take me walking through the meadows and over the fells of Upper Teesdale. As Site Manager of the 20,000-acre (8,000-ha) Moor House and Upper Teesdale National Nature Reserve, there isn't much that Chris doesn't know about these magnificent and beautiful uplands, the damp slopes and hollows of the Pennine moors, the rare sugar limestone that supports the fragile arctic-alpine flora, the pavements of limestone blocks and sheltered cracks, the acid patches of bog and the traditionally farmed hay meadows. Nowadays this mosaic of habitats is properly recognised for what it is – a unique landscape in which flourish plants that are among our most senior floral residents, communities that are a throwback to a slowly unfreezing, post-glacial Britain.

By ten o'clock next morning, after a log-like sleep at Langdon Beck, I was down in the river meadows with Chris McCarty, watching lapwings flapping against the stiff spring wind and rain. Seeing the two humans approaching, they had become agitated on account of their newly hatched chicks crouching in the lee of sedge clumps. In creaking voices the parent birds cried their folk name – *pee-wit! pee-wit!* 'Holding their numbers well this year,' remarked Chris as I steadied my binoculars against the gusts. 'And listen! That's a sound you don't hear too often.' Through the incessant complaining of the lapwings I made out a background whirr. 'See the snipe? He's drumming – look, just over our heads!' A small dark body was diving groundwards, long bill extended in front like an aeroplane skid. 'It's all to impress the ladies,' said Chris. 'He holds out his tail feathers, and the air drums them as it rushes by.'

Like most of the northern dales, Upper Teesdale lies separated into very distinct agricultural strata. The green valley-bottom pastures known as inbye land give way to rougher 'intake' land further up the dale sides. This olive-coloured higher land is boggy and wet, lightly grazed to prevent its cover becoming too wild and dense – ideal conditions for wading birds such as snipe and redshank to nest and rear their young. Beyond the intake wall, darker and rougher country rises to the open heather moorland that rolls away across the fell tops.

Swollen with the night's downpour, the Tees roared and rumbled in its stony bed. Milky curtains of rain came swishing through the dale as we tramped the meadows among the nesting lapwing, the redshank and plover. Under the tuition of Chris McCarty, I found myself wandering from one floral treat to the next like a child in a sweetshop. The rain-sodden pastures beside the Tees, at first glance composed of thick grass, revealed themselves on closer inspection to be a rich salad of herbs known as a Northern Hay Meadow community. Such species-rich upland meadows (there can be upwards of 30 plant species in one square yard) form one of the rarest habitats in these islands, said Chris – there are fewer than 3,000 acres (1,215ha) still intact in the whole of the UK. Left unblasted by chemicals, and allowed to lie uncut until their flowers have set seed, the riverside fields yield pink and white milkmaids, shiny marsh marigolds, slender purple spikes of early marsh orchid and the acid yellow balls of the rare globeflower. Also here were widespread rosettes of butterwort, the violet-like flowers trembling on long stalks, the pale green leaves pitted with circular glands. These extrude a glue to entice insects. When the butterwort's sensors detect that two or three struggling flies have been trapped, the edges of the leaf turn up and roll together. Then strong digestive juices get to work on liquidising the entombed victims.

As Chris and I crossed the racing Tees by way of the footbridge at Cronkley and began to climb towards the intake land, we started to spot the delicate arctic-alpine flowers on ledges and in crevices of the rocks among tattered juniper bushes. I got down on my knees and crawled along, transfixed by their fragile beauty. Mountain pansies, boldly coloured purple flowers with a broad lower lip of yellow striped with black; one or two tiny Teesdale violets; and then the glorious bird's-eye primroses, deep pink, with an intense yellow eye glowing at the heart of each flower. Why had they clung on here, in this particular dale?

'Well,' said Chris, 'arctic-alpine flora are directly threatened by climate change. They have to have things cool. Their natural reaction to a warmer environment is to lower their temperature, either by going north, or by climbing up the hill. But they can't go north because the conditions north of

Swollen with the night's downpour, the Tees roared and rumbled in its stony bed. Milky curtains of rain came swishing through the dale as we tramped the meadows among the nesting lapwing, the redshank and plover.

Above **The view from Cronkley Fell as the River Tees curves round the foot of Falcon Clints**

Above right **Delicate, rare and beautiful: the bird's eye primrose is just one of Upper Teesdale's many springtime glories**

Teesdale aren't right for them, and they already are at the top of the hill. So they thrive here essentially because of lack of competition. The climate in Upper Teesdale stays cold and wet till late on in spring, which most British flowers can't deal with Having said that – these moors are seeing 25 per cent less frost and snow in winter than they did only ten years ago. The formation of the Whin Sill is the other main factor. That tongue of hot lava pushed into the limestone like a sausage into a hotdog roll, and when it did, it baked the surrounding rocks into crystals full of minerals – sugar limestone, we call it – see?' He scooped up a palm full of glittering crystals like dull little diamonds. 'They've got exactly the balance of nutrients that the arctic-alpines need. A huge slice of luck, and it gave us this fabulous flora.'

Chris got to his feet and swept an arm over the dale. 'Everything that's here, this whole landscape, looks so – I don't know, sort of peaceful and settled, don't you think? But it took fantastic events, forces it's really hard to get your head round, to form it. The last Ice Age, for example. You have to imagine a sheet of ice *a mile thick* grinding through this dale. I mean, can you picture that?'

I put my head back and stared up into the watery heavens. A lapwing was tumbling overhead, perhaps 50ft (15m) above the ground, already small against the sky. I tried to visualise the bird ten times as high, a dot almost out of ken; then the wrinkled, rock-streaked upper surface of the vanished glacier, rearing at least ten times taller than that – far higher than Ben Nevis. The sheer scale of it; the bitter cold, the crack of ice, the whine of an arctic wind. The absence of any man as the behemoth of ice moved over the barren rocks of Teesdale.

'At the end of the last Ice Age those glaciers left behind a great carpet of crumbled rock and gravel as they shrank back northwards. That's why we've got these thick banks above the river on each side. And those little rounded hillocks down in the bottom of the dale, drumlins as we call them – they're just more of this glacier-borne gravel, washed into shape by huge floods of racing meltwater when the Tees would have filled half the dale. What a sight that must have been!' And what a roaring beast of a sound, I thought to myself as we moved on.

We climbed the well-worn track of the Pennine Way above Cronkley Farm. On the fell top of Bracken Rigg a rough circle of stones poked through the turf of a low circular embankment – the boundary bank of a Bronze Age dwelling. The hut doorway faced southwest, away from the quarter out of which the bitterest winter weather would blow. Here we turned aside along the Green Trod, a link in the great chain of ancient cattle-droving roads that lies forgotten across so much of upland Britain. The Green Trod runs straight and true down Teesdale, ribboning over the backs of the fells. Back before the days of refrigeration and wheeled transport for beasts, black Scottish cattle passed this way under the capable stewardship of professional drovers. The animals were small and hardy, and they needed to be; their journey, scarcely believable nowadays, brought them on the hoof from the Highland glens where they were reared, 200 miles to Appleby in Westmorland, then over the Pennines by way of the Green Trod and Upper Teesdale, down to the great livestock markets at York and Northallerton. Sold there to graziers, they would be driven on to fatten for slaughter in the sweet grazing meadows of the south.

As for the drovers, those 'great stalwart hirsute men, shaggy and uncultured and wild, who look like bears as they lounge heavily along', they were much maligned, much misunderstood. A drove comprised between 100 and 400 cattle, moved along by up to eight men and their dogs. A drover reckoned to cover 15 or 20 miles a day, and might walk the cattle many hundreds of miles to market. He wore heavy homespun and a broad-brimmed hat, and soaped his brown paper leggings against the weather and the soles of his rough woollen stockings against blisters. He often slept out of doors with the animals, or in the outhouses of farms whose sign of welcome to drovers was a spinney of three Scots pine trees.

With his ragged beard and weather-stained clothes, a drover might look like a wild man and an outlaw, but in fact he was generally a sober and reliable person who exercised huge responsibility looking after other men's fortunes on the hoof, bringing those fortunes converted into gold coins back to his clients, often carrying other commissions, messages and mail between the cattle breeders and dealers, the graziers and the small-town bankers who formed his network of business contacts. A drover expected to work and live hard, and he often died hard, too, in an accident at a flooded ford or on a slippery cliff edge, or of a painful illness on some remote hillside. His heyday ended in the mid-19th century; roads were better, steamships and railways slashed journey times for travelling beasts, and lowland farmers bred bigger, fatter cattle of their own. The drover passed into history, unlamented, soon forgotten.

Beside the hissing jet of White Force waterfall Chris and I ate our sandwiches under the ruined gable of an old mine shop, a bothy where lead miners once sheltered between shifts in the levels of White Force's mine. Then it was on up the long nape of Cronkley Fell, up the dolerite cliffs and crags to the ancient fenced and walled enclosures that lay across the broad summit. The sugar limestone was spattered with white stars of spring sandwort – a plant so indicative of the presence of lead that it was once known as 'leadwort'. Thousands of bird's-eye primroses trembled in the wind. Seeded in this rich pink carpet, trumpet-shaped spring gentians of a celestial royal blue vibrated as if blowing a silent paean to spring.

Right **High Force: in a furious outburst of peat-stained water, the River Tees crashes down the 70-ft dolerite step of the Whin Sill in the full majesty of springtime spate**

Down by the roaring Tees we turned back along the river bank, walking silently now. A redshank stood sentinel on a fence post, spitting out its sharp warning, *chip! chip!* The scratchy cries of the nesting lapwings recalled the creaking of fracturing ice, and I thought of the glaciers melting away northwards 10,000 years ago, in retreat from the deep valley they had gouged, leaving behind a naked landscape ready for seeding with the ancestors of Teesdale's gentians and violets, pink primroses and gaudy pansies. John Hillaby summed it all up to perfection: 'For me Teesdale was more beautiful than I could have imagined; certainly more strange and evocative than I could have foreseen.'

On Wat Garth footbridge I said goodbye to Chris McCarty and went on down the dale. The dolerite step of High Force, when I reached it, was a hurling maelstrom of rain-driven water. The peat-stained Tees went crashing over the black cliff in a single mighty sluice of creamy yellow water, a furious and thunderous outrush that fell 70ft (20m) like a hammer into a basin misty with spray and brilliant with miniature rainbows. I walked the bank among rowan trees foaming with blossom and gin-scented juniper bushes, feeling the rocks beneath my boots quake and shudder with the force of the torrent.

In the late afternoon I came down into Middleton-in-Teesdale. It was sheep sale day, and farmers around the dale were still gathered at the mart on the outskirts of town. Fifty or so men sat round the auction ring, faces under flat caps gloomy or quizzical according to type. 'The two yows are Neville Nixon's,' murmured the ring attendant to the auctioneer, 'and the tup's from Howgill.' A young boy helped to marshal the sheep into the ring, his small hands grabbing horns, ears and noses as confidently as the big red fists of his father. 'Get down, now,' said one of the attendants to another youngster who was clambering up the railing, and gave him a gentle clap on the backside.

In Middleton, after dumping my pack at a B&B, I went out to run one particular pub to earth. I walked straight past the King's Head twice before I could believe that this neat and decent little establishment – now renamed Forresters Hotel – was the place that I remembered. Back more than 30 years ago, when Dad and I had made our first expedition up the Pennine Way, the King's Head had been the grimmest pub in Middleton, a peeling shack of a place, done out before the war in matt black paint and chinoiserie wallpaper and never since refurbished. I'd chosen it, like every other pub we stayed in during that week's walking, from the *Good Beer Guide*. Consequently we found ourselves drinking well all week, but sleeping hard.

The King's Head was the roughest of the lot, by a country mile. It squatted by the road with a cramped, ominous look. The 21-inch TV screen, enormous in that era, stood a foot from the dining table and operated at a volume that precluded conversation. None of the guests dared to turn it down, much less off. The bedrooms lay under the eaves, and were approached by a staircase whose ceiling dropped suddenly to a clearance of less than 2ft (0.6m) above a hairpin bend. Dad and I were obliged to crawl round this obstacle on hands and knees, one behind the other, like a couple of soaks who'd had a skinful apiece. Our room and the one next to it shared a single unshaded bulb, which hung from the ceiling in the other chamber. Our allowance of its sickly, low-wattage light was admitted to our gloomy den by a square aperture high in the corner of the hardboard wall that separated us from our fellow guests, an enormous elderly couple 'retired

Above **The meadows along the River Tees between High Force and Middleton-in-Teesdale are separated by drystone walls, very characteristic of the Pennine hills**

Above right **When Robert Bainbridge, Chief Officer of the London Lead Company, retired in 1877, LLC employees raised £262.15s.5d. Bainbridge used part of it to build this ornate fountain in Middleton-in-Teesdale**

Left **Juniper bushes grow wild on the fell slopes above the River Tees**

from trade' in Birmingham. They couldn't have been friendlier, the 20-stone lady offering with tremendous gusto to give Dad a rub-down if we could find her a drop of oil to sweeten her hands. Dad didn't take her up on the suggestion, but it certainly cheered him up.

Out on the southern edge of town I stood watching a smeary magenta sunset over the moors. Another of the great landscape shifts of this journey was in prospect tomorrow morning. A couple of miles after quitting Middleton I would be exchanging the light and cheerful limestone of the dales, all bright spring flowers, silvery stone farms and spectacular river valley formations, for the dun colours and harsh scenery of the Pennines' most characteristic material – millstone grit. The industrial north, with all its dourness, its hardness and its blackly humorous people, would gather to enfold me like a fly in a leaf of butterwort for the next ten days or more. I had no illusions about the struggles of the path awaiting me, the slogging and the squelching on the gritstone moors. But with a head still reeling with the glories of Upper Teesdale and spirits buoyed by the lightness of limestone, I found I was actually looking forward to it: the vast sweep of the moors, the cut of the wind, the low-crawling flora in beds of acid green sphagnum, the hunched mill towns with their cobbled packhorse bridges, the cramped dark pubs with pungent local bitters. Thinking of that, I turned back towards the town, fancying I could already hear the musical hiss and crash of Cameron's Strongarm jetting from a hand-pulled pump into the first pint glass of the evening.

... with a head still reeling with the glories of Upper Teesdale and spirits buoyed by the lightness of limestone.

15

Tunes and Trails of Cheviot

Alistair Anderson is teaching a group of musicians in a room in Gateshead. The master of the concertina and Northumbrian smallpipes encourages his students to listen critically to a recording of the Border shepherd and fiddle player Willie Taylor playing the Linhope Lope.

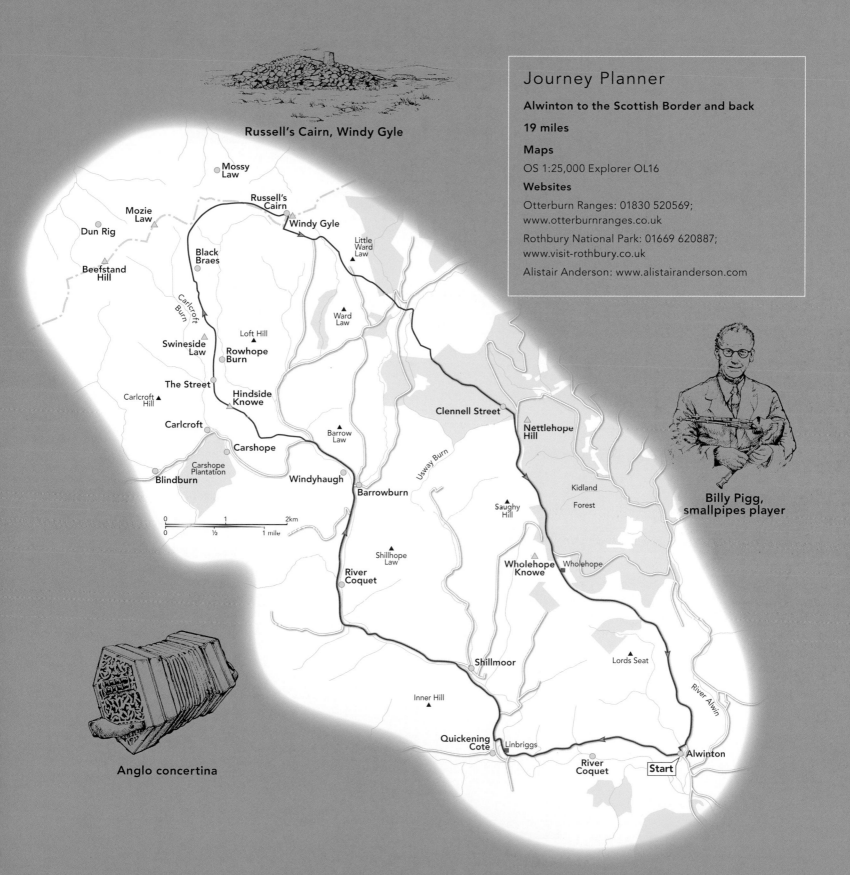

Russell's Cairn, Windy Gyle

Journey Planner

Alwinton to the Scottish Border and back

19 miles

Maps

OS 1:25,000 Explorer OL16

Websites

Otterburn Ranges: 01830 520569;
www.otterburnranges.co.uk

Rothbury National Park: 01669 620887;
www.visit-rothbury.co.uk

Alistair Anderson: www.alistairanderson.com

Mossy Law

Russell's Cairn

Windy Gyle

Little Ward Law

Mozie Law

Dun Rig

Black Braes

Beefstand Hill

Carlcroft Burn

Ward Law

Loft Hill

Swineside Law

Rowhope Burn

The Street

Carlcroft Hill

Hindside Knowe

Clennell Street

Nettlehope Hill

Carlcroft

Barrow Law

Carshope

Kidland Forest

Carshope Plantation

Windyhaugh

Usway Burn

Blindburn

Barrowburn

Saughy Hill

Billy Pigg, smallpipes player

Wholehope Knowe

Wholehope

0   1   2km
0   ½   1 mile

Shillhope Law

River Coquet

Inner Hill

Shillmoor

Lords Seat

River Alwin

Quickening Cote

Linbriggs

River Coquet

Start

Alwinton

Anglo concertina

'Is he putting in an extra note there?' queries Alistair Anderson. 'Yes, I think he's kicking up from that semi-quaver below,' says the flute player, carefully. 'And he's cutting the E short,' suggests the banjo player, 'and that's what makes it sound so snappy.' Alistair nods approval. 'I'm inclined to agree. And he's leaving that big C in mid-air, do you hear?' To demonstrate he swings his own concertina high in a patent flourish, as if shaking out the note into its new state of eminence.

The librarian, two teachers, car mechanic, schoolgirl and unemployed builder smile, then go quiet and still as the recording scampers on. 'Nipping along, isn't he?' remarks Alistair. 'Probably late for a visit to Nancy that night. Don't forget, Will lived a good two hours' walk away from her.' It is the comment of a man who knew the old guard of Northumbrian traditional music as well as he knows today's players; someone very familiar with the moorland tracks and farm roads of the Cheviot Hills where these wonderful hornpipes, rants and waltzes belong.

Setting off up the road through Upper Coquetdale from the little farming settlement of Alwinton, I pictured Alistair, his lean face with its dryly humorous expression, his upright stance and energetic demeanour, the little dancer's steps he takes as he plays, the way he bends and straightens like a well-tempered blade, swinging the concertina or sweeping it round in circles to push the tune away to where his listeners can catch it out of the ether. It's impossible to imagine a better ambassador for Northumbrian music and for the wild, rolling Cheviot Hills from which it flows so copiously. If it hadn't been for Alistair and like-minded young friends and fellow musicians back in the 1960s and '70s, this ancient spring of music inextricably linked with a particular landscape might well have dried up and vanished under the glaring heat and light of pop music. The Cheviots and their people would have been disastrously the poorer.

The border between England and Scotland runs a crooked course along the heights of the Cheviots, and many old roads cross it: Clennell Street, Salter's Road, Pass Path, Gamel's Path, the Roman soldiers' marching highway of Dere Street, and the winding route known simply as The Street, which threads the narrowing cleft of Coquetdale beside the shallow, noisily rushing River Coquet. I stepped out briskly enough along The Street with some 20 miles to cover on this autumn day. Grassy hillsides rose on either hand, the long smooth slopes so characteristic of the Cheviots scattered with the circular stone enclosures of bields, or sheep pens, lined with wire fences and dotted with clusters of sheep. Solid, low-built farmhouses punctuated the long miles of road tramping. Quickening Cote and Shillmoor, Barrowburn and Windyhaugh, Carshope, Carlscroft and Blindburn – evocative names for wind-bitten, hard graft farms in an all but treeless landscape with little shelter from wind and rain.

With a splash and a throaty roar an army personnel carrier passed me on the road near Windyhaugh. A group of soldiers stared out of the open back of the truck, rigid with boredom. One nodded to me, his mate raised a laconic thumb, and they vanished round the bend in a cloud of slate-blue diesel smoke. How many other soldiers were up on the tops or down in the clefts today? The Cheviots form the northern quarter of Northumberland National Park, and the army has

training rights over a big swathe of the hills. Walking the Cheviots, one becomes accustomed to being overtaken by grizzled tough guys in camouflage toting 60lb packs; also to the sight of their greenhorn comrades limping in their slipstream in too-big boots. Often it seems that there are more jeeps than sheep, more squaddies than farmers in these hills. Sheep rearing today has proved too unprofitable for many of the Coquetdale farmers. In Upper Coquetdale there are locked doors and sagging roofs among the farms where a teenage Alistair Anderson was handed the gift that informed his whole life and work.

At a bend of the valley just beyond Barrowburn, The Street leaves the course of the tarmac road and forges ahead up the flanks of Hindside Knowe and Swineside Law, a broad grassy track climbing steadily into the remote uplands of Cheviot. I climbed with it, whistling the Barrowburn Reel as the miles slipped away under my boots. In my mind's ear ran Alistair's Northumberland-inflected voice, a conversation unrolling in a Gateshead bar as I savoured a nice hoppy pint of Deuchars, and Alistair sipped his abstemious glass of water.

...'I grew up in the 1950s and '60s in the shipbuilding district of Wallsend, by the Tyne in the east end of Newcastle. Among Wallsend lads at that time, if you did a sport, it was football – end of story. And if you got into playing music, it was pop or R&B; there were the Animals,

Above **A characteristic Cheviot view, with rounded hills rolling away from the lush flat meadows of the river valley**

Left **Farmhouse music: in front of the kitchen dresser, Northumbrian smallpipes players get lost in the tune**

playing the clubs in town and setting the example. Well, I didn't like football. But my mother loved to walk, and she loved plants. So I came to the Cheviots with her at first, looking for plants and birds, and later on with the local rambling and climbing clubs, and bicycling here with my school friend Dave Richardson. Anything to get out of Wallsend!

'... I began to get interested in folk music, trying out tunes on my father's mandolin and then on a friend's granny's concertina that was kept locked up behind glass in a cabinet in her front room. I thought, "Hey, I can get a tune out of this!" Finding what tunes to play was a real problem, though. Books or records of Northumbrian tunes – they were hard to come by. I'd come home from the folk club trying to hold the tune in my head. Newcastle Central Library had a battered old copy of the *Northumbrian Minstrelsy*, an absolute treasury of local tunes, and Dave and I virtually copied out that whole book by hand!

'.. I really got my awakening when a teacher's wife took me to meet Billy Pigg at Hepple Woodside, his farm in Coquetdale. The Northumbrian smallpipes had never died out, but around that time they very nearly did. People in the hill farms, the stronghold of the pipes, were watching TV in the evenings rather than gathering in the back kitchen to play music. You were down to the last half-dozen really great players, and the greatest was Billy Pigg. He was a very hospitable man, very tolerant of this enthusiastic teenager, and absolutely brilliant on the pipes. Very open, and would share his music with anyone. I was taken to other farms, and other players. The drop scones on the griddle, the big pots of tea, the dogs, the kindness… And finding you could play something yourself. It was a big, big thing for me.

'... Visiting those farms, you'd find yourself in contact with people untouched by the 1944 Education Act. Some of them were very, very bright, but just happened to have spent all their lives in manual labour. I became aware of music not as an incidental pleasure, but as something that naturally flowed through their lives. Also I felt there was a strong connection between the Cheviot landscape they worked and lived in, and the music they made and played there. But it's a very vague and nebulous thing, and not something I could put into words.'

High on Black Braes, I followed The Street through dark stands of heather, looking down to my right into the steep cleft of the Rowhope Burn. A cold northwest wind out of Scotland blew into my face, fluttering my shirt and tugging at my hair. Sheer exhilaration took hold of me, the kind of inexpressible bliss that visits a walker from time to time in high and lonely places. Up at the Border fence I sat on the step of a stile, staring a long time over the pale, sun-streaked whalebacks of the hills, rehearsing their names from memory and the map: Mossy Law, Big Dun Rig, Mozie Law, Beefstand Hill. Then I turned my back on the breeze and let it bowl me along the Border up the miry track of the Pennine Way.

The last time I trod this path it had been in thick mist and warm, freckling rain. Today all lay clear and cold, with cloud shadows racing sun patches across the slopes. As always in these hills, the names on the map enchanted my inner ear: Foulstep Sike and Goat Cleuch, Windy Gyle and Split the Deil. Evocative names for ominous places, where more blood was spilt than was ever recorded. Clan set-tos and 'frays', full-scale battles between English and Scots, throat-slittings by sheep-rustlers, lonely murders by footpads and masterless men. These wild hills were debatable lands all through the Middle Ages and long after, contested between two neighbouring nations and fought over between a dozen neighbouring families, a place where national law did not run and every man looked out for himself and his kin.

On Russell's Cairn I sat and let an hour go hang. The butt end of the afternoon remained for the long descent down Clennell Street to Alwinton by way of Murder Cleugh and Drummer's Well, Nettlehope Hill and Wholehope Knowe. I stretched out in the grass, the tune on my lips now changed to a Billy Pigg classic, 'The Wild Hills of Wannies'. If Alistair Anderson were home at this moment and not out on tour elsewhere in the wilds of the world, he'd be setting off even

'In the end, the music lifts everybody up. You can leave a ceilidh thinking, "That's the best night I've ever had", in a way that you just wouldn't if you'd been listening to classical music played by an equally inexpert group of musicians.'

Left **Rank, ragged and magnificent: approaching downwind, you can smell the wild goats of Cheviot long before you catch sight of them**

Above right **Stony river, green pasture, whaleback hill, birch and sycamore, a lonely farmhouse down in the dale – the keynotes of the Cheviot Hills**

now for some village hall or farm up in the hills, to talk of his beloved music, perhaps, or to lead some shepherd's child through the first steps on a lifelong musical road.

'This music has worked for all these years, and it's still working. People are really not all that different from the way they were. It gives people a chance to join in without rehearsals or any formality. It makes a bond between players who've only got ordinary skills, and that benefits communities, I very strongly feel – and schools, too. It's essential that Northumbrian schools offer Northumbrian material that's geographically and culturally rooted in the area, so the children will develop a feeling for the place they live. That's very important, especially in these days of faceless, could-be-anywhere estates.

'... In the end, the music lifts everybody up. You can leave a ceilidh thinking, "That's the best night I've ever had", in a way that you just wouldn't if you'd been listening to classical music played by an equally inexpert group of musicians. And the reason is that these players are from the same community and the same place, playing with and for people they know. I would love to see it get to the stage one day where to walk down the street with a set of pipes or a concertina in your hand would be as natural as carrying a tennis racquet or a fishing rod.'

16

Upheaval and Renewal in the Hills of South Armagh

'Paddy Collins? Oh, he's been offered a mint of money to sell that house of his to the road makers. But he's kind of determined, Paddy. They'll have to drag him out of it feet first!'

Newry to Crossmaglen and back around the Ring of Gullion

33 miles

Maps

OS of Northern Ireland 1:50,000 Discoverer 29

Books

An Illustrated Guide to Walking the Ring of Gullion Way, available at tourist information centres

Websites

Ring of Gullion Way: www.walkni.com/Walk.aspx?ID=46

www.ni-environment.gov.uk/places_to_visit_home/aonb/aonb_gullion.htm

Fionn MacCumhaill and Cúchulainn: www.shee-eire.com

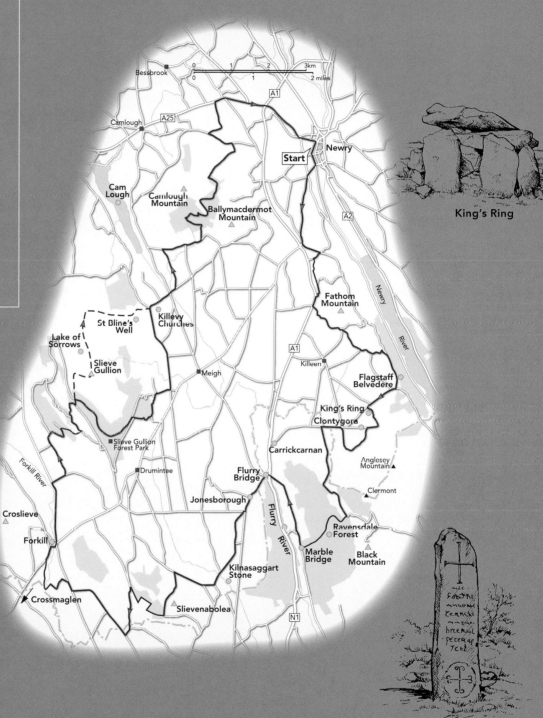

King's Ring

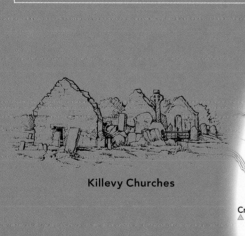

Killevy Churches

Kilnasaggart Standing Stone

All Newry was tickled to death just now by the story of bold Paddy Collins and his defiance of a seemingly inexorable fate at the hands of the road builders who were in the process of constructing a bypass to take the main A1 Belfast–Dublin road clear of the town. They'd upped their offer many times, so the story said. But Paddy Collins had held out stubbornly. Now a general recession had hit, the offers had dried up, and Paddy was stuck in his unwanted house in the ghostly shadow of the as-yet-unbuilt flyover. There was the house, stark and lonely among construction vehicles and monstrous piles of rubble on the southern outskirt of Newry as I took the back road to Flagstaff early in the morning.

Now that 40 years of the Troubles had finally come to an end, Northern Ireland was desperate for a change of profile in the eyes of the outside world. Images of masked gunmen, of bombs and bitter tears, intransigent politicians and grieving families had defined the Province for far too long, and nowhere more markedly than in the green drumlin county of South Armagh – 'bandit country' to the media, 'where we live' to its residents. Among the many initiatives for revitalising Ireland's most passionately Republican region, and for attracting the oxygen of outside interest, one in particular had caught my eyes: the laying out of a 33-mile circular walking route, the Ring of Gullion Way. This up-and-down long-distance path would introduce walkers to the cream of some superb countryside; and, just as important, would put them alongside some of the island's most welcoming and dryly humorous people.

'Fabulous views from Flagstaff,' Newry friends had told me. 'Make sure you look down at the Newry Canal as well as over the border at the Mournes, now!' The canal was definitely there, a

Right **Yin and yang at Clontygora: two bordering stones in the courtyard of the Stone Age tomb known as the King's Ring**

Below **The view from the lower slopes of Slieve Gullion: neatly hedged farmland girdles the mountain, running out to the encircling volcanic hills of the Ring of Gullion**

narrow stretch of water far below the lane that climbed to the Flagstaff viewing point. But when I raised my eyes, the famed Mountains of Mourne were nowhere to be seen. Thick mist, rolling in from Carlingford Lough, had wrapped them up and stolen them away.

As I stood looking out fruitlessly from the Flagstaff belvedere, the rumble of unseen traffic on the A2 coast road came up through the murk, along with the clanking of an invisible tractor and trailer a couple of fields away. It was eerie marching down the road with the world more than a stone's throw away rubbed out of sight. Instead of grand vistas over Northern Ireland and across into the Republic, intimate details of the border farms came forward to grab my attention: small rushy fields with the circular raths, or ancient ring forts, that senior locals still talk of as fairy rings; heaps of pale boulders dragged together to clear the rocky fields; groups of fat cream-coloured cattle lying down, each in a personally warmed and dried bed of grass, staring me out with bovine fixity as I walked by.

Down in Clontygora a group of big grey stones in a laneside field drew my attention. I turned off the road and stopped in my tracks. The King's Ring was something to behold. The scores of huge, hand-smoothed stones that made up this mighty Stone Age tomb gave a weight and solemnity to the landscape. The thick jambs of the north-facing portal and the kerbstones of the main burial chambers held up a tilted capstone and other massive roofing slabs. Altogether the monument put me in mind of a great lobster, the tail represented by further burial chambers and kerbstones stretched out southward, the curved claws formed by standing stones walling in a grassy 'courtyard' where rituals associated with collective burials and the cult of death were played out some 5,500 years ago. One pair of courtyard stones seemed to have been chosen and placed close together for their yin-yang effect – an archetypally masculine slab, square-cut and broad with a pointed apex 7ft (2m) high, and a curvaceous consort stone as broad-hipped and slender-waisted as a Henry Moore female.

Such scenes – the beautifully maintained field monuments, the wet pastures and piles of cleared stones – had changed

hardly at all since I first ventured on foot through South Armagh in 1994. The new houses that lay at the top of preposterously long driveways were another matter. In the intervening 15 years the 'Celtic Tiger' had bounded in, laid about it with a merciless lack of respect, swept the chosen off to undreamed-of success, and spat the half-chewed remnants of the old and failed to the four winds. Gone were the modest butt-and-ben houses whose trails of chimney smoke had betokened day-long occupation by women, children, old folk, relations and friends. Vanished, too, were the gateways of churned tractor mud, the bent backs in the fields behind the house. In their place a rash of 'Irish hacienda' ranches had drifted in on the tiger's slipstream to settle all over the lanes of Louth and Armagh on both sides of the border. Prosperity had produced strange fruit. Here were bungalows the size and complexity of mini-mansions, their grounds lit by elaborate cast-iron candelabra, replete with picturesque farm carts, gnomes, convoluted runs of railings, windmills and watermills and bridges. Every kind of exotic plant had been deployed up the 100-yard driveways – exotic shrubs, bonsai trees, Himalayan heathers, anything but native Irish species. Double and triple car ports, tons of pale limestone gravel; dormer windows and arcades a-go-go; deeply recessed entrance gates; eagle-topped pillars. Everything was as blowsy, big and bouncy as could be.

In conversations over garden walls and bar counters as I walked through South Armagh, the story behind the establishment of the new Border plutocracy was fleshed out for me. Any local who could manage it had been employed in the building trade south of the border during the fat years when the Celtic Tiger was at full gallop and the construction business was booming like never before. Hard work, huge money. Many more were engaged in the other traditional Border trade: smuggling. Diesel used to be the big one – it was cheaper in the Republic. The fuel was dyed green in the south, red in the north, to try to scupper smugglers by means of spot inspections of fuel tanks. Tankers from the south would pull up to the border and stretch a hose across to the bowsers and tractors waiting on the northern side. Southern cigarettes were cheaper, too. There were subsidies to claim every time a sheep or cow moved between Republic and Province, and many beasts spent a good portion of their lives in transit if what the stories said was true.

Nothing stopped the Border free-traders, until the IRA declared a ceasefire in 1994 and the Loyalist paramilitaries followed suit. There were plenty of stumbles, plenty of falls along the way over the next four years, but after the Good Friday Agreement of 1998 came a more permanent sense of hope and an upsurge in prosperity on both sides of the national fence. Customs posts were demolished all along the border, and smuggling lost much of its point. But many folk had grown very rich. They couldn't bank their greasy money for fear of questions about its provenance. So they stuck it into bricks and mortar instead.

I couldn't quite buy into this vision of the border country as entirely given over to tack and bling. And once the mist had lifted enough to reveal the farms further up the mountain, I saw that here change had been only skin deep. The mist rolled away like cannon smoke from Anglesey Mountain and Clermont. Up on their higher contours lay the poor farms. Here still stood the ragged barns of corrugated tin painted in fading green and red, starveacre houses spattered to the windows with mud and dung, scratchy hedges and boggy gateways where dogs rushed out to snarl the stranger away.

The farmer who hurried out of his barn high above Clontygora to shush his dog came on across the yard to lean on the gate and light the stub of a cigarette. 'All built on family land, them flashy new houses, and most of 'em built with easy money. Two or three 4X4s at the door! Thirty thousand pound kitchens going into them houses, and the women can't even cook!' His tone was rich with contempt and sly amusement. 'Holidays, now; they're always on the holidays, and if 'twas your neighbours going away for a week, then you yourself wouldn't come home under two! But now the banks aren't lending, and the mortgages on some of them houses are through the roof. No-one can afford to buy 'em, and the owners won't sell 'em – family land, you see! So they're up the creek, we'll say.'

He glanced around him at the unpainted sheds and broken walls of his yard, the rusty bed-heads filling hedge gaps, the signs of rock-bottom farming. 'I've been in it 50 years, and I'm still here. And they'll soon be back to this themselves.' The satisfaction in his voice was like the purr of a well-pleased old tom cat.

Far right **The stream that tumbles off Black Mountain through a miniature gorge to join the Flurry River**

Right **Higher up the mountain, many of the border farms have missed out on the extravagant refurbishments of the 'Celtic Tiger' years**

Hereabouts the border between Northern Ireland and the Republic saws back and forth. In former times there would have been a patrol of British soldiers or the Royal Ulster Constabulary, a check-point or a road block to hold the traveller up at every crossing of the frontier. Today the Ring of Gullion Way slips imperceptibly in and out of the Republic. Between Clontygora and Carrickcarnan I crossed the border without even knowing it. By the time I realised I was no longer walking in Northern Ireland, I was high up on the bleak plateau of the Black Mountain and looking for the way into Ravensdale Forest.

The mountain road wriggled between dark heathery slopes loud with bees and thick with stands of conifers that hissed and tossed in the wind like a troubled sea. The ill-sited waymark posts of the Ring of Gullion Way had me scratching my head, but at last I picked up the route and plunged off down the forest paths. A stream, undignified by any map name, went rushing through a rocky little gorge between mossy beech trees, and I followed it down to the Flurry River beyond Marble Bridge. Across the river the newly built N1 dual carriageway sizzled and roared, but the old narrow road I joined on the Flurry's east bank ran slow and quiet.

A farmer's wife was scratching the stomach of a tiny terrier beside a curious thick-walled barn with mock arrow-slits for windows. What was the story of the building?

'It was the coach house of Ravensdale House, just down there along the valley,' said the woman. 'Lord Clanborough, you know. The house was pulled down long since, and he and herself are buried in the wee church below.' Was the family missed in the locality? The innocent question sparked fury, sudden and unlooked for. 'Oh Jesus, no! Them was terrible days! Men worked all day long for nothing.' She blazed out at me, vehemently. 'Listen, there was an old man lived up the mountain, and he told my husband of a feller. This man had been walking up and down behind a plough and horses all day, and he stopped for a smoke. And the man that was over him came running across the field and grabbed the pipe out of his mouth and smashed it against the wall. "You're not paid to smoke," he said.'

The woman gulped in righteous indignation over these hundred-year-old wrongs. 'Another feller, his children came down to him in the field with a can of porridge for his lunch, and they were barefoot like all the children were back then, and they ran on the grass to spare their feet. Next day didn't the Lady order them to come to her, and she gave them a terrible telling off for daring to walk on the grass. Oh, desperate days! It's best they're gone!'

The banks along the road to Flurry Bridge were lined with spring flowers – stitchwort, bluebells, self-heal and dandelions along with primroses and violets still bravely pushing their faces up to the sun. It was a shock to come to the brink of the N1 and find that Flurry Bridge had been sliced in half by a roaring river of traffic. I crossed back into the North over the Flurry River and looked back across the village, a shell of a place with huge hotels and roadhouses struggling for a living, boarded-up shops and an empty, derelict chapel in a weed-festooned graveyard. Up in Jonesborough, the first village into Northern Ireland, the first thing I saw was a pair of roadside memorials – one to an 18-year-old IRA volunteer 'murdered by Crown Forces in 1975', the other to two young girls shot by soldiers. Fresh flowers in front of each tablet showed that memories were long here.

The Ring of Gullion Way led south from Jonesborough along a peach of a country lane, its stone walls topped with hedges and bright with enormous gorse bushes in full flower. Between the gaps Slieve Gullion sailed on the northwest skyline, a great dark lump of a mountain with a ridge crest raised against the clouds. The day before I had been up there with Ron Murray, strong walker and long talker, absorbing legends of Fionn MacCumhaill and facts of a most extraordinary geology. I gave the mountain a salute with my walking stick. Tomorrow I aimed to climb it again and wander those peaty paths alone on my way back to Newry.

The ginger horse and his donkey companion in the field beside the Kilnasaggart Stone didn't so much as look up from their grazing as I passed them by. The stone is a remarkable thing, and must have attracted attention and speculation ever since Ternoc, son of Little Ceran, incised a dedication to St Peter the Apostle on the 7ft- (2m-) high granite pillar and erected it some 1,300 years ago beside the Slighe Midhlachra, the ancient road through the Pass of Moyry. Either Ternoc or those who came after him carved ten crosses in the face of the pillar, some curlicued, others straight-ended. Invisible under the turf around this stone lie the burial places of believers who lived and died in Ireland's Golden Age of Christianity. Later folk looked for other meanings in the stone. A tier of parallel cuts on one flank, produced by the whetting of countless knife blades, was taken by generations of savants to be a message in Ogham script, that hard-to-decipher Dark Ages code. Others, less scholarly, pushed the pillar over in hopes of finding the crock of gold that everyone knew lay buried beneath it. They came away with empty pockets and a full measure of bad luck, and pious hands soon set up the Kilnasaggart Stone in its rightful place once more.

The Pass of Moyry was always liable to be contended. Anyone who controlled this 'Gap of the North' in the mountains was master of the high road between south and north. When Lord Mountjoy was busy subduing the O'Neill chiefs of the region in 1601 in the name of Queen Elizabeth I, he built a block-like castle on the heights above the Slighe Midhlachra, as much to serve as a statement of intent as to provide shelter and lookout for soldiers. I ate my cheese-and-coleslaw sandwich

in its shadow, and pushed on south and west through these often debated lands. The view ahead opened out over 20 miles to the hills of the Cooley Peninsula and a gleam of sea in Dundalk Bay, a prospect that entranced me all the way down to Forkill.

I hardly recognised the village, and it took some time to realise why. In 1994 Forkill had been subdued, if not crushed, by a gigantic fortified police station, tellingly known as 'the Barracks', with great steel fences, observation turrets and towering aerials. Today there was no sign of it. Nothing remained but a patch of bare ground, like a bald spot in a bushy thatch of grass and trees. The session in the side bar of the Welcome Inn was as vigorous as ever I remembered it, though. Four button accordions, a banjo, a guitar and a couple of fiddles made the air hum. I'd armed myself with a fistful of harmonicas – just in case – and here was the opportunity to join in once more with that irresistible exercise of democracy in action, a session of Irish music. All ages, all stages are welcome. As long as you are restrained enough not to spoil the tune, you're in. The only time we all fell silent was when round-faced 13-year-old Micheál Mullins put down his accordion and picked up his tin whistle. Oh my God, and then some. If ever a boy had songbirds in his fingertips, it was young Micheál. Eyes fixed dreamily in front of himself, fingers rising and falling like hummingbird wings, he had us under strong magic. The silence after he'd finished his long variations was punctuated by little grunts of delight from the listeners, and I saw people literally shaking themselves free of the spell, like dogs upon waking. What power, and how modestly wielded. Micheál simply grinned as if it were nothing. To him, maybe, it was.

I slept that night in Aidan Murtagh's pub in Crossmaglen, southwest of Forkill, a couple of miles at most from County Monaghan and the Irish Republic. It was good to see Aidan again, as waspish of wit and warm of hospitality as ever. Things had changed a long way in 'Cross', he told me, and walking around the big border village I soon saw that for myself.

Crossmaglen lay under a miasma of notoriety throughout the Troubles. It was the most vehemently Republican village in the whole of the North, the nerve-centre of South Armagh's 'bandit country', a place where British soldiers could expect to come under attack at any time by the IRA. Blinkered Marxism was assumed to underlie the hard-line stance of the local activists. 'Planet Crossmaglen,' said people you talked to in Belfast or Derry or Enniskillen. 'It's another world down there.'

Before I set out to walk through the area in 1994, a couple of months after the IRA had announced their first suspension of hostilities, I'd made two telephone calls, one to the British Army in Bessbrook Barracks, the other to the local Sinn Fein councillor, Jim McAllister, just to let everyone know who I was and what I was up to.

'I'll give the lads a heads-up on you,' a clipped military voice in Bessbrook had stated. From the Sinn Fein office in Crossmaglen, Jim's weary voice came down the line: 'Call in, and I'll give you The Tour.' The Tour had consisted of a whistle-stop circuit of Republican monuments and memorials in Jim's clapped-out little car, followed by lunch in his house, salted with rhetoric

Above **There have been huge changes in South Armagh since the signing of the Good Friday Agreement in 1998 and the subsequent fading of the Troubles – but some old symbols are still in evidence around the back country lanes**

Left **Crock of gold or Christian believers – the Kilnasaggart Stone marks their burial spot**

and peppered with poetry. The sight of a young soldier on patrol, backing past the Sinn Fein office on the corner of the square with cradled gun and crackling earpiece, provoked a snort and a muttered 'What's he doing in our village?' Jim didn't really believe that peace had arrived, couldn't really allow himself to think it until the last British soldier had gone from the giant ugly barracks behind Crossmaglen's big village square.

Today the big bronze monument to Republican dead still dominates the square, a young man straining for the skies with clenched fists and upturned face. But the dour defensive tower towards which he used to stare has gone from its position between the houses. No soldiers patrol the streets; few officers of the Police Service of Northern Ireland, either. I found the little Sinn Fein office locked and semi-derelict, the 'Disband The RUC!' poster fallen from its walls to lie crumpled and dusty on the floor. The fierce Republican polemic that graffitists had once painted up on Crossmaglen's walls was all cleaned away. The big Chinook helicopters that had hovered over the village night and day were seen and heard no more. In 1994 I'd spent a morning chatting to a class of 10-year-old children at St Patrick's primary school, and they had all confessed to anxiety nightmares, to fears of shots and explosions, to sleepless nights as the Chinooks clattered overhead, to bullying from older children if they were seen responding to friendly overtures from a soldier. All that seemed like a bad dream now.

Only a few weeks before my Ring of Gullion Way walk, dissident Republicans had murdered two soldiers and a policeman in two separate incidents elsewhere in the Province. Ten years ago, that might have caused retaliatory shock-waves vicious enough to shake the whole structure of the peace process to pieces. But things held together now. Political leaders from both sides of the divide stood side by side in public to condemn the killers. News reports during my stay in Crossmaglen were of Loyalist representatives visiting the Roman Catholic Bishop of Armagh to pledge that there'd be no going back to the bad old days. People in Crossmaglen could hardly believe their ears. It was true, though. The new leaf seemed to have been well and truly turned.

Next morning I beat the rain up Slieve Gullion by a short head. Blue patches sailed in a layered sky of cloud and wind. The slippery climb up the granite boulder steps and peat slides of the southwest shoulder was effortful enough, but once at the crest I was able to sit down and take in a quite stupendous view. The long mouth of Carlingford Lough opened in the east, the wide jaw of Dundalk Bay to the southeast. The peaks of the Mountains of Mourne stood up north of Black Mountain's forest-clothed bulk. Away north on the edge of sight, slipping between marching regiments of rain, stood the high wedge of the holy mountain of Slemish where St Patrick languished as a captive shepherd boy in his youth some 16 centuries ago. The direction-finder at the summit gave the distances. Slemish was 54 miles off, the Wicklow Hills – tiny lumps of familiar profile – 62 miles to the south. This was a 100-mile view at the very least. So many superlative mountain shapes claimed attention in the distance that it took time to focus in on the almost perfect ring of hills, crumpled and ancient in appearance, that surrounded the summit I stood on. From the heights of Slieve Gullion the view encompassed rugged Croslieve above Forkill, three-humped Slieve Bolea in the south, the peaks of Fathom and Ballymacdermot dwarfed by the Mourne Mountains looking over their shoulders. Camlough Mountain to the north, big and dark with trees, stood separated from its little sister Sturgan by Cam Lough's long arm of steely-grey water. Slievenacappel, the Mountain of the Horse, rode tall and tumbled in the west. It was a magnificent view over a petrified landscape of mind-boggling volcanic violence.

The original volcano of silt and shale, squeezed and baked into granite by fabulous subterranean forces, was formed perhaps 400 million years ago. But earth continued to rumble and boil under the covers. Some 40 million years ago – not much more than yesterday in geological time – the great caldera, or cauldron-shaped bowl, underneath the volcano

Left **The big bronze monument to Republican dead in the village square at Crossmaglen leaves local allegiances in little doubt**

Below **View looking north from the slopes of Slieve Gullion, over Sturgan and Camlough Mountain towards the low-lying farmlands of North Armagh**

collapsed, pushing out enormous ripples of molten rock as it crumpled in on itself. This ring of magma, several thousand feet high and 10 miles across, solidified in a tangled mass of cooling rock of various types – dolerite, felsite, gabbro – but also others such as breccia, tuff and volcanic glass. Of this treasury of variegated rock, ground down by 40 million years of weathering, the hills of the Ring of Gullion are made. Slieve Gullion itself, the centrepiece of the Ring, is a slightly different kettle of fish. Layers of granite and basalt, normally uneasy bedfellows, make up this king of a mountain, which like its surrounding courtiers has been reduced by weathering to a fraction of its former height. At some 1,700ft (518m) it stands proudly, dominating its landscape, with the level plains of the Republic's midlands stretching off southwest to infinity.

The direction pointer on the south summit stood on a miniature hill of loose stones. In the side of the boulder heap was a low doorway with a rough and massive stone lintel, like something in a Beatrix Potter illustration. I stooped down and crawled inside. A single octagonal chamber lay at the heart of the mound, with a blocked recess in its further wall and a roof hatch to let in the light. Archaeologists know this monument as the highest passage grave in Ireland, a Stone Age burial chamber constructed on the peak around 2,500BC

to command a magnificent prospect to all quarters. Spinners of tales say it is the enchanted house of the Cailleach Beara.

Slieve Gullion is laden with legends. It is Sliabh Chulainn in Irish, the mountain of Chulainn, the god-like blacksmith who lived and worked up here in a great grim castle. The child prodigy Setanta came to the mountain one day, and was attacked by the smith's savage mastiff. Setanta hefted the hurling stick he was carrying, and smacked his sliotar, or hurley ball, so hard at the hound that it became stuck in the brute's throat and choked it to death. Chulainn was not best pleased. To appease the smith's fury, Setanta offered to guard the castle in the dog's stead. From that day out he was known as Cúchulainn, the Hound of Chulainn, and grew up to be the greatest hero and defender that Ulster ever knew.

Mighty Cúchulainn may have been, but no-one could ever outdo the giant Fionn MacCumhaill – Finn McCool to some – in the mightiness stakes. Walking on from the Cailleach Beara's house along the spine of Slieve Gullion, I came to the Lake of Sorrows where Fionn and the Cailleach had their famous encounter. It seems that Fionn came hunting here ahead of the Fianna, his faithful band of warriors. On the shore of the lake he met a beautiful young girl, weeping sadly. 'I have dropped my gold ring in the lake and can't get it,' she lamented. Quick as a flash the gallant hero dived in to retrieve the ring. But as he sprang out of the water – lo! His reflection showed him a wrinkled old man with white hair and enfeebled frame. Gone, too, was the lovely maiden. In her place crouched the fearsome, hag-like Cailleach Beara, cackling with glee at having overcome the mightiest warrior of them all.

When the Fianna arrived on the scene and heard from Fionn what had befallen him, action and not lamentation was their response. Fionn's son Oisín ran the length of Ireland to collect his father's great hunting dog Bran. The keen-nosed hound soon smelt out the house in the stones where the witch had run to hide. Dragging her out, the Fianna forced her to restore their leader to health and vigour, unharmed by his disorientating experience.

I sat for a while on a rock beside the Lake of Sorrows, careful to keep my feet from the enchanted ripples. On the shore, half in and half out of the water, lay a stone the size and shape of a tractor wheel, pierced through the centre with a narrow hole – the Cailleach Beara's millstone, according to lore. A miller once had the audacity to remove it from the witch's dwelling and roll it down the mountainside for use in his mill. But so much bad luck attended him that he determined to return it to the house in the stones. Easier said than done. His donkey managed to haul it as far as the Lake of Sorrows, where the poor beast collapsed and died, leaving the cursed millstone to lie for ever more where it came to rest.

I should have come off Slieve Gullion at its northern end, but somehow I missed the way and ended up descending the eastern slopes to the holy well of St Bline. I could hear the gurgle of the water from a long way off. In a square stone basin under a white-painted shrine it pulsed and rippled, sending a burst of silvery bubbles across the surface every few seconds. Freshly picked daffodils lay on the steps of the shrine among ripples of water spilling from the agitated well. A babble of young voices came up the hill as I walked on, and soon I met their owners, a couple of classes of eight-year-olds, pink-cheeked and high-spirited, being shepherded up to the Holy Well by their teachers. 'Young monkeys,' winked the lady bringing up the rear. 'But quite nice ones!'

After the glories of Slieve Gullion, everything seemed a little tame to me. I spared the ancient churches at Killevy a glance or two. Then I stepped out for the forest road across Camlough Mountain. In air heavy with the scent of newly felled pine trees I swung over the summit of Camlough and down towards Newry once more. The views were wide, the lanes full of flowers, but I paid them little heed – not with Fionn MacCumhaill and his imperishable Fianna for a band of imaginary marching companions.

In air heavy with the scent of newly felled pine trees I swung over the summit of Camlough and down towards Newry once more. The views were wide, the lanes full of flowers...

The Road to the Isles

Part One

A hearty bunch of Glaswegian walkers in breeches and bare legs was descending from the train at Bridge of Orchy station as I climbed on board. Laughing, hoisting knapsacks and scuffing their boots in the platform gravel, the hikers looked delighted to be out in the sharpish breeze of this beautiful clear day in the Scottish mountains. After months of enforced inactivity in this Foot and Mouth-blighted year of 2001, I knew exactly how they felt.

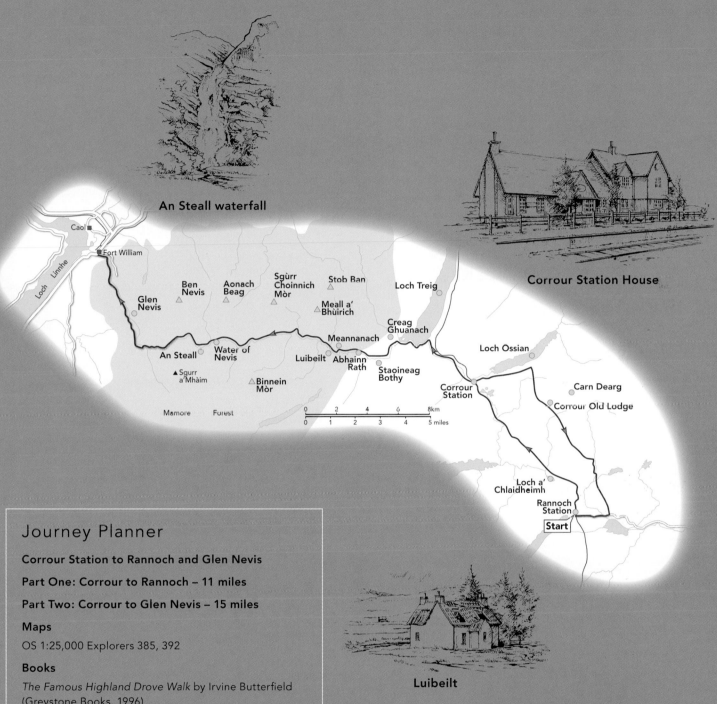

An Steall waterfall

Corrour Station House

Loch Linnhe

Caol

Fort William

Glen Nevis

Ben Nevis

Aonach Beag

Sgùrr Choinnich Mòr

Stob Ban

Loch Treig

Meall a' Bhùirich

Creag Ghuanach

Loch Ossian

Meannanach

An Steall

Water of Nevis

Luibeilt

Abhainn Rath

Staoineag Bothy

Corrour Station

Carn Dearg

Corrour Old Lodge

Sgurr a' Mhàim

Binnein Mòr

Mamore Forest

0   2   4   6   8km

0   1   2   3   4   5 miles

Loch a' Chlaidheimh

Rannoch Station

Start

Luibeilt

Journey Planner

Corrour Station to Rannoch and Glen Nevis

Part One: Corrour to Rannoch – 11 miles

Part Two: Corrour to Glen Nevis – 15 miles

Maps

OS 1:25,000 Explorers 385, 392

Books

The Famous Highland Drove Walk by Irvine Butterfield (Greystone Books, 1996)

Websites

Corrour Station House accommodation/refreshments: 01397 732236; www.corrourstationhouse.co.uk

Corrour Estate: 01397 732200; www.corrour.co.uk for information. Courtesy call before walking during deer stalking season (1 Aug–20 Oct) would be appreciated

The two-car sprinter rattled north across the eastern edge of Rannoch Moor, sending a herd of red deer bouncing away from a loch beside the railway line. Cloud shadows dimmed the moor colours to sombre tans and olives; then the sun slid through again and spread thick gold across heather and grass. The light train gave a gentle spring every now and then, a reminder that when the West Highland Line was built across Rannoch Moor in the 1890s the engineers had to float the track on bundles of brushwood. The treacherous peat, up to 20ft (6m) thick in parts, was far too yielding for any conventional hard foundation.

At Rannoch station, out in the wilds, Steve Duncan and Irvine Butterfield hopped on. I'd been keenly looking forward to walking with this pair – fresh-faced Steve from the Perthshire tourist board, bursting with enthusiasm for the hills, and stocky white-bearded Irvine, a deep well of knowledge of Scottish landscape and culture. A Skipton-born man with a rich Dales accent, author of a clutch of well-respected books, Irvine had forgotten more than I had ever learned about the mountains and moors of Scotland. By 1971, the year I left university, Irvine had already climbed all 277 of the Scottish 'Munros' or 3,000ft (915m) mountains, a feat achieved by every lycra-clad bulge bagger these days, but a rare triumph back then. He wrote a best seller about it, too – The High Mountains of Britain and Ireland – the bible of Munro-climbers ever since.

'Loch a' Chlaidheimh, the Loch of the Sword,' Irvine said, pointing out of the train window. 'Now there's a great story attached to that, about the time the Earl of Atholl and Lochiel of the Camerons of Lochaber had a quarrel about which of them the land around the loch belonged to. Both chiefs wanted to try and settle it without bloodshed, so they agreed to meet by Loch a' Chlaidheimh to talk things out, just the two of them. But… both had hidden men in the heather, naturally, just in case things went wrong. Well, these guys jumped up and faced each other, and it looked as if the dispute would have to be settled the good old way. But then Atholl broke the tension: he threw his sword into the loch, saying the land would belong to Lochiel and Lochaber until the sword should be found.

'Anyway, in 1826 a boy actually fished Atholl's sword out of Loch a' Chlaidheimh. But no one wanted to stir things up – especially the Lochaber people who owned the land! So they took the sword off the boy and chucked it back in the loch again – where it still is.'

Corrour is the remotest railway station in Scotland, marooned below the mountains at the northern edge of Rannoch Moor, 10 miles at least from the nearest tarmac road. We left the train and struck out along a rough dirt road, making for Loch Ossian in its cradle of mountains. We were heading south, back towards Rannoch station, a walk of 10 miles or more in some of Scotland's most bleakly beautiful country, along the ancient track known to generations of cattle thieves and drovers as Rathad nan Eilean, the Road to the Isles. 'As step I wi' my cromach tae the Isles,' sang Harry Lauder in his 'Road To The Isles' smash hit song, and Irvine was wielding his own fine cromach with a carved ram's horn crook as we crunched down to the lonely youth hostel by the lake.

The Road to the Isles left the stony lochside road and ran parallel to it before plunging abruptly away southward. The three of us trod a firm green track founded on a bed of stone, with rough

Left **Looking east from the bedroom window at Corrour Station House over Loch Coir' a' Bhric Beag on a dark, stormy morning**

Right **Two Highland drovers on the road take five for a brew-up, while their cattle graze nearby**

stone culverts carrying burns beneath it. This was no casual cattle path wandering through the heather, but a proper moorland road maintained down the centuries by the drovers who depended on it for their livelihoods. As Irvine told the tale, these hardy men were the lynchpin that held the economics of Highland society together from medieval times until the fallout from Culloden and the coming of the railways consigned them to history.

'The owners of the cattle would have to trust the drovers, firstly to take their cattle safely for hundreds of miles from the Western Highlands down to the great trysts, or markets, at Crieff and Falkirk, secondly to get the best price they could from the dealers, and lastly to bring the money back home again. Sometimes the cattle would be taken on for fattening as far as Norfolk, a journey of getting on for six or seven hundred miles. Most of them became salt beef for the Army or the Navy; the Napoleonic wars did the owners and drovers a very good turn, economically.'

I looked round the bleak scene: the rolling empty moor, stripped hundreds of years ago of the great Wood of Caledon that once covered its 60 square miles; the inhospitable granite humps of the mountains; ragged edges of lonely lochs. Where would the drovers find shelter for the night? 'Oh,' said Irvine, 'there'd be stances along the way, rough-and-ready inns with a patch of grass. The men could have a dram and put their heads down while the cattle grazed. But when I see this landscape I think of winter and other travellers on the track, in a blinding snowstorm maybe, or lost in mist. Rannoch doesn't always look like it does today, you know!'

That was a true word. When a party of engineering experts including Robert McAlpine set out in January 1889 to walk the 40 miles from Spean Bridge to Inveroran across the moor, they became separated in mist. Benighted and lost, with one of the party helpless with exhaustion, they had to be rescued. 'An inconceivable solitude,' wrote Dr John MacCulloch in 1811, 'a dreary and joyless land of bogs, a land of desolation and grey darkness.' The authors of the West Highland Way official guide, Bob Aitken and Roger Smith, remark dryly of Rannoch Moor: 'In rain or snow with low cloud driving before a gale, it tends to promote the conviction that Hell need not be hot.'

Today, though, all was sweet on Rannoch as we followed the green ribbon of the Road to the Isles. We stopped to picnic on a rock, watching sun and cloud shadows sweep each other majestically from the flanks of Carn Dearg, the Red Rock. 'I was in the glen at the back of it at the weekend,' Steve said, 'and I couldn't hear a sound. Complete silence – how rare is that nowadays?' We sat listening. The scratchy song of a pipit, a faint sigh of wind in grass – that was all.

In the afternoon we explored the ruins of Corrour Old Lodge, a wilderness of grey stone walls above the track. Then we went on, with Irvine and Steve deep in the peak-naming game. 'Garbh Meall? Well, if it is, that must be Meall Chomraidh in front.' – 'No, that's Meall a' Bhobuir, I think.' I was more than content to walk in ignorance, with snow-streaked mountains filling every far view and late afternoon sunshine flooding gloriously across the moor.

Above **Jack Frost's genius: pebbles on an icy morning along the Road to the Isles, appearing to burst through a skein of spun glass**

Right **Half a mile north of Corrour Station the West Highland line tops out at Corrour Summit on a bleak and barren stretch of Rannoch Moor**

Part Two

Eight years and many thousands of miles had gone under my boots when I stood once more on the short gravelled platform at Corrour station. The world of Scottish mountaineering was in mourning for Irvine Butterfield, whose death had just been announced. I pictured his jutting white beard and ram's horn cromach, and heard his Dales-bred voice naming the peaks along the Road to the Isles. This time I was aiming to trace the Road the other way from Corrour, due west through the passes between Mamore Forest and the Aonach range under Ben Nevis, walking upriver beside the waters of the Abhainn Rath, then across the boggy watershed to find and follow the Water of Nevis down through its dark gorge to Glen Nevis in the shadow of Britain's tallest mountain. I'd have a good companion for this trip, too, in the energetic shape of Richard Spencer, a retired army officer very active in the interests of the Mountaineering Council of Scotland and of the Mountain Bothy Association.

The Corrour Estate sees the lonely railway station on its property as a great asset, and operates the Station House B&B and Restaurant alongside the railway platform and signal box. Hikers and climbers know and treasure this little oasis of warmth and welcome in the middle of Rannoch Moor. You have to book early to secure one of the creaky rooms with the incomparable views of moor, lochan and mountain. And a wise walker makes a friend of Beth Campbell, who runs the place and is a wellspring of good advice and practical help. Once I'd got outside a plate of her lamb casserole and a pint or two of hand-pulled bitter, I settled down with map and notes to wait for morning.

It dawned cold and threatening, with the sun struggling to look through an angry sky. Two Canada geese sailed on the lochan outside my window, and rain slashed heavily across the panes. But by the time Richard Spencer and his black labrador Guy turned up, the east wind had blown the worst of the weather off west along the Road to the Isles.

We started out to follow in the wake of the rain, with Richard setting a clinking pace across the hurdles that had been laid over the squelchy bogs beside the railway line. At first I had to save my breath to keep up with him, but as we descended the stony way towards the foot of Loch Treig, the 'Forsaken Loch', there was time to talk and swap some morsels of life history. Richard had served in many corners of the world with the Army – he had 'soldier' written all over him, in fact, with his upright carriage and air of no-nonsense determination. 'Just a hill walker,' he modestly described himself, but since leaving the Army in 1995 he'd siphoned off some of his abundant energy by completing a full house of Munro summits. Mountain bothies, surveys of mountaineers, this committee and that council in the service of mountaineers and hill walkers: Richard's finger was in many mountain pies. Today's 15-mile crossing of the moors would be a doddle to

him, I knew – even more so to his constant companion Guy, who had been to the top of more Munros than most human hill walkers in his few short years of existence.

The Road to the Isles climbed steadily from the loch side into a peaty moorland, following the course of the Abhainn Rath through a narrow pass below the tumbled slopes of Creag Ghuanach. A hut stood under the trees on the far bank of the river. 'Staoineag Bothy, where I spent last night,' said Richard. 'Think it's time for a brew.' Suiting action to words, he made for a well-spaced line of stepping stones. I copied his athletic strides and leaps from boulder to boulder across the river, and followed him into the dark, smoke-perfumed hut. Richard got out his camping stove, brewed himself a steaming, milkless mug of tea and hoisted the large pack he'd left on the floor to await his return after collecting me

Left **The view from the Road to the Isles looking northward up Loch Treig, the lonely and beautiful 'Forsaken Loch'**

Below **Richard Spencer and Guy stride out beside the Abhainn Rath on the approach to the watershed**

Below right **A refuge in the wilderness: the bothy of Meannanach, high up in the boggy wilderness of the watershed, has sheltered many a benighted traveller on the Road to the Isles**

from Corrour. 'It'll slow me down a bit,' he said as we recrossed the Abhainn Rath and forged on west up the river bank. Maybe it did, a little tiny bit.

In a mile or so the hill slopes opened out and fell back on either hand, and we found ourselves up at the watershed between Abhainn Rath and Water of Nevis. In common with all watersheds under high mountains it was a boggy and squelchy piece of ground, in which the old drovers' road wound and snaked, climbing and falling, not well made and drained as in the moors east of Corrour, but a disconnected succession of stony sections interspersed with rushy wastes, ankle-deep sphagnum bogs and swathes of thick heather. This was tiring ground demanding concentration, and I was grateful to have a companion like Richard who knew where he was going and went there purposefully. We passed the ruin of Luibeilt cottage under its redundant shelter trees, and the remote bothy of Meannanach, prized by walkers who enjoy a silent night in a lonely setting. The peak of Binnein Mòr, still streaked with snow patches, looked over the shoulders of Mamore far ahead, and the rounded hump of Meall a' Bhùirich was our guide to the north. We strode on across heather and bog to ford the Abhainn Rath where it came bouncing and chattering down from its high corrie under Stob Ban, the White Point.

Fifteen minutes to sit and eat a sandwich, with the river sparkling at our feet. Guy devoured a bone-shaped dry biscuit and curled up, nose on tail, for a short nap. 'Putting up the Zs,' said Richard fondly as he contemplated his colleague. Then we were up and on, with better ground underfoot as we came alongside the infant Water of Nevis and followed it on a long westward descent. Mighty mountains stood on our right hand: the pyramid of Sgùrr Choinnich Mòr, the tall banded rock wall of Aonach Beag, and then the towering grey whalehead of Ben Nevis itself, rising in a curve more powerful than graceful through patchy snowfields to a flat top at 4,405ft (1,343m). Minute dots of figures moved across the summit, from which fearsome faces fell south in long, plunging cliffs. Ben Nevis is scarcely a beautiful mountain,

but what it has, in spades, is dignity and massive presence. Walking in its shadow, I wondered if the generations of drovers and robbers, travellers and swordsmen on the old track had looked up at its grey whalehead with equal wonder and delight.

Beauty might not be part of the great mountain's charm, but the glen of the Water of Nevis that curves at its feet is a beautiful sight in the eyes of any walker descending the Road to the Isles from the east. Like a scene in a painting the sinuating river lies cradled in a flat bed of meadows of a tender, pastoral green quite unlike anything seen along the moorland track. There is a high waterfall, An Steall, hissing down a 200-ft (60-m) rock slide, an isolated hut perfectly placed for the camera, and a swinging footbridge made of three slender wires that you can dare if intrepid or foolhardy

enough. Hut, meadows and fall make up a scene of rustic tranquillity, in startling contrast to the severity of the narrow gorge that follows. Twisting and turning up a stumbly staircase of dark rocks, rough and jagged, the path climbs high over the Water of Nevis and the thread-like bed of hollows, basins and channels it has carved for itself through the rock. The gorge makes a supremely dramatic and completely unexpected finale to the open moorland trek that precedes it, a proper *coup de théâtre* to end the long day.

In the car park at the head of Glen Nevis we found Richard's van. 'Something to rinse out your mouth?' he queried, producing a bottle of Pinot Grigio from the cluttered interior. I raised the silver tassie in a toast to Richard and Guy, to all who forged and follow the Road to the Isles, and to the wandering shade of Irvine Butterfield.

Mighty mountains stood on our right hand: the pyramid of Sgùrr Choinnich Mòr, the tall banded rock wall of Aonach Beag, and then the towering grey whalehead of Ben Nevis itself, rising in a curve more powerful than graceful through patchy snowfields to a flat top at 4,405ft (1,343m).

Right **Green and flat, the meadows of the glen that lies at the foot of An Steall waterfall are balm to the eyes of descending walkers sated with bog, heather and rough mountainsides**

Left **You need a good head for heights and a rock-steady nerve to cross the three-wire footbridge over the Water of Nevis**

18

A Winter Wander on the Spey

A cold blue day in the skirts of the Cairngorm mountains at the start of the year – but not just any day. It was the morning after the 250th birthday of Scotland's fine and favourite son, the 'heav'n-taught ploughman' Robert Burns.

Tugnet Ice House

Journey Planner

Nethy Bridge to Spey Bay

50 miles

The Speyside Way runs 70 miles northeast from Aviemore to Buckie on the Moray Firth, via Boat of Garten, Nethy Bridge, Grantown-on-Spey, Ballindalloch, Charlestown of Aberlour, Craigellachie, Fochabers and Spey Bay

Maps

OS Landrangers 36, 28; Explorers 403, 419, 424; Harvey's 'Speyside Way' (1:40,000); Stirling Surveys 'Speyside Way'

Book

The Speyside Way by Jacquetta Megarry and Jim Strachan (Rucksack Readers)

Website

www.moray.org/area/speyway/webpages/swhome.htm

Atlantic salmon

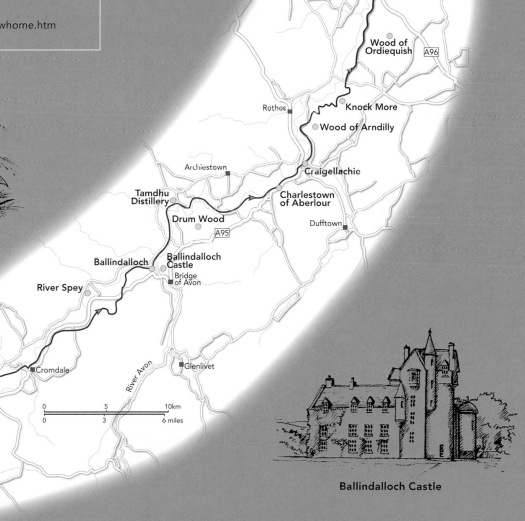

Kingston on Spey
Tugnet
Spey Bay
Garmouth
A96
Mosstodloch
Gordon Castle
Fochabers
Wood of Ordiequish
A96
Rothes
Knock More
Wood of Arndilly
Archiestown
Craigellachie
Tamdhu Distillery
Charlestown of Aberlour
Drum Wood
Dufftown
A95
Ballindalloch
Castle
Ballindalloch
Bridge of Avon
River Spey
Glenlivet
River Avon
Grantown-on-Spey
Cromdale
Dulnain Bridge
0   5   10km
0   3   6 miles
A95
Nethy Bridge
Start
Boat of Garten

Ballindalloch Castle

' ... But to our tale: - Ae market-night,
Tam had got planted unco right;
Fast by an ingle, bleezing finely,
Wi' reaming swats, that drank divinely,
And at his elbow, Souter Johnny,
His ancient, trusty, drouthy crony;
Tam lo'ed him like a vera brither—
They had been fou for weeks thegither!
The night drave on wi' sangs and clatter
And ay the ale was growing better ... '

Last night I had gone out through the streets of Aviemore in high hopes of finding a few Souter Johnnies of my own, boon companions with whom to quote 'Tam O'Shanter' and quaff to the glory of Burns until the wee hours. No such luck. No fiddler raised a stave, no piper a skirl through the length and breadth of the town. There wasn't even a decent party in honour of the randy rhymer of Alloway. The skiers were all in bed, exhausted after a long day's play in the heaviest snow the Cairngorms had seen for two decades. The German, Japanese and Geordie visitors in the Indian restaurants and hotel lounges couldn't have given two raps about Rabbie. Snow-bound Aviemore lay deathly quiet. I had

a few pale and hoppy pints of Deuchars in the Old Bridge Inn, and walked the frosty ways back to my Inverdruie lodgings a sadder if not entirely a soberer man.

Approaching Nethy Bridge not long after sunrise, the whole panorama of the central Cairngorms lay open and breathtaking ten miles off, blasted with snow and storms. The deep, dramatic canyon of Strath Nethy slashed south into the face of the massif, where a series of gigantic snow-whitened steps rose between the tent-like pyramid of Bynack More and the long white shoulder of Cairn Gorm, climbing above lesser peaks and ridges into a cap of swirling blizzards under a sky of ominous yellow. It seemed unbelievable that such ferocious weather could be raging over mountains only half an hour's drive away, while across here in Strathspey the sun was striking softly between the trees.

Down on the old railway footpath, with a dusty thudding at the back of my skull and sun-sparkle from the frosted grasses shooting dazzlingly into my eyes, I wondered whether Robert Burns, a man for the bottle after the bottle before if ever there was one, was not enjoying a quiet laugh at my expense somewhere beyond the blue, blue sky. Ten minutes after

Left **In parts the Speyside Way is landscaped into scenic curves, disguising its origins as the trackbed of the Strathspey Railway**

Right **Knockando station, seen here in the early 20th century, was typical of the Strathspey Railway stations of the era, always kept in spick and span order**

setting off along the Speyside Way, flat on my back with a bump on my head after skidding on a deep-frozen pebble, I was sure of it. I lay back in the broom bushes and had a damn good laugh at myself, always the best cure for the morning-after blues.

I'd long been planning this winter walk from the mountains to the sea. A superb long-distance path, the Speyside Way had its genesis back in the 1980s, as someone's canny notion of what to do with the disused Strathspey Railway. This famous route, the Spey Valley's local line, was opened in 1863, and ran from Boat of Garten (where it branched away from the Highland Railway's Inverness-Perth line) down to Craigellachie, a snaking 36-mile journey that closely hugged the River Spey. There it split, one branch running east through Dufftown to Keith and on to Aberdeen, the other forging south to Elgin and thence westward to Inverness. As a money-making concern the Strathspey Railway always struggled, with much of its income (and motive power for its drivers and firemen, it sometimes seemed) dependent on the whisky distilleries that were scattered up Strathspey and its side glens. Much loved but little used, like so many rural railways after the advent of motor transport, the Strathspey Railway was closed to passengers on 18 October 1965. The same day saw the demise of its local rival, the Highland Railway's Aviemore to Forres branch line. Whisky traffic trickled on for a few more years, but by 1971 the whole system had been shut down, leaving Strathspey bereft of all railway communications.

Now the question had to be faced: what to do with the trackbed of the former railway? Instead of carving it up and selling it off piecemeal, the local authority bought it from British Railways with the intention of using it as the backbone of the Speyside Way, a long-distance footpath which, it was hoped and dreamed, would one day run from the majestic heights of the Cairngorms northwards for 65 miles down the full length of Strathspey to the meeting of river and sea in Spey Bay on the Moray coast. It took 30 years for the dream to come to fruition. Below Craigellachie the Keith and Elgin branches of the Strathspey Railway diverge from the river; from here it is a mixture of forestry roads, country lanes and meadow paths that carry a walker on the final day's journey down to the long, salmon-haunted estuary of the Spey. The northern part of the route was opened back in 1981, and I walked it southwards in a wet summer shortly afterwards, a long upriver slog from Spey Bay for 30 miles to the castle of Ballindalloch where the path petered out. This winter walk would be a different affair entirely, going downstream with the flow of the Spey on a more established and better marked path, a walk from snowy mountains down to a frost-bound coast, with the hope of glimpsing a salmon swimming in fresh and early from the open Atlantic on its epic spawning run.

Recovering my senses after my crash-landing, I got to my feet and went along the icy path, gingerly feeling the lump on my skull. The trackbed of the Strathspey Railway led purposefully on, twisting this way and that, keeping the northwest wind in its eye. The cold breeze sang up the valley, nipping my ears, streaming tears down my cheeks and filling my beard with tiny diamonds of ice. The last notes of the Burns Night blues were blowing away, and I took pleasure in swinging out strongly. Soon the Spey came chuckling up and fell into line beside the path, to keep step with me all the way north to the pebbles in Spey Bay.

The Spey is a noble river – there is no better term to catch its liveliness, its largeness and grandeur as it carves and moulds its wide-floored strath. In one stretch it rushes in glassy shallows with tremendous vigour, chattering over a rocky bed; the next moment it deepens and darkens to surge round a bend with slow, muscular strength. As a salmon river it is one of Scotland's greatest. The Atlantic salmon that leave the Spey as tiny smolts a few inches long return to their parent river after years of cruising the deep ocean as big fish of 30lb weight or more, gleaming in dull silver and humpbacked with sea-fed muscle. They are intent on reaching the headwaters of the very burn in which they first hatched, to spawn on the redds, or gravel shallows, where thousands of eggs tumble from the females and are fertilised by the males in a milky cloud of milt. To reach this salmon nirvana the fish must run the gauntlet of predatory sea creatures such as porpoise, killer whale and seal, of deep sea trawlers, of net fishermen and anglers in the rivers, and of man-made pollution, in addition to the disease and accidents that nature and chance happenings visit on them. It is a tough call, and getting tougher. Fewer and fewer Atlantic salmon are coming back to Britain's rivers. Some observers think they may be falling prey to ruthless and lawless netting off Greenland and other Atlantic feeding grounds; others wonder whether a rise in ocean temperatures is decimating the shrimp and squid which they eat while at sea, or driving the food source north beyond the salmon's range. The figures show a persistently downward trend. In the lifetime of the Speyside Way, the number of salmon returning to the River Spey has halved. And the Spey is one of the rivers least affected so far by the decline in salmon numbers. As for how these wonderful and extraordinary creatures navigate themselves so precisely, not only back to Scotland and the Moray Firth but to the mouth of the Spey itself, and on upriver until they identify and ascend the stream of their birth – that remains a mystery.

The Speyside Way ran through thickets of silver birch, the low winter sun brilliant on the trunks blotched in black and silver. The view west across the river was of lumpy fells cloaked in snow. Eastward and south lay the Forest of Abernethy, part modern plantation and part ancient growth, concealing one of the finest mountain prospects in Scotland. A flock of yellowfaced birds with black caps was bouncing in the topmost branches beside the path; I thought at first they were greenfinches, but the binoculars suggested the chirpy little seed-eaters called siskins.

By mid-afternoon I was well past Grantown-on-Spey. Squeezed onto ledges cut out of precipitous hillsides in the narrow strip of land between the river and the A95 trunk road, the old line was a testimony to the art of the Victorian railway engineer and the craft of the navvy. The hummocky pastures lay frosted into a pale sage green, the track itself nibbled by sheep into a velvet nap like a rustic billiard table. Black-faced ewes lifted their heads and watched

Above right **The Spey is one of Scotland's chief salmon rivers. The big fish make their way upstream early in the New Year to spawn in the headwaters where they themselves were hatched**

Right **Fishermen of all kinds find sport along the Spey**

Far right **The 50-yd (45-m) Taminurie Tunnel at Craigellachie is – rather remarkably for a railway in such a hilly region – the only tunnel on the Strathspey line**

me walk by, their fleeces mottled with hanging icicles that made a gentle, faery tinkling as the sheep shifted stance with a faint crunch of icy grass under their hooves. The early exhilaration of setting out on a long walk had drained away now. I plodded the last few miles of the winter day through the narrowing valley, over bogland where frozen tuffets of heather and moss were bound fast in miniature lagoons of ice. Silver birches stood like trees in a Japanese print, each thread-like black twig sharply outlined in the cold still air. In spite of the stark beauty of the valley, it was an effort to put one foot in front of the other with nearly 20 miles of hard, stony ground trodden today, and it was a weary and hungry walker who trudged off the track and down the road at nightfall to find a bed at Ballindalloch.

It is wonderful what a good night's sleep after many miles of walking will do for a body. Nine o'clock next morning found me on the slippery railway path once more, staring across the river at the Rapunzel-style tower of Ballindalloch Castle. Ballindalloch, haunted by a Green Lady, was built by the Macpherson-Grant family (they still live here) in Tudor times in the haugh, or pasture, where the rivers Spey and Avon mingle their streams. Construction actually started on the adjacent hillside of Dalnapot, stories say – but Someone did not approve. Each midnight a fearsome tempest would arise and blow the builders' handiwork into the Spey. The dead silence that followed would be then broken by a wild,

unearthly howl of laughter. The Laird of Ballindalloch was a stubborn man, however. Dalnapot Hill he had selected for his castle, and Dalnapot Hill it should be. After several weeks having his building materials hauled daily out of the Spey, the Laird decided one night to hide with his servant on the construction site, in order to see exactly what went on. Midnight struck, the storm roared up, timbers and stones went tumbling once more into the river, and the Laird was hurled with his servant into a holly bush. As they lay among the prickles, a fearsome laugh went bellowing through the strath, followed by a terrific shriek: 'Build in the cow-haugh!' The chastened landowner did as he was bid, and Ballindalloch Castle was troubled no more by the Powers of Darkness.

The A95, which yesterday had been bound closer than a clinging lover to the Speyside line, now cast the old railway off and followed its own fancy north through the pass of Carron towards an afternoon reunion on the outskirts of Charlestown of Aberlour. The Strathspey Railway, freed of its younger and louder counterpart, wound through a beautiful stretch of valley landscape. The dramas of the high Cairngorms lay far behind now, and I found myself in thickly wooded back country where buzzards mewed overhead and the Spey snaked at the feet of forested promontories that marched down one behind another from the heights of Drum Wood. The river rushed and fussed over its shallows, a sibilant backdrop to all other sounds in the strath.

A breath of sweet and malty air came down on the wind, a hiss and hum and a jet of steam from behind the trees. The tall buildings of a distillery appeared ahead, just off the old line; a set of buildings I recognised. 'Tamdhu,' said the softly spoken and diffident Head Brewer when I ran him to earth in the shadows among the duty-free stores. 'Ah, so you have tasted our whisky before. Well, we still make Tamdhu here, we still malt all our barley here, and it's still as good as ever.' He gave me a modest, half-averted smile. 'But the company that owns us now doesn't really promote us in this country. They've Highland Park and The Macallan, you see, both very popular here at home, so…'

I recalled buying a bottle of Tamdhu direct from the distillery 25 years ago – the sweet tang of it, the dark hint of peat smoke implicit in the afterburn. A great desire to celebrate the poet Burns suddenly seized me. Could I obtain a bottle?

'Aye, well, you'll have to go to France for that. They have almost all of it there nowadays, the lucky beggars.'

Single malt whisky and Speyside go together like a song and a dram. It's to do with the quality of the local burn water, with the enthusiasm of individual clan chiefs who encouraged the distilleries to set up, with taxes and levies, fashion and happenstance. Whatever the causes, Strathspey and its tributary glens are stuffed with distilleries small and local in character, huge and international in reputation. Beyond Tamdhu (smoky, honeyish) the Speyside Way passed Knockando (pale, sweet), Cardhu (smooth, subtle) and many more distilleries I couldn't put a name to. Each lay deathly quiet, gently hissing steam, seemingly deserted. In among the brambles and grasses ran the tracks of sidings along which a dozen varieties of Highland nectar once trundled onto the Strathspey Railway at the start of their journey to the glasses of discerning drinkers across the world. The old railway ran on down the valley, slipping from one miasma of malty, alcoholic air to the next, passing weatherboarded station buildings on

platforms that still held their blue and white nameplates. The metal gates that blocked the line here and there against the wandering sheep were ice cold to the touch, and milky panes of ice glazed the tractor and bicycle ruts along the path.

Charlestown of Aberlour lay clustered round its castellated church tower, a one-street, two-storey town of low granite houses. School was out, and the teenagers of Charlestown scuffled and shoved each other round the door of the carry-out shop. Down on the river bank in afternoon sunlight I watched the local fishermen – anticipating the season by a week or two, perhaps – at their craft, selecting flies as discerningly as a gourmet choosing between one sauce and another, tying them on with enviable economy of movement, whipping rod and line extravagantly back and forth, then with the subtlest flick of the wrist gracefully laying fold upon fold of white line on the surface of the clear blue Spey.

At the onset of dusk I secured a bed at Craigellachie in Clan Grant country (clan war-cry: 'Stand fast, Craigellachie!'). Next day was to be an 18-miler. I didn't really want to walk so far on a short January day, but didn't really see how I could avoid it. So the following morning I hit the trail early, a long and snaking track through the woods of Arndilly and Knock More, then more of the same in the skirts of the Wood of Ordiequish. At least there was no problem with wayfinding. Although the trackbed of the Speyside Railway had performed its split at

Above **Low winter sun strikes gleams out of the many winding channels of the River Spey as it approaches Tugnet and its meeting with the North Sea**

Right **The pebbly shores of Spey Bay, where powerful tides push both inland and seaward at the narrow mouth of the River Spey**

... two cormorants opened their wings and stood sentinel on the far spit, hazed by the winter light like birds on a silk screen, and I was happy enough with that.

Craigellachie and quit the bonnie braes of Strathspey, I had forestry roads and country lanes, not to mention superb high views downriver, to speed me on to Fochabers, another distillery town on the Spey.

In the 1770s the 4th Duke of Gordon, Alexander Gordon, decided to extend the grounds of his residence, Castle Gordon. So he simply demolished the old village that stood in his way, and replaced it with the new town of Fochabers. Just downstream of the town, where the river began to widen into its five-mile-long estuary, I passed the demesnes of Gordon Castle in mid-afternoon. When the castle was founded in the 1470s it stood in the midst of the great Bog o' Gight. Successive Gordon clan chiefs went by the nickname of 'The Gudeman o' the Bog', until the 4th Duke, an energetic agricultural improver, had the estuarine marsh drained and turned into good productive land. Alexander Gordon seems to have been a typically autocratic nobleman, but one of his tenants, Alexander Milne, refused to knuckle under. History seems not quite sure about Alexander Milne's act of defiance. Some stories say he was a schoolboy who rebelled when the Duke decreed that all the boys of Fochabers should submit to an identical haircut; others declare that he was serving the Duke as a footman, and was dismissed for declining to wear his own hair short under his powdered wig. Whatever the truth of it, Milne emigrated to America, made a fortune, lived till he was 97, and had the last laugh by leaving $100,000 in his will to found Milne's Free School in Fochabers, independent of the Gordons who had stirred him to revolt all those years before.

On again with low light behind me and an ever-widening prospect of river, flood islands and marshy margins ahead. In the shadow of the old triple-vaulted ice house at Tugnet, the evocatively named former net-fishing station at the river mouth, the Spey went headlong to its meeting with the sea. A royal blue scour of fresh water surged powerfully from a wide pool through a narrow gap only a few yards wide between shingle spits, then pushed on out to sea for 50 turbulent yards before the in-pressing might of the salt tide drove it back on itself in a confusion of agitated wavelets and haphazard bursts of spray. I found a seat at the water's edge on a tree trunk that the sea had stripped of its bark, salted white and cast up on the pebbles. I sat gloved, hatted and scarved, with boots off, sore feet gradually numbing in the ice-cold, ice-blue water of the firth. No dull silver salmon flank broke the tumbled water of the river mouth, though I kept watch in hopes until the sun went down. But two cormorants opened their wings and stood sentinel on the far spit, hazed by the winter light like birds on a silk screen, and I was happy enough with that.

The Flow Country

The 10.38 from Inverness to Wick moved out on time under a blue sky piled with soft white clouds – coastal weather. I had the binoculars on the table, just in case. I'd come this way before, on the clickety-clack single-track line of the Sutherland & Caithness Railway to the northernmost corner of mainland Britain, and had regretted my lack of aids to eyesight on that occasion as red deer, harriers, merlins and otters cavorted all across the wild landscape outside the carriage windows, just beyond the capacity of my blurry vision.

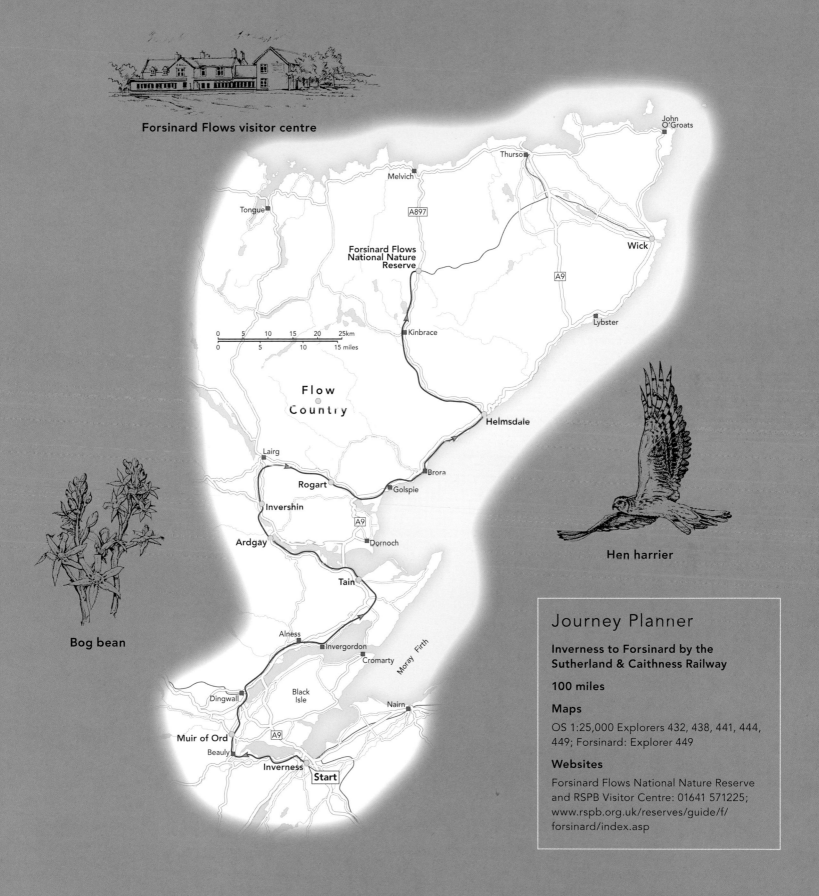

Forsinard Flows visitor centre

John O'Groats

Thurso

Melvich

A897

Tongue

Wick

Forsinard Flows
National Nature
Reserve

A9

Kinbrace

Lybster

0 5 10 15 20 25km
0   5   10   15 miles

Flow
Country

Helmsdale

Lairg

Brora

Rogart

Golspie

Invershin

A9

Ardgay

Dornoch

Bog bean

Hen harrier

Tain

Alness

Invergordon

Moray Firth

Cromarty

Dingwall

Black
Isle

Nairn

Muir of Ord

A9

Beauly

Inverness

Start

Journey Planner

**Inverness to Forsinard by the
Sutherland & Caithness Railway**

100 miles

Maps

OS 1:25,000 Explorers 432, 438, 441, 444,
449; Forsinard: Explorer 449

Websites

Forsinard Flows National Nature Reserve
and RSPB Visitor Centre: 01641 571225;
www.rspb.org.uk/reserves/guide/f/
forsinard/index.asp

This time I was determined to savour to the hilt the journey up the beautiful northeast coast of Scotland and on inland through the wide wet boglands of Sutherland and Caithness that carry the suitably liquid name of the Flow Country.

This Flow Country occupies a lozenge-shaped block of northern Scotland. A million acres of blanket bog lie spread here. The bog is about 98 per cent water, yet you can walk across it without sinking in more than an inch or two. Starved of nutrients, all but the uppermost layer is dead matter, yet those few sodden inches of sphagnum moss – a plant capable of retaining up to 20 times its own weight of water – support a large, lively and thriving population of birds, animals, insects, water creatures and invertebrates. The Flow Country has been described as a wet desert, and is Britain's own tundra. In terms of ecological importance it has been ranked with the Amazon rainforest and with the bush landscapes of Serengeti. Yet few know of it, and fewer care for it. Desolate, boring, dead, ugly, monotonous: over the years I have heard all these disparaging judgements on this most extraordinary wilderness.

Lucky for me that I had the binoculars on the table, for ironically the biggest ornithological treat of the day was handed to me while we were still leaving the bounds of Inverness. I was glancing out across the Caledonian Canal sea lock at Clachnaharry when I saw a large bird, mostly white with some dark patches, passing across the mud flats with powerful, deliberate wing beats. I got the glasses on it. Oh, my Lord! A hen harrier! The sun lit up its white belly as it spread dark wings to haul itself upright in the air, stretching white legs downwards like a ballet dancer poised on points, the sharp-faced little head ducked between the shoulders as it scanned the flats for some movement. After a few seconds the stance relaxed, the legs went back, the shoulders came forward and the long wings resumed the steady beating of level flight. I took that spectacle – rightly, as it happened – as an omen of a special day ahead.

Below left A female hen harrier swoops down, alert for anything – one of the ornithological incentives to keep your binoculars handy on a ride up the Sutherland & Caithness Railway

Below 'Did Ah tell ye the wan aboot the sodger who widnae wear a kilt?' – lighthearted murals at Invergordon Station recall the era of World War II

Right Liquid gold of both kinds: an oil rig out in Invergordon Bay, and closer at hand, whisky barrels in the yard of Whyte & Mackay's distillery

The train moved leisurely by the sea past green meadows loaded with red and white cattle, fat sheep and the late spring crop of lambs. A buzzard got up and flew heavily away from the capsized hulk of a ewe that lay on grass strewn with torn wool, two lambs glancing at the train from the shelter of her corpse. A fisherman knee-deep in the River Peffer, the white scribble of his line coiling out across the water at a flick of his wrist. A skeletal oil rig in Invergordon Bay. A mountain of barrels in the Whyte & Mackay distillery yard. Oak trees in the hills, thicker with lichen streamers than with leaves. A succession of stations: Muir of Ord, Tain, Ardgay. Request stops at Invershin and Rogart where no-one came and no-one went. In Rogart station yard a veteran bus painted cream and scarlet, with 'Sutherland Transport' lettered along the side – someone's restoration comedy, or tragedy. Helmsdale huddled around the sturdy walls of its fishing harbour, under cliffs smothered in gorse flowers so brilliantly yellow it hurt the eye to look at them. And then the long, slow ascent of the Strath of Kildonan, with wilder country moving in to replace the green fields, red deer outnumbering sheep, and lumpy hills rising into mountains as we topped the 500-ft (150-m) climb and levelled out across an immense dun-coloured expanse of treeless, houseless, empty-seeming bog, the so-called badlands of the Flow Country.

If you are looking for absolute loneliness, a complete absence of human clatter (apart from the occasional unearthly howl of an RAF jet) and a salutary sense of your own insignificance, the Flow Country peatlands of northern Scotland are the place to come. Altogether about two per cent of Britain's land surface is contained in the vast blanket bogs and craggy remote mountains that fill the rhombus-shaped tip of Scotland, hemmed in by dark granite cliffs and rough seas. This giant agglomeration of sphagnum and other mosses, its gently undulating surface pushing up here and there into conical peaks, has been getting on with its own natural business since the last Ice Age came to an end, long before man put in any significant appearance. The cool, wet climate of the region keeps the bog moist, the underlying acid gneiss rock stops the sphagnum rotting down into fertile soil. Only along the narrow straths, or river valleys, do any settlements penetrate the interior; almost all the crofts and villages lie scattered around the perimeter. This vast, sombre desolation is crossed by one single-track railway line, a couple of roads and a loose skein of tracks.

The Flow Country is the nearest Britain comes to a desert – albeit a wet and species-rich one. That's why, during the latter half of the 20th century, it came to be seen as a useless wasteland just waiting to be turned into profit. Thousands of acres were destroyed through commercial peat-cutting, with powerful harvesting machines slicing up the bog for horticultural fertiliser. In the 1980s and early '90s about ten per cent of the Flow Country was planted with conifers. Many of the blocks of woodland were sold on to investors who had little or no idea how much damage their nice little Scottish nest egg was creating: draining the bogs of their life-sustaining water, ploughing them up, poisoning them and their wildlife with pesticides and herbicides, destroying the unique local habitat.

The RSPB, recognising the value of the Flow Country not only to birds but as a whole ecosystem, mounted a national appeal, raised about £1.5 million, and in February 1995 bought the 17,580-acre (7,114-ha) Forsinard Estate at the heart of the region. Since then they have more than doubled their holding. Nowadays the Forsinard Flows National Nature Reserve encompasses nearly 40,000 acres (16,000ha) of 'wet desert', with public access based on the little visitor centre and exhibition in the Forsinard station buildings, now owned by the RSPB.

Twice a week Reserve Warden Colin Mair takes anyone who cares to turn up for a tramp over the bogs. I found him waiting, neat and business-like, in the visitor centre when I climbed down from the train at Forsinard. His wellington boots and waterproof trousers told me all I needed to know about what conditions would be like underfoot. The reserve possesses a couple of well-marked circular trails, paved with flagstones in places to help visitors across the wetter patches. The walk Colin leads is nothing like that. Wet boots, peat-smeared trousers and plenty of contact with sodden sphagnum and bog pool water are guaranteed. Chalked up on a blackboard in the visitor centre were some of the birds spotted around Forsinard in the past month. They included greenshank, golden plover, siskin, cuckoo, black-throated and red-throated diver, osprey, hen harrier, short-eared owl and golden eagle. 'Can't promise anything,' smiled Colin as we set out west across the bog, 'but we've a good chance of one or two of them, anyway'.

In fact there were few bird sightings for us today, but I didn't care – not with the sharp eyes and well-stocked mind of Colin to enrich the walk. For an aiming point and focus we had the 1,900-ft (580-m) peak of Ben Griam Beg and its neighbouring hills. Rain came sweeping intermittently through the gaps in the range, gathering everything up in its dark grey skirts, but we felt only the swirl of its outermost hem. Somehow our portion of the bog slipped between the showers, gilded with sunshine or shadowed under rolling fields of cloud. Near at hand there was enough to occupy a life-time of observation, let alone a few short hours.

'This place has been this way for maybe 8,000 years,' Colin said, sweeping a hand over the bog that stretched to the horizon on all sides. 'A bit of a warm-up about 5,000 years ago allowed

Right **Bring your binoculars, keep quiet and still, watch the skies and – most important of all – be lucky, and you may see golden eagles at Forsinard**

Centre right **Rooted killers of the sphagnum bogs: sundews trap insects in a mesh of sticky hairs, then digest them**

Far right **The shallow, peaty lochans of the Flow Country are good places to find bogbean; the delicate pink and white flowers are at their best from April to June**

Left **Colin Mair, Warden at the RSPB's Forsinard Flows National Nature Reserve, examines a 4,000-year-old pine branch that has been perfectly preserved in the sphagnum bog**

some forest to get established – Scots pine, birch, alder, the sort of thing that grows naturally up here. Then it all cooled off again, and the bog moved in. But the remnants of those trees are still here,' and he stooped to pick up a dried-out pine branch, twisted and flaky, tinder-delicate to the touch. 'Probably grew and was felled 4,000 years ago.'

By the shattered and tumbledown snow-fence stood three red deer hinds, watching us uncertainly. We leaped the narrow Catsack Burn and squelched away across the acid green and russet sphagnum. Deep-pink lousewort flowers lay uncurling. Crisp grey branchlets of reindeer lichen, *Cladonia portentosa*, clung to the sphagnum among tiny sundew plants embedded in the wet matrix of the bog. Close to, the sundews revealed themselves as cobra-headed, and deadly as cobras, too, for struggling among the sticky hairs fringing the scarlet heads were blue or white marbled flies in their death throes, feebly kicking before their dissolution and digestion by the insectivorous plants. I dug my fingers deep into the sphagnum beside one of these silent slaughterhouses and felt my fingers slide through feathery moss and cold water into the soft embrace of the peat below. Withdrawing my hand, I found black silt lining each fingernail. 'Three metres deep, the peat here,' commented Colin, 'and it's twice as thick in many other parts of the reserve. Here, smell this bog myrtle.' He held out an unremarkable-looking plant with fleshy little buds. I pinched them and dipped nose to fingers to savour a spicy fragrance that wouldn't have gone amiss in a bowl of venison stew. Nearby a fat balloon of opaque membrane, with a hole at one end, was tethered to a sprig of heather by tiny liens. 'Egg-case of the emperor moth – that's a handsome creature with great big eye markings on its trailing wings. Never seen one on the reserve, but I know they're here somewhere!'

We climbed a slope and came suddenly on a maze of gleaming lochans, among whose jigsaw shapes we stepped by way of isthmuses of sodden sphagnum and heather. Thick tuffets of grey-green moss stood clear of the sphagnum. The dark peaty pools, interconnected by narrow spillways, were spattered with pale pink stars of flowering bogbean. 'A visitor from the Western Isles told me they boil bogbean up and drink the brew as a medicine for arthritis,' Colin remarked. 'Very, very bitter, she said.'

On the reverse slope of the hill we came on Gull Loch, a long fleet of steel-grey water bristling with sedge. If we were in luck, Colin had said, we might see a rare red-throated diver here, possibly its even rarer black-throated cousin, a handsome waterbird with a jauntily striped neck and a wail of a song. But no divers were there for us today. Instead we saw a solitary greenshank take off and fly quickly across the sky on black-tipped wings, the sun lighting its white back against slate-grey rain-clouds. A sharply echoing *piu! piu!* came back to us, as we stood and watched the fleeing bird.

That poignant cry, not as mournful as a curlew's call, but wilder and more haunting here in the horizon-lapping spaces of the Flows, seemed a fitting solo against the unending chorus of lark song pouring down out of the enormous bogland sky.

20

Out Stack

'Don't you worry,' the red-haired, multiple-pierced driver of the North Isles bus advised me at the end of a tangled recitation of ferry and bus connections. 'The only thing you need to remember is… don't panic.' That was the last thing I was going to do. This was Shetland, after all.

Journey Planner

Through Shetland mainland, Yell and Unst to the prow of Britain

65 miles

Maps

OS 1:20,000 Explorers 466, 467, 468, 469, 470

Websites

www.shetland-heritage.co.uk

Ferry and bus timetables:
www.shetland.gov.uk/ferries

Shetland's traditional music:
www.scotlandsmusic.com/
shetlandfiddlestyle.htm

Up-Helly-Aa midwinter festival (last Tuesday of January):
www.up-helly-aa.org.uk

Isle of Yell: www.//en.wikipedia.org/wiki/Yell,_Shetland

Isle of Unst: www.unst.org

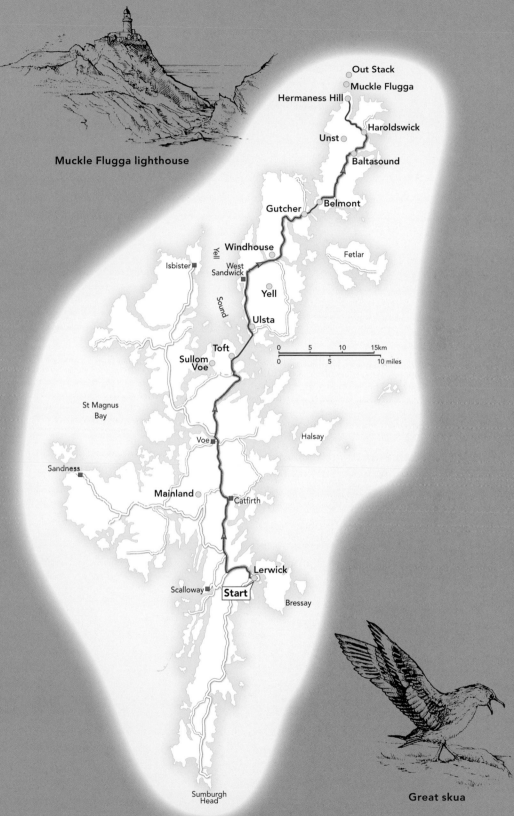

Muckle Flugga lighthouse

Out Stack

Muckle Flugga

Hermaness Hill

Unst

Haroldswick

Baltasound

Belmont

Gutcher

Windhouse

Isbister

West Sandwick

Yell

Fetlar

Ulsta

Sound

Toft

Sullom Voe

St Magnus Bay

Voe

Halsay

Sandness

Mainland

Catfirth

Lerwick

Scalloway

Start

Bressay

Sumburgh Head

0 5 10 15km
0 5 10 miles

Longship prow

Great skua

From the air the Shetland archipelago resembles an addled egg broken on a rough stone floor. The three main islands – Shetland Mainland, Yell and Unst – lie in a ragged-rimmed splash of green and brown, flung northwards in line across a sea that's sometimes royal blue, more often a granite grey flecked with white. These are the most northerly islands in Britain, the wildest and windiest, the most remote in situation. The capital of Shetland, stone-built Lerwick, is only 200 miles from Bergen on the Norwegian coast – the same distance as it is from Aberdeen. With its deep cut inlets (hereabouts called voes) and huddled fishing communities, Shetland feels more Norse than Scottish, and the native islanders look that way too. Broad giants with plenty of red in their cheeks and beards share the stone-paved streets of Lerwick with short dark natives with snub noses and sapphire-blue eyes. Summers are short, and so are summer nights, the 'simmer dim' during which the sun never goes properly to bed in these high latitudes. Winter, by contrast, lasts half the year, a long season of truncated days and endless wind.

Towards the end of January the Shetlanders blow their great annual raspberry in the face of winter and exorcise the northern blues when they celebrate Up Helly Aa, a fabulous feast of Viking songs, flaring torches, burning longships and heroic feats of all-night quaffing and dancing. The islanders' capacity for drinking is legendary, the energy and bounce of their fiddle music could fell an ox, their hospitality is unstinting. They run their lives more by the season than by the clock, and anyone expecting plans to unroll to any rigid timetable on any given day in the islands can look forward only to frustration. 'Go with the flow' might be tattooed on the inside of every Shetlander's skull, and visitors who leave the panic button at home are all the happier for it.

Left **One of a number of stained glass windows in Lerwick Town Hall, which tell the history of Shetland**

Top right **Up Helly Aa midwinter celebration: guisers encircle a purpose-built Viking longship before launching their torches and setting her ablaze**

Bottom right **Cut peats lie neatly stacked in long rows; each block is cleverly balanced against its neighbours, allowing the air to circulate and dry it to produce a fuel that burns hot and slow**

The little North Isles bus began its northward run through Shetland Mainland under the milky blue sky that early summer brings to the islands. I sat back, watching the road unroll and picturing in my mind's eye the journeys and the seasons that had preceded this one: the fog-wreathed cliffs of Cornwall, a thousand miles and a whole world away, the frozen track of the Ridgeway bound fast in snow and ice, primroses along the canals of Birmingham and Stoke-on-Trent, sun-streaked sands of Gower, the sodden moors and sentinel mountains of the Road to the Isles through central Scotland. And now the culmination – this jolting ride by bus and ferry to the outermost tip of Shetland, as far from Land's End as it is possible to travel within these British Isles.

Lapwings and oystercatchers were wheeling over the low-rolling, dun-coloured moors, treeless and wind-scoured. The peat underlying the heather and grass formed shelves with dark rims, seeming to wash across the hills in wave-like ripples petrified in mid-flow. A solitary man laboured on his peat bank, slicing down on the black face of the peat with a tushkar, or narrow-bladed cutter, driven firmly by stabs of his gumboot. The foot-long blocks he'd cut lay stacked for drying along the bank. A turn of the road and he was out of sight. Narrow inlets indented the shores, steely-grey fjords striped with the floating cages of fish farms. Solitary croft houses lay like white sugar cubes on long green hillsides, each one shadowed by the ghost of a long abandoned forerunner in tumbled grey stone. Since my last visit some 20 years before, a Scandinavian twist seemed to have entered Shetland architecture. There were new houses clad in pine weatherboarding, and others painted brightly in turquoise, lilac, mustard-yellow, carmine – a style borrowed from the Faroe Islanders, I guessed.

An intense orange flare above a hill showed the location of the North Sea oil terminal at Sullom Voe, out of sight beyond a broad ridge. More than any other factor during the 20th century, it was the announcement in August 1972 of the discovery of the Brent oil field a hundred miles northeast of Shetland that revolutionised economic and social life in the islands. The Shetland Islands Council had the wit and foresight to buy up the land round Sullom Voe and lease it to the various companies involved with the oil terminal

that sprang up there. The resulting revenue funded new roads, new schools and hospitals, new community halls, improvements to the fishing fleet and the island crofts. It also brought a huge social dislocation as some Shetland people became dissatisfied with the old ways of earning a living, as well as with the old courtesies and customs, habits of visiting lonely neighbours and taking time for others.

The Sullom Voe flare dropped behind, and the bus went swooping down to a short pier at Toft on the northeast coast of Mainland. The jolly driver squeezed us onto the tightly packed deck of the ferry and we rumbled across the sound to Ulsta on the southern coast of the island of Yell.

In spite of its defiant name, Yell lies quiet. This large island, 20 miles from toe to tip, must be one of the least visited and least appreciated in Britain. There's nothing especially memorable about Yell on first acquaintance. Empty moors open and rolling, spring-sodden peat bogs packed with

acid-loving flowers, seal-haunted geos and long miles of solitary cliffs where no-one goes: these are the sum of Yell's subtle charms, irresistible to anyone who loves to walk and walk and be away from everything and everyone. The road shows you some of it, ridges like the backs of deep sea waves, smooth and mottled, forbidding and bare; the house of North Haa standing foursquare to the winds beside a garden defended from the gales by an uncompromising stone wall; peat banks exploited more widely than in Mainland. And at the head of Whale Firth the wonderfully stark, battlemented ruin of Windhouse high against the sky, its roof in holes, the blank eyes of its windows staring blindly over one's head.

Windhouse is a fantastically haunted place. One of many grisly tales speaks of a benighted sailor, victim of a shipwreck, who turned up one Christmas Eve only to find the inhabitants quitting the house for fear of spending the night there. Undaunted, the sailor bedded down in Windhouse all alone. At dead of night he was woken by a fearsome shriek or growl,

Left **A typical Shetland landscape: treeless slopes of bog and grass sweeping down to the shore, croft houses tucked well down out of the weather, and the sea close at hand**

Below **The Yell ferry *Bigga* bustles across Bluemull Sound from Gutcher to pick up passengers from Belmont Pier on the southern tip of Unst**

Below right **Baltasound, Isle of Unst: the pinkest (and most northerly) bus shelter in Britain**

and found himself attacked by a trow – a Shetland-style troll. Our hero grabbed his trusty axe, hacked the monster to death, and then went back to bed to resume his slumbers. Next morning, all the sailor could find of the ghastly visitor was a huge, slippery pile of blubber.

As much as what one sees with the physical eye, it is the outlandish images conjured up by the Norse place names on the OS Explorer map that invest Shetland's landscape with magic. Klyptir of Garth, Trollakeldas Houlla, Crying Taing, Muckle Swart Houll; Sneugie of Dalsetter and the Black Geo of Gerherda; Eegittle, Aastack, Tittynans Hill and Point of Whack. I savoured their angular poetry and cantering beat as the bus descended to Gutcher (a toad-like croak in the inner ear) and the ferry to the Isle of Unst.

Unst is the most northerly island in Britain. It is rockier, steeper, more rough and rugged than comparatively gentle Yell. Ancient boulders lie thick across the pastures, cliffs fall several hundred feet into wild seas, and big hills roll up ahead on the horizon as you travel north from Belmont pier in the chugging old minibus to Baltasound. Tall grey clouds were building as the bus jerked to a halt outside the Baltasound Hotel. I stepped down into a stern, no-nonsense half-gale that pushed right on through me and out the other side. Along the stony shores of Baltasound new houses huddled together in the wind and rain like a flock of sheep, and I could see exactly why the architect had set them so protectively close together. It was a relief to stretch my bus-numbed nether quarters and make for the hotel bar and the delectable products of the island's Valhalla Brewery – 'Britain's Most Northerly Brewery', naturally.

Summer dawns come early to Unst, and make it hard to go on sleeping. By five o'clock next morning I was on a borrowed bike, pedalling the road to Haroldswick. The day was starting grey, but a whole world of pink was waiting for me just around the corner from the hotel, in the shape of the gayest bus shelter in Britain – and the most northerly, of course. The shelter had

been all done out by some humorous hand with pink cushions, pink curtains, and pink roses in a planter. There were pink teddies to cuddle, a pink mug, a pink feather duster, and a pile of pink-jacketed chick lit to while away the hours between the buses: Jackie Collins, Catherine Cookson, and a basque-ripper entitled *Step On it, Cupid* by the improbably named Lorelei Mathias. A final touch of perfection was the business card of a London Tube Health and Safety Manager, Mr Neil Pepper, MBE, FRGS, FZSL. Who needs LSD on Unst, when they can step into an alternative reality such as this? And – uncomfortable thought – where else in Britain would such a delightful ensemble remain unvandalised?

I biked like a man in a dream between ditches crammed with shining yellow kingcups and fields ringing with the mournful voices of oystercatcher, golden plover and snipe, down along the voe of Harold's Wick where a full-sized Viking longship raised an exquisitely carved prow to the cloudy sky.

Up above Burra Firth I leaned the bike against a fence and climbed the long wet path onto the nape of Hermaness Hill. Memories of 20 years before came thick and fast. Here were the great skuas, 'bonxies' to all Shetlanders, big speckled birds harshly croaking maledictions as they pointed their long wings skyward to show me a warning flash of bright white armpit. The last time I'd climbed this hill the bonxies had been well on with their nesting, and one big individual had made a dead set at me, parting my hair with his webbed feet and clacking his bill an inch or so from my nose with a blood-curdling screech and a stink of fishy breath. No such incivilities today; the bonxies let me go with hard words rather than aerial bombardment.

Left **Beware the bonxie! The great skuas of Hermaness are liable to press home low-level attacks if you stray too near their nests in the breeding season**

Right **Superb interwoven patterns on the prow of a Viking longship, built in Norway for a transatlantic voyage and now being restored at Haroldswick after years of abandonment in Shetland**

... I was exactly where I had planned and longed to be: standing at the very prow of the great ship Britain, with Out Stack off the port bow, and nothing but a thousand miles of sea between me and the Arctic ice.

I climbed past the lochans of Southers Brecks, on up to the crown of Hermaness Hill. A glance over my shoulder showed Burra Firth clouded out, the hill path a wraith in drifting mist. But it wasn't the backward view that occupied me now. I was waiting for a first glimpse of Out Stack.

My previous visit to Unst had coincided with an exhibition on Sir John Franklin's desperate and doomed expedition to search for the fabled northwest Passage to India and China. Franklin's two ships *Erebus* and *Terror* set sail from the River Thames with 134 souls on 19 May, 1845; they were seen in Baffin Bay a couple of months later, and then they simply disappeared. Sir John's devoted wife, Lady Jane Franklin, became a celebrity in the years that followed, raising money for one expedition after another to go to the rescue of her husband and his men. She became an expert in publicity, too. In perhaps the most bizarre stunt of all, she travelled to Shetland in order to be seen praying for Sir John's safe return as far north as possible. She came to Unst, and had herself taken out in a boat to the row of dramatically canted rock stacks that stand out of the sea beyond Unst's most northerly headland. I had never forgotten the extraordinary thrill of seeing these sharp, 100-ft (30-m) high blades of gleaming rock appear one by one beyond the brow of Hermaness. It had been the most memorable of many wonders during that first trip through the Northern Isles. And now, descending northwards down the dark green slope towards the last cliffs in Britain, I saw them appear once more in line astern, those sloping sea stacks so often thought and dreamed of in the intervening years, definitive sea blocks to close off the British Isles, with a cumbersome and irresistible poetry to their names: Vesta Skerry, Rumblings, Tipta Skerry, and Muckle Flugga with its lighthouse perched dizzyingly at the very apex of the rock.

Out beyond Muckle Flugga, separated by half a mile of heaving sea as dark as ink, rose the grey dome of Out Stack, a blunt name for a blunt round button of stone quite unlike its tall and striking neighbours. Lady Jane Franklin had scrambled up Out Stack from her boat, and knelt on the harsh rock to pray for Sir John. 'She stood on the Out Stack,' wrote the 19th-century Shetland author Jessie Saxby, 'and said, "Send love on the wings of a prayer", quite silent with tears falling slowly and her hands stretched out toward the north.' Some folk nowadays assert that that never really happened – couldn't have happened, given the restrictive clothes of Victorian ladies and the hazards of landing from a pitching boat.

Well, pshaw to them. There was magic in the moment for me, in the perfection of that singular image, on this day in particular. It was the morning of my 60th birthday, the last day of my journeyings for this book, and I was exactly where I had planned and longed to be: standing at the very prow of the great ship Britain, with Out Stack off the port bow, and just a thousand miles of sea between me and the Arctic ice.

Left **Looking back over Muckle Flugga and the other great rock stacks that close off Britain, with the green brow of Hermaness beyond**

Index

Page numbers in *italic* refer to the illustrations

A

Abhainn Rath 213, 214–15, *215*
Abney Park Cemetery 79, 81, *81*, 85
Acton Bridge *142*
Aitken, Bob 212
Alfred the Great, King 44–6, *45*
Alfred Memorial 44–5
Alfred Tower 59–60, *59*
Alkborough 152
Alkborough Flats 152–3, *153*
Alwinton 186, 190
An Steall 216, *217*
Anderson, Alistair 184, 186, 187–8, 190–1
Andover 56–7
Antonioni, Michelangelo 82
Aonach Beag 213, 215
Arncliffe Viaduct 84
Arthur, King 49, 60
Askham-in-Furness 167
Athelney 44
Atholl, Earl of 210–11
Atlantic Ocean 21, 223, 224
Aviemore 222
Avon, River (Dartmoor) 33
Avon, River (Scotland) 226

B

Bainbridge, Robert *181*
Balham 83
Ballindalloch Castle 223, 226, *226*
Ballowall Barrow 19, *19*, 20
Ballymacdermot 203
Baltasound 247–8, *247*
Barlaston *143*, 144–5
Barle Valley 34–6
Barrow-in-Furness 164–6, *166*, 167
Barton 154
Barton Clay Pits 153
Basingstoke 55–6
Beckenham Place Park 85
Bedford, 4th Earl of 105, 106

Ben Griam Beg *237*, 238
Ben Nevis 213, 215–16
Bennett, Arnold *146*
Berwick St James 58
Berwyn, Cadair 126–9, *129*
Berwyn Hills 122–31
Binnein Mòr 215
Birmingham 134–9, 141, 245
Birmingham Canal Navigation 137, 138
Black Country 11, 136–7, 139
Black Death 60
Black Dog 34
Black Mountain 199, *199*, 203
Bluemull Sound *247*
Boat of Garten 223
bog, Flow Country 234, 236–9, *237*
bogbean 239, *239*
Bojewyan 22
Bond, James 90
Booth, William 81
Borlase, William Copeland 19, *19*
Borrow, George 11, 124–5, 129, 131
Boscaswell 22
Boswarthen 24
bottle kilns 146, *146*
Bracken Rigg 178
Brent, River 79, 80, 84
Brent oil field 245–6
Brentford 84, 85
Bridge of Orchy 208
Brill, Edith 54
Brilleaux, Lee 70–1, *71*, 73
Brindley, James 136, 137, 138, 139, 141, 145
The Brisons 18-19
British Army 186–7, *188*, 201–2, 212, 214
Broadwindsor 61
Bronwen, Cadair 128, 129
Bronze Age 20, 22, 54, 58, 59, 97, 178
Brooke, Rupert 25, 102–3
Broughton Burrows 119
Brush Hill 94
Buckley, Rev William 116

Burns, Robert 220, 222, 227
Burnt Fen 106
Burra Firth 248, 251
Burrow Mump 45–6, *45*
Burrowbridge 44
Burry Holme *118*
Burslem 146
Butterdon Hill 31
Butterfield, Irvine 210–12, 213, 216
butterwort 176
Bwlch Nant Rhyd Wilym *127*, 128
Bynack More 222

C

Cadbury Castle 60, *60*
Cailleach Beara 204–5
Cairngorms 220, 222, 223, 226
Caledonian Canal 234
Cam, River 103, 105
Cam Lough 203
Cambridge 102–3, *102*, *103*
Camlough Mountain 203, *203*, 205
Campbell, Beth 213
canals *136*, 137–47, *138*, *139*, *141–3*
Canary Wharf 81, 82, *82*
Canterbury 55
Canvey Island 64, 69, *69*, 70–3, *72–3*
Cape Cornwall 20–1
Capital Ring 78–85, *78–80*
Cardhu 227
Carlingford Lough 197, 203
Carn Dearg 212
Carn Gloose 19
Carn Porth 25
Carrickcarnan 199
Cartmel 164, *164*
Cartmel peninsula 163–4
Castell Dinas Bran 131
Castlewood 82, 85
cattle drovers 178, 211–12, *211*
Cauldron Snout 174, *174*
Ceiriog, Afon 126, 127

The Chains 37
Chapel Island 164
Chapmansford 56
Charles I, King 154
Charles II, King 66
Charlestown of Aberlour 226, 228
Charnage Down 59
Chequers 95, *95*
Cheviot Hills 11, 184–91
Chilterns 88, 90, 93–4, *93*
Chinnor 94
Chlaidheimh, Loch a' 210–11
Chulainn 204
Chûn Downs 22
Chûn Quoit 22–4
Clachnaharry 234
Clannaborough 34
The Cliff 152
Clontygora 197, *197*, 199
clootie trees 23, 24
Coalhouse Point 68
Coir' a' Bhric Beag, Loch *210*
Collier, Rev. Henry 59
Collins, Paddy 194, 196
Cooley Peninsula 201
Coombe Hill 95, *95*
Coquet, River 186, *189*
Coquetdale 186–7
Cornwall 11, 14–25, 54
Corrour 210, 211, 213, *213*
Corrour Old Lodge 212
Corscombe 60–1
Coryton oil refinery 68
Cove, River 25
Cox, Ka 25
Craigellachie 223, 225, 228–9
Creag Ghuanach 214
Cronkley Fell 176, *177*, 178
Croppenburgh, Joos van 73
Croslieve 203
Crossmaglen 201–2, *202*
Crowley, Aleister 25
Crystal Palace 83
Cúchulainn 204
Curry Rivel 42

D

Dartmoor 11, 28–34, *30*, 37
de le Hey, Serena 46
Dee, River 126, 127, 129, 131
Deep Cutting Junction 137
Defoe, Daniel 67
Denver Sluice 107
Dickens, Charles 64, 72, 73
Dirty Corner 56
Disgynfa, Afon 124, *125*, 126–7, *126*
Docklands, London 82
Dr Feelgood 70–1, *71*, 72
Dorchester 48–9
Downham Market 107
Doyle, Arthur Conan 31, 32, 37, 64
drainage, Fens 104–5, *104*, 106
Drayton, Michael 106
Drewsteignton 31
drovers 178, 211–12, *211*
Duddon, River 11, 163
Duddon Estuary 167–8
Duncan, Steve 210–12
Dundalk Bay 201, 203

E

eagle, golden 238, *239*
Easington 157
East Coker 60
Edward Longshanks, King 154
Eltham 78
Eltham Common 82, 85
Eltham Palace 79
Ely 105–6
Enclosures 92–3
English Channel 21, 54
Essex 64–73
Etruria 145, 147
Exmoor 11, 28–31, 34–7
Eyston, George *138*

F

Fairfax, Governor 154
Falcon Clints *177*
Far Ings Nature Reserve 153–4
Farnham 54
Fathom 203
Fen Rivers Way 103
Fenland 100–7

Fielder, Richard 105
Fionn MacCumhaill 204–5
Five Lanes End 55, *55*
Flagstaff 196–7
Fleming, Ian 90
Flow Country 11, 232–9, *237*, *238*
Flurry Bridge 200
Flurry River 199, *199*, 200
Fobbing Marshes 69
Fochabers 229
Fonthill Bishop 59
Forda 34
Forest of Abernethy 224
Forkill 201, 203
Forsinard Flows National Nature Reserve 237–8, *237–9*
Franklin, Lady Jane 251
Franklin, Sir John 251
Freeth, John 134, 136, 137
Furness Abbey 164, *165*, 166
Furness peninsula 164
Furness Railway 162, 164, *164*, 166, 167–8

G

Gas Street Basin, Birmingham 134, *136*, 137
Gateshead 184, 187
Gentleman Adventurers 104
Giles Wood 94
Glastonbury Tor 42, 45, *48*, 49, 60
Glen Nevis 213, 216
goats, wild *190*
Goodmerhill Wood 95
Gordon, 4th Duke of 229
Gordon Castle 229
Goring 90
Gower Peninsula 110–19, 245
Goxhill Haven 154
Grand Junction Canal 97
Grand Union Canal 84, 85
granite 25, 25
Granta, River 102
Grantchester 102–3, *102, 103*
Gravesend 66
Great Haywood Junction 141, 142
Great Ouse 11, 103, 105, 106, 107
Green Trod 178
Greenford 79, 80, 84

The Greenway 78, 79, 82, 85
Grim's Ditch 90
Gull Loch 239
Gutcher 247, *247*
Gwybr of Llanrhaeadr 127, *129*

H

Hackney 78
Hackney Marshes 81
Hadleigh Ray 69, 73
Hadrian's Wall 174
Halstock 60
Ham Hill 42
Ham Wall 49
Hampstead Garden Suburb 80, 85
Haroldswick 247, *249*
harrier, hen 234, *234*, 238
Harrow-on-the-Hill 80
Harroway 52–61, *55*
Hawkridge 34
Haws Bank 166
Hedon 156, *157*
Helmsdale 236, *236*
Hem Heath colliery 145
Hempton Wainhill 94
Henry IV, King 156, 157
Henry VIII, King 66
Herbert, Sir George 114
Hereward the Wake 105
Hermaness Hill 248, *250*, 251
High Force *179*, 180
Highgate 78, 80
Highgate Wood 85
Highlands 208–16
Hillaby, John 174, 180
Hittisleigh Barton 34
Hoar Oak Water 37
Hoare, Henry 59
Hodbarrow 169
holy wells 23, 24, 205
Horsa 80
Horsenden Hill 79, 80, 85
The Hound of the Baskervilles (Doyle) 31, *31*
Hudson, W.H. 16–18
Hull 152, 154–6, *156*
Humber, River 11, 141, 150–7, *155*
Humber Bridge 154, *155*
Hunstanton 97

Huntingdon Cross 33
Huntingdon Warren 33, 33

I

Ice Age 177, 180, 236
Icknield Way 96–7
Industrial Revolution 92, 136, 153
Invergordon *234*
Invergordon Bay *235*, 236
IRA 198, 200, 201, *201*
Irish Republic 199
Irish Sea 21, 163
Iron Age 54, 59, 60, 61, 90
Isleworth 84, 85
Ivinghoe Beacon 90, 91, 96–7, *97*

J

Jack Wood 82–3, 85
James II, King 46–8
Jefferies, Richard 34, 36
Jeffreys, Judge 48–9
Johnson, Paul 146
Johnson, Robert 31, 32
Johnson, Wilko 64, 70–1, *71*, 72
Jones, Eilys and Aeron 128–9
Jonesborough 200
Julian's Bower 152, *152*

K

Kent, River 162, 163
Killevy 205
Kilmington 59
Kilnasaggart Stone 200, *200*
kilns, bottle 146, *146*
Kilnsea Cross 156, 157, *157*
King's Head, Middleton-in-Teesdale 180–1
King's Lynn 103, 107
King's Ring 197, *197*
Kingsettle Hill 59–60
Kingston Wood 94
Knockando 223, 227
Knowstone 30
Kynochtown estate 68

L

Lake District 160, 163
Lake of Sorrows 204–5, *204*
Lambert's Castle 61
Land's End 10, 16, *16–18*, 245
Langmoor Rhyne 46–8
Lanyon Quoit 22, *23*
Lauder, Harry 211
Lawrence, D.H. 25
Lea, River 78, 81
Lee Navigation towpath 85
Leftlake Mires 32
Lerwick 244, *244*
Levant tin and copper mine *20*, 21
Leven, River 163
Lincolnshire 150–3, 156
Liverpool 137, 142
Llandrillo 129, 130, 131
Llangennith 119
Llangollen 131
Lluncaws, Llyn 127, *129*
Llynon, Afon 128
Lochiel of the Camerons 210–11
London 76–85
London & Birmingham Railway 97
London Walking Forum 78
Long Horse Island 73
Long Sutton 54–5
longship, Viking 248, *249*
Longships lighthouse 17, 18–19, *18*
Loughor Estuary 119
Lower Cadsden 94–5
Lyme Regis 61
Lynmouth 30

M

McAllister, Jim 201–2
McAlpine, Robert 212
McCarty, Chris 175–80
MacCulloch, Dr John 212
Macpherson-Grant family 226
Madron Well 24
Mair, Colin 238–9, *238*
Mamore 215
Mamore Forest 213
Mansel family 114
Marazion 54

Margaret of Antioch, St 69–70, *70*
Marshwood 61
Martin, Keble 33, *33*
Matthews, Stanley 145
'Mattins Corner' 33, *33*
mazes 152, *152*
Meall a' Bhùirich 215
Meannanach 215, *215*
Meare 49
Mên-an-Tol ('Stone with the Hole') *23*, 24–5
Mere Down 59
Mersey, River 141, 142
Middleton, Ian 155–6
Middleton-in-Teesdale 180–1, *181*
Midlands 11, 134–47
Millom 168–9, *168*
Milne, Alexander 229
mining, tin 19–21, 54
Moel Felen 126
Moel Fferna 130
Moel Sych 127, 128, 129
Monmouth, Duke of 46–9
Moray Firth 223, 224
Morchard Bishop 34
Morecambe Bay 160–9, *162–3*
Mountjoy, Lord 200
Mourne, Mountains of 196–7, 203
Muchelney 42
Mucking Flats 68
Muckle Flugga *250*, 251
Mullins, Micheál 201
'Munros' 210, 214
Murray, Ron 200
Murtagh, Aidan 201
Musgrove, L.A. 46, *47*
music 184, 186–91, *186*, *188*, 201
Mutton Brook 80, 85

N

Nant y Pandy 131
National Trust *20*
Nethy Bridge 222
New Holland 154
New Main Line 137, 138–40, *138*
Newry 196, 205

Newry Canal 196–7
Nicholaston Woods 114
Nicholson, Norman 11, 168–9
Normanton Down 58
North Downs Way 54
North Haa 246
North Sea 73, 152, 157
Northern Ireland 194–205
Northumberland National Park 186–7, *188*
Northumbria 184–91
Nuffield 90
Nuffield, Lord 90

O

Oath 43
oil, North Sea 245–6
Ossian, Loch 211
Ouse, River 152
Out Stack 251
Overton 56
Overton Hill 90, 97
Owen, Wilfred 96
Oxleas Wood 82–3, *83*, 85
Oxwich Burrows 114, 116
Oxwich Castle 114–16, *114*

P

Parkland Railway Walk, London 78, 85
Parrett, River 43
Pass of Moyry 200–1
Patrick, St 203
Patrington 157
Paull Holme Sands 156
Paviland Cave 116, *117*
peat 245, *245*, 246
peat bogs, Flow Country 236–9, *237*
Peddar's Way 97
Peffer, River 236
Pen Creigiau'r 130
Pen-y-Crug 114
Pendeen 22
Pendeen Watch lighthouse 21
Penmaen Burrows 114
Pennard Castle 112–13, *113*
Pennard Pill 112, *112*
Pennine Way 174, 175, 178, 180, 190
Pennines 172

pennywort *34*
Penwith 14, 16–25
Penzance 24
Perivale 78, 80, 85
Petersham Meadows 84, 85
Piel Island 166–7
Pigg, Billy 188, *188*, 190
Pilsdon Pen 61
Pinkworthy Pond *30*
Pistyll Rhaeadr 124–5, *125*, *126*, 129
Pitsea 69
Pitstone Hill 97
Pobbles Beach 112
Port-Eynon Bay 116
Porthmeor Beach 25
Potteries 11, 144, 145–7
Preston Park 80
primrose, bird's eye 176, *177*, 178
Princes Risborough 94
Pulpit Hill 95

Q

Quarley Hill 56
Queen's Wood 80, 85
Quiller-Couch, Mabel and Lillian 24

R

Ramsden, James 166
Rannoch Moor 11, 210–12, *213*
Ravensdale Forest 199
Red Hill 42
Redlake 32
Redlake tramway 31–2
reeds 105
Rhossili Beach *118*, 119
Richard I, King 154
Richard II, King 156
Richmond 84, *84*, 85
Richmond Park *78*, 83–4, 85
The Ridgeway 88–97, *93*, 245
Ring of Gullion 11, 204
Ring of Gullion Way 196, 199–200
Road to the Isles 211–16, *212*, *214*, *215*, 245
Robinson, Cedric 160, 162–3
Robinson, Walter ('Wayfarer') 128

Rogart 236
Rolle Bridge 36
Rosemergy 25
RSPB 237–8
Russell's Cairn 190

S

St Bline 205
St Ives 21, 25
Salisbury Plain 57, 97
salmon 223, 224, 225
Saxby, Jessie 251
Scilly, Isles of 17
Scorriton 33
Scotland 208–16, 220–9, 232–9, 242–51
Scott, George Gilbert 81
Seaton 54, 61, 61
Sedgemoor, Battle of (1685) 48
Sennen Cove 18
Setanta 204
Severn, River 137, 141
Severndroog Castle 79, 82, 85
Sgùrr Choinnich Mòr 215
Shepton Montague 60
Shetland Isles 10, 11, 242–51
Shillmoor farmhouse 189
Shirburn Hill 94
Shugborough Hall 144, 144
Silverdale 163
Simonsbath 36
Sinn Fein 201–2
skua, great 248, 248
Slemish 203
Slieve Bolea 203
Slieve Gullion 196, 200, 203, 203, 204–5, 204
Slievenacappel 203
Slighe Midhlachra 200–1
smallpipes, Northumbrian 184, 186–91, 186, 188
Smith, Roger 212
snipe 175, 175
Sollas, William 116
Somerset Levels 11, 42–9, 44
South Armagh 11, 194–205
South Crofty mine 20
South Lakelands 11, 160–9
Sowy River 44
Spencer, Richard 213–16, 215

Spey, River 220, 223–6, 225, 228, 229, 229
Spey Bay 223, 224, 229
Speyside Way 222, 223–9
Spilman, John 157
Spurn Point 156, 157, 157
Stafford 142
Staffordshire and Worcestershire Canal 141–3, 141–3
Stathe 43
Steeple Langford 58–9
Stewart Aqueduct 138
Stoke Newington 81, 81
Stoke-on-Trent 144, 145–7, 245
Stone 144
Stone Age 22, 54, 90, 97, 197, 204
stone monuments 22–5, 23, 200, 200
stone walls 127, 127, 181
Stonehenge 57–8, 58
Stourport-on-Severn 141
Stratford 82
Strath of Kildonan 236
Strath Nethy 222
Strathspey 222
Strathspey Railway 222, 223–9, 225
The Street 186-7, 189, 190
Sturgan 203, 203
Sullom Voe 245–6
sundew 239, 239
Sunk Island 156–7
Sutherland and Caithness 234
Sutherland & Caithness Railway 232, 234–6
Swansea 112
Swyncombe 91, 91

T

Tamdhu whisky 227
Taminurie Tunnel 225
Tarka the Otter (Williamson) 30, 36, 37, 37
Tarr Steps 31, 34, 35
Taylor, Willie 184, 186
Tees, River 172, 174, 174, 176, 177, 179, 180
Teesdale 172–81
Teesmouth 172

Telford, Thomas 138, 138, 139
Thames, River 90, 141, 251
Thames Estuary 11, 64–73
Thames Flood Barrier 82, 82
Thames Path 84, 85
Thomas, Dylan 119
Thompson, Francis 32
Tilbury Fort 66–7, 66
Timperley, H W 54
tin mining 19–21, 54
Tipton 139, 139
Tixall 142–3
Toft 246
tombs, prehistoric 22–4, 23, 114, 197, 197, 204, 204
Tregerthen 25
Tregiffian Vean 18
Treig, Loch 214, 214
Trent, River 144, 152
Trent & Mersey Canal 141–2, 143, 144–7, 146
Tring 97
Trinity House 16
Tugnet 229
Two Moors Way 28–37

U

Ulsta 246
UNESCO World Heritage Sites 21
Unst 11, 244, 247–51, 247
Up Helly Aa 244, 245
Upware 105

V

'Vale of Deadly Nightshade' 164
Vange Marshes 69
Vermuyden, Cornelius 105, 106, 107, 156–7

W

Wales 11, 110–19, 122–31
walls, stone 127, 127, 181
Wallsend 187–8
Walney Island 166
Walthamstow 78, 81
Wandsworth Common 83
The Wash 97, 102, 103, 107

Water of Nevis 213, 215, 216, 216
Watlington Hill 94
Watts, Isaac 81
Wayfarer's Pass 129
Weatherdon Hill 31
Wedgwood, Josiah 144–5, 145, 147
Well 54
wells, holy 23, 24, 205
Wembley 80
Wendover 95–6
West Highland Line 210, 213
West Highland Way 212
West Sedgemoor 42–3
Western Beacon 31
Westernend Shaw 91
Westonzoyland 46, 49
Weyhill Fair 56, 57, 57
Whale Firth 246
Whin Sill 174, 177, 179
whisky 227, 235, 236
White Force 178
White Sheet Hill 59
Whiteford Burrows 119
Whitesand Bay 18
Whitton 153
Whyte & Mackay 235, 236
Wicklow Hills 203
Widecombe-in-the-Moor 30, 31
William of Orange 154
Williams, Ron 130–1
Williamson, Henry 37, 37
willows 46, 47
Wimbledon Common 83, 85
Winchester 55
Windhouse 246–7
windpumps, Fens 104
Withypool 36
Wolverhampton 137, 138, 140, 141, 142
Woolwich 79, 82
Wordsworth, William 11, 167
Worm's Head 116–19, 119
The Wra reef 21
Wylye, River 58

Z

Zennor 25, 25
Zennor Head 25

Acknowledgements

The Automobile Association would like to thank the following photographers, companies and picture libraries for their assistance in the preparation of this book. Abbreviations for the picture credits are as follows – (t) top; (b) bottom; (l) left; (r) right; (c) centre; (dps) double page spread; (AA) AA World Travel Library

1 J Somerville; **4-5** Andrew Doggett/Alamy; **8** Richard Cannon; **9** AA/James Tims; **11**tl J Somerville; **11**tr C Somerville; **12-13** AA/Chris Warren; **14** AA/Peter Trenchard; **16** AA/Rupert Tenison; **17** AA/Caroline Jones; **18** Private Collection/The Stapleton Collection/The Bridgeman Art Library; **19** David Chapman/Alamy; **20** AA/Roger Moss; **23**tl C Somerville; **23**tr C Somerville; **23**b David Noble Photography/Alamy; **25** AA/John Wood; **26-27** AA/Guy Edwardes; **28** C Somerville; **30** John Warburton-Lee Photography/Alamy; **31** Everett Collection/Rex Features; **33**tl Terry Hurt; **33**tr C Somerville; **34** AA/Nigel Hicks; **35** AA/Nigel Hicks; **36** C Somerville; **37**tl ITV/Rex Features; **37**tr C Somerville; **38-39** AA/Richard Ireland; **40** C Somerville; **42**bl AA/Michael Moody; **42**br J Somerville; **43** C Somerville; **44** AA/Richard Ireland; **45**tl The Print Collector/Alamy; **45**br C Somerville; **47**t C Somerville; **47**bl C Somerville; **47**br C Somerville; **48** AA/James Tims; **50-51** Derek Stone/Alamy; **52** AA/Michael Moody; **55**t C Somerville; **55**b C Somerville; **56**t Worldwide Picture Library/Alamy; **57** Mary Evans Picture Library; **58** AA/Michael Moody; **59**tl C Somerville; **59**tr AA/Michael Moody; **60** Skyscan/Corbis; **61** Brian Gibbs/Collections; **62-63** C Somerville; **64** C Somerville; **66**bl Skyscan/Corbis; **66**br AA/John Miller; **67** C Somerville; **68** snappdragon/Alamy; **69** C Somerville; **70** Mary Evans Picture Library; **71** Photo by Estate Of Keith Morris/Redferns/Getty Images; **72**tl Photodisc; **72**tr Jon Combe; **73** Raymond Kleboe/Picture Post/Getty Images; **74-75** James Osmond Photography/Alamy; **76** C Somerville; **78** AA/Neil Setchfield; **79** Paul Carstairs/Alamy; **80**tl AA/Michael Moody; **80**tr Gregory Wrona/Alamy; **81**t C Somerville; **81**b Stephen Markeson/Alamy; **82** AA/Leigh Hatts; **83**bl C Somerville; **83**br AA/James Hatts; **84** AA/Neil Setchfield; **86-87** AA/Bob Johnson; **88** C Somerville; **91**t Travel Ink/Alamy; **91**b Getty Images/Photodisc; **92** C Somerville; **93**l Yale Center for British Art, Paul Mellon Collection, USA/The Bridgeman Art Library; **93**r C Somerville; **95** AA/Michael Moody; **96-97** Richard Roscoe; **98-99** AA/M Birkitt; **100** C Somerville; **102** cambpix/Alamy; **103**tl AA/Michael Moody; **103**tr C Somerville; **104** AA/Tom Mackie; **105** Museum of English Rural Life; **107**tl C Somerville; **107**tr C Somerville; **108-109** AA/Michael Moody; **110** AA/Derek Croucher; **112** C Somerville; **113** C Somerville; **114**bl M Schaef/Photolibrary; **114**br The Photolibrary Wales/Alamy; **115** AA/Caroline Jones; **117** Andrew Davies/Photolibarywales.com; **118** AA/Harry Williams; **119** C Somerville; **120-121** C Somerville; **122** C Somerville; **125** AA/Derek Croucher; **126**tl C Somerville; **126**tr C Somerville; **127** C Somerville; **129** Julian Cartwright/Alamy; **130** AA/Nick Jenkins; **131** AA/Nick Jenkins; **132-133** AA/Caroline Jones; **134** C Somerville/Wedgwood Museum Trust; **136** AA/Caroline Jones; **138** C Somerville; **139** Derek Pratt - Waterways Photo Library; **141**l C Somerville; **141**r AA/Michael Moody; **142** C Somerville; **143** C Somerville; **144** AA/Jonathon Welsh; **145** Mary Evans Picture Library; **146**bl Mary Evans Picture Library; **146**br C Somerville; **147** C Somerville; **148-149** C Somerville; **150** fotolincs/Alamy; **152** Ashley Cooper/Alamy; **153** C Somerville; **155** AA/Graham Rowatt; **156** Mary Evans Picture Library; **157**bl Neil Holmes Freelance Digital/Alamy; **157**br C Somerville; **156-157** AA/Anna Mockford & Nick Bonetti; **158** Ashley Cooper/Corbis; **160** C Somerville; **161** Darren Staples/Reuters/Corbis; **162**bl National Railway Museum/Science & Society Picture Library; **162**br AA/E A Bowness; **163** AA/E A Bowness; **164**tl The Francis Frith Collection/Corbis; **164**tr Ashley Cooper/Corbis; **165** Hulton-Deutsch Collection/Corbis; **166** The Print Collector/Alamy; **167** Neil Barks/Alamy; **168-169** AA/Roger Coulam; **170** C Somerville; **172** David Taylor Photography/Alamy; **173**t Andy Sands/Nature Picture Library; **173**b Leslie Garland Picture Library/Alamy; **174** AA/Roger Coulam; **175**tl C Somerville; **175**tr C Somerville; **177** C Somerville; **178** C Somerville; **179**tl AA/Roger Coulam; **179**tr Wayne Hutchinson/FLPA; **182-183** Graeme Peacock; **184** Paul Harris/Northumberland County Council; **186** Paul Harris/Northumberland County Council; **187** AA/Graham Rowatt; **188**tl Troy GB images/Alamy; **188**br Society of Antiquaries of Newcastle upon Tyne; **189** Graeme Peacock; **190** C Somerville; **191** AA/Derek Forss; **192-193** The Irish Image Collection/Photolibrary; **194** C Somerville; **196** C Somerville; **197** C Somerville; **199**tl C Somerville; **199**tr C Somerville; **200** C Somerville; **201** C Somerville; **202** C Somerville; **203** The Irish Image Collection/Photolibrary; **204**tl Ron Murray; **204**tr C Somerville; **206-207** AA/Stephen Whitehorne; **208** Phil Seale/Alamy; **210** C Somerville; **211** Mary Evans Picture Library; **212** background Andy Hockridge/Alamy; **212** inset Andy Hockridge/Alamy; **213** Milepost 92½ - railphotolibrary.com; **214** C Somerville; **215**bl C Somerville; **215**br C Somerville; **216** Christian Hand/Imagebroker/FLPA; **217** AA/Jim Henderson; **218-219** AA/Jonathan Smith; **220** Photodisc; **222** Mike Taylor/Stock Scotland; **223** Tamdhu Distillery/The Edrington Group; **225**t John Kelly Photography (UK); **225**bl AA/Ronnie Weir; **225**br John Gray; **226**tl John Pringle/Scottish Viewpoint www.scottishviewpoint.com; **226**tr AA/Jonathan Smith; **227** AA/Sue Anderson; **228** C Somerville; **229** AA/Michael Taylor; **230-231** Oaktree Photographic/Alamy; **232** C Somerville; **234**bl Arco Images GmbH/Alamy; **234**br Colin Hugill/Alamy; **235** Shenval/Alamy; **236** C Somerville; **237** C Somerville; **238** C Somerville; **239**tl AA/Mark Hamblin; **239**tc C Somerville; **239**tr C Somerville; **240-241** Patrick Dieudonne/Robert Harding; **242** Grant Dixon/lonelyplanetimages.com; **244** Richard Cummins/lonelyplanetimages.com; **245**t Scottish Viewpoint/Alamy; **245**b TopFoto/Doug Houghton; **246** TopFoto/John Corbett; **247**bl C Somerville; **247**br C Somerville; **248** Patrick Dieudonne/Robert Harding; **249** C Somerville; **250** Adrian Warren/www.lastrefuge.co.uk

Every effort has been made to trace the copyright holders, and we apologise in advance for any accidental errors. We would be happy to apply the corrections in the following edition of this publication.